PERFORMANCE EVALUATION OF PUBLIC ENTERPRISES

PERFORMANCE EVALUATION OF PUBLIC ENTERPRISES

An Annotated Bibliography

By

R.K. Mishra

ANMOL PUBLICATIONS PVT. LTD.
NEW DELHI - 110 002 (INDIA)

ANMOL PUBLICATIONS PVT. LTD.
4374/4B, Ansari Road, Daryaganj
New Delhi - 110 002
Ph.: 23261597, 23278000
Visit us at: www.anmolpublications.com

Performance Evaluation of Public Enterprises

First Edition, 2003

ISBN 81-261-1550-5

PRINTED IN INDIA

Published by J.L. Kumar for Anmol Publications Pvt. Ltd., New Delhi - 110 002 and Printed at Tarun Offset Printers, (Delhi)

Dedicated to

Professor Laxmi Narain

"A Distinguished Academician, Researcher & Authority on Public Enterprise"

Contents

	Preface	ix
	Abbreviations	xi
1.	Public Enterprise Performance: 1991-92 to 2001-02	1
2.	Research on Management of Public Enterprises in India	28
3.	Performance Evaluation of Public Enterprises in India	74
4.	Annotated Bibliography	105
	Appendix I: Committee on Public Undertakings (COPU)	169
	Appendix II: Report of the Committee to Review Policy for Public Enterprises [Arjun Sengupta Committee Report]: A Summary	203
	Appendix III: Report of the Committee on Disinvestment of Shares in Public Sector Enterprises	215
	Appendix IV: Report of the Comptroller and Auditor General of India	238
	Annexures	276
	Index	284

Preface

Public enterprises despite the ongoing wave of privatisation, continue to remain an important part of the Indian economy. Their width and depth is such that hardly any aspect of the lifeline of the Indian masses remain can be beyond their influence. It is thus very clear that their performance will continue to be a major determinant for the success of the Indian economy. Public enterprise performance has been a matter of intense debate right from the independence of the country. Both the doctrinaire and pragmatic approaches have been used while assessing the performance of public enterprises. As the users of public enterprise system have been multiple and varied, the performance assessment results have also been widely varying and contradictory. The present work brings together the essence of published writings in the form of books, research papers, articles, and official/non-official reports relating to public enterprise performance in India. The sole objective of the present work is to provide relevant inputs on performance of public enterprise for a more informed assessment of such enterprises.

A two-fold approach has been followed in completing this work. First, a general overview of public enterprise performance in India has been provided as the backdrop of the study followed by an extensive paper on survey of researches relating to these enterprises containing a discussion on the contours of new research vistas and another concept paper on the theory of performance appraisal on public enterprises in India. Second, a wide range of annotations have been presented to focus the thrust of various studies on performance and accountability of public enterprises.

In this work, the author has been helped and inspired by many eminent scholars of public enterprises who have dominated this field of study in India during the last five decades and are held in high esteem on the international academic scene. We are confident that the annotations of their work will create a new genre of scholars who will continue this sound tradition built up by them. In particular, we have been inspired by the living legends such as Prof. V.V. Ramanadham, Prof. Laxmi Narain, Prof. Om Prakash, Dr. C. Rangarajan Mr. T.L. Sankar, Dr. Y.V.Reddy, Dr. Nitish Sen Gupta, Dr. Prajapati Trivedi, Shri. Arjun Sen Gupta and Dr. Pradeep N Khandwala, C S Venkataratnam. Their writings are a rich mine of information and analysis and provide deep insights into the whole spectrum of performance of public enterprises.

Prof. Laxmi Narain has single handedly pursued studies on public enterprises, trained by Late Prof. W. A. Robson, Father of Public Enterprise, based at London School of Economics and Political Science, is among the leading scholars who set the tradition of research on public enterprises in India. He has been researching on public enterprises over last five decades. There is hardly any aspect of public enterprise which has not been researched by him. Today, he has become the last word on public enterprise in India and is popularly known as POPE (Professor of Public Enterprise). This book is dedicated to him as a mark of deep respect to his penetrating scholarship.

—R. K. Mishra

Abbreviations

BICP	Bureau of Industrial Costs and Prices
BPE	Bureau of Public Enterprise
COPU	Committee on Public Undertakings
CPEs	Central Public Enterprises
CPUs	Central Public Undertakings
EC	Estimates Committee
ICPE	International Centre for Public Enterprises
IMF	International Monetary Fund
IPE	Institute of Public Enterprise
IPR	Industrial Policy Resolution
LBS	London Business School
PAC	Public Accounts Committee
PEs	Public Enterprises
SLPEs	State Level Public Enterprises
WB	World Bank

Chapter I

Public Enterprise Performance: 1991-92 to 2001-02

The purpose of this paper is to bead together various statements of the government on public enterprise (PE) during the liberalisation era to develop a comprehensive perspective of PE policy in India, portray PE performance and examine the role that these enterprises can play in future with an appropriate reformulation by the government of its policy.

PE Policy

In any scheme of economic liberalisation, a proper sequencing of reforms is very vital. It may be observed that to begin with reforms around the world were initiated with PE restructuring. India did not pay any heed to this critical dimension of reform. Not to mention, the first generation economic reforms, there is no clarity about the approach to be adopted with regard to PE restructuring as a part of second generation reforms. The reforms in their first stage have more or less been limited to the central government. Consequently, the talk about reforming the PE has veered around only the central PEs (CPEs), leaving out of its scope a vast number of state level PEs (SLPEs), municipal enterprises and cooperatives with a majority shareholding of the government. Besides the impact of coalition politics, the lack of bureaucratic will has been the principal cause of shying away from formulating a transparent PE reform policy.

Policy Measures in 1990s

Between 1990 and 1999 there have been frequent changes in the government, barring July 1991 to June 1996 during which period a minority government was at the helm of affairs.

The year 1990 saw two governments, both of which were the by-products of coalition. During the year, the thought of employee stock ownership in public enterprises gained momentum and worker's participation in management assumed ascendancy. The concept of regulated growth in investment in public enterprise marked its emergence.

Between 1991 - 1996

The fiscal crisis reached its peak in 1991 and the government had to approach global financial institutions for stabilisation and structural adjustment. As a part of the conditionalities imposed, the government had to announce some important measures to restructure public enterprises.

Portfolio

It was decided to review the portfolio of public sector investments with a view to focus on strategic, hi-tech and essential infrastructure. Consequently, enterprises which were operating in competitive sectors of the economy where the private sector had registered its emphatic presence were decided to be hived-off. This policy pronouncement provided a forceful hint to public enterprises to review their spectrum of activities with the objective of unloading non-core and peripheral functions. It was expected that the follow up of this measure would result in making public enterprises lean and mean. The government felt that a selective public enterprise portfolio would bring down the transactions cost, improve the quality of control and add to the efficiency of the public enterprise system.

Reference to the Board for Industrial and Financial Reconstruction (BIFR)

At the beginning of the 1990s itself, a large number of public enterprises had fallen sick. They constituted about 25 per cent of the then operating public enterprises. The trends in the financial results of the remaining public enterprises revealed the likelihood of more public enterprises falling sick. The government did not have an exit policy for public enterprises and it refrained from following the path adopted by the private sector. It, therefore, decided to use the BIFR route, which provided a fair opportunity to public enterprises to evolve suitable revival packages and implement them or else wind up with a social safety net. Unlike the private sector which throws away the baby with the bathwater, the government suggested public enterprises to have a human face. Each enterprise was directed to formulate its own social safety net comprising voluntary retirement, and retaining and redeployment schemes for workers. The government made an announcement to set up the National Renewal Fund (NRF), the finances for which had to be gathered from global agencies, while part of the proceeds were to come from disinvestments.

Mobilisation of Funds, Disinvestments and Public Participation

The 1990s started with a severe resource crunch. In February 1990 the coffers of the government did not have adequate money to pay for the employees' salaries. This was an adequate hint about the shape of things to come. The constant increase in social sector spending and the move to curtail fiscal deficits did not leave much scope for public enterprise to depend on the government for funding. The government permitted public enterprises to access international capital markets and make forays into the Indian capital market.

The partial disinvestment in public enterprises was introduced as a double-edged sword aimed to reduce, on the one hand, the fiscal deficits of the government, and enhance the degree of 'publicness' in public enterprises, on the other, through wider participation in their shareholdings by general investing public, banks, mutual funds, workers and financial institutions.

Up-gradation of Technology

For the introduction of the state-of-the-art technology, it was decided that public enterprises would be given a free hand and the funds for such upgradation would come from the disinvestment proceeds or restructuring packages approved by the global financial institutions.

Governing Boards

It was realised that strengthening the institution of the Governing Boards was necessary in order to professionalise public enterprises and make them effective business entities. A number of steps were suggested for revamp. It was decided that the number of government nominees was not to exceed two. Further, part-time directors were expected to bring in a breath of fresh air to the public enterprises and were to have a greater say. More room was made for the representation of professionals, who were expected to provide sound business advice. The representation of different interest groups also received attention and the worker's representation on the Boards was accepted in principle.

Accountability and Autonomy

To solve this tangle, the government emphasised the need for widening and deepening the concept of Memorandum of Understanding (MoU). It wanted the contracts to be negotiated well in advance and subsequent delegation and decentralisation of powers within the enterprise. It advocated sincere involvement of public enterprises in the formulation and implementation of MoU to thwart unnecessary public criticism on the count of public accountability, conferment of greater autonomy to these enterprises gradually over a period of time with regard to matters concerning capital expenditure, mobilisation of funds, formulation of incentive schemes, joint ventures, etc.

1997

The Janata Dal government, during this period, initiated some important measures and made public its unambiguous stand of speeding up the disinvestment process through majority stake in shareholdings.

Disinvestment Commission

The government set up through an executive order, the Disinvestment Commission which was responsible for reporting its scheme on the disinvestment of select public enterprises. It was also empowered, among other things, to suggest to the government the appointment of global advisors.

Navratnas and Miniratnas

In order to prepare giant public enterprises for global competition and enable them to assume the role of Indian multinationals, the government identified 9 enterprises (namely, Bharat Heavy Electricals Limited, Steel Authority of India Limited, Mahanagar Telephone Nigam Limited, Videsh Sanchar Nigam Limited, National Thermal Power Corporation, Bharat Petroleum Corporation Ltd., Hindustan Petroleum Corporation Ltd., Indian Oil Corporation Ltd, Indian Petrochemicals Corporation Ltd., Oil & Natural Gas Corporation) as navaratnas and 97 enterprises as miniratnas, based on their record with regard to constant profitability and size of capital. Later, the list of navaratnas was extended from 9 to 11 to accommodate MTNL and VSNL. Subsequently, the number of miniratnas was scaled down from 97 to 45. The rationale behind identification of these enterprises as navaratnas and miniratnas was to increase their economic and operational autonomy in proportion to their financial and commercial success, as also to provide them special leverage to face competition in Indian and global markets by freeing them from bureaucratic and procedural hurdles.

Guidelines

The government appointed the Vittal Committee to examine the guidelines issued to public enterprises from time to time. The Vittal Committee suggested that 762 guidelines out of the 892 issued to public enterprises be slashed. However, the Government abolished 696 guidelines.

Distribution of Dividends

The profit-making public enterprises had to declare 30 per cent of the net profits as dividends as opposed to the earlier practice of capitalising profits.

1998

The coalition government during this year had to do a lot of tight rope walking with the left front and had to therefore adopt a mild posture with regard to off-loading public enterprises from its portfolio.

Rehabilitation Package

The government decided to prepare rehabilitation packages for sick public enterprises to give them a chance for revival instead of going for their quiet closure / privatisation.

Redefining the scope of the Disinvestment Commission

The government wanted the Commission to make suggestions regarding disinvestments of only those enterprises which it referred to the commission. The Commission was divested of its powers to recommend the names of global advisors.

1999

The rightist government of the day is in all preparedness to accelerate the tempo of the disinvestment programme and reduce the scope of public enterprise activities in the Indian economy.

Privatisation

For the first time, during the 1990s, the government in its budget presented to the parliament used the word 'privatisation'. The government went all out to show its commitment to privatise public enterprises and restore the powers of the Disinvestment Commission.

Competition

The government initiated the process of evolving a competition policy. It exhorted public enterprises to be competitive.

Salaries and Wages

While accepting the Mohan Committee report on wage revision in public enterprises, the government left it to each and every public enterprise to examine its paying capacity to meet the burden arising out of its implementation. The government categorised public enterprise into 3 divisions: public enterprises earning profits continuously for three years; public enterprises recording mixed performance; and public enterprises suffering from sickness. Those enterprises which were consistently earning profits could implement the revision, the mixed performance enterprises were required to take the approval of the respective ministries and the sick enterprises had to get the burden of implementation incorporated in the rehabilitation packages.

We propose below to critically evaluate the success in the implementation of these measures and assess their overall impact on the functioning of public enterprises.

Policy Measures: 2000-2002

The government decided to discontinue the National Renewal Fund (NRF) in its present form and place the funds required for retraining/rehabilitation of employees who had availed VRS under the Department of Public Enterprises (DPE). The DPE would involve itself in this work from 2001-2002 with a plan fund of Rs.11.50 crore. It would be concerned with the employees of the Central Public Enterprises (CPEs). The Ministry of Labour and the Ministry of Small Scale Industries would concern themselves with the employees of State Level Public Enterprises (SLPEs).

The Committee of Secretaries decided to declare a deadline for the closure of sick non-revivable PEs and provide a window for VRS/ voluntary separation scheme (VSS), which if non-availed by a worker would entitle him to the normal retrenchment compensation.

Budget: 2000-2001

In the budget presented to the Parliament for the fiscal year 2000-2001, the government decided to bring down its equity in all non-strategic PEs to 26 per cent or lower, if necessary. The government further announced that the entire receipts from disinvestment and privatisation will be used for meeting expenditure in social sectors, restructuring of PEs and retiring public debt. The newly setup Department of Disinvestment for providing thrust to the process of disinvestment, is now headed by a full-fledged Minister for Disinvestment.

The Disinvestment Commission was reconstituted in 2001 with part time and full time members with the mandate to examine disinvestment possibilities in the specific enterprises and assess the disinvestment scenario in general.

Budget: 2001-2002

The government continued with its earlier policy on PE. A target of realising an amount of Rs.12,000crore through disinvestment in PEs was setup in this budget. Out of this, an amount of Rs.7,000 crore was to be used for providing restructuring assistance to PEs, safety net to workers, reduction of debt burden, and the sum of Rs.5000 crore were to be used to provide additional budgetary support for the Plan in the infrastructure sector.

Performance

That PEs have done commendably well both before and after economic liberalisation is a very widely known fact. Though the ideologues favouring economic reforms have always rated PE performance below the mark. Table-1 showing public sector contribution in total industrial production gives a different picture. The table points out a clear cut hold of public sector on the industrial economy. In this context, it is significant to note that the development experts have been advising to give a fresh thought of providing new impetus to manufacturing in the absence of which the services dominated structure of the Indian economy cannot satisfy the employment and growth demands.

Table-1

Public Sector's Contribution in Total Industrial Production

Item	*National Production (NP)*		*Public Sector's Production (PSP)*		*PSP to NP (%)*	
	1968-69	2000-01	1968-69	2000-01	1968-69	2000-01
Fuel (Million Tonnes)						
Coal	71.40	309.63	12.61	300.52	17.66	97.05
Lignite	3.98	22.95	3.98	22.95	100.00	100.00
Petroleum (Million Tonnes)						
Crude Oil	6.06	32.43	3.08	28.34	50.83	87.39

(Contd.)

Natural Gas	NA	29.48	NA	25.88	NA	87.79
Refined Crude	16.55	103.44	8.09	70.97	48.88	68.61
Basic Metals (Million Tonnes)						
Finished Steel	4.58	29.70	2.55	9.61	55.68	32.35
Non-Ferrous Metals (000 Tonnes)						
Aluminium	125.63	642.84	Nil	317.18	Nil	49.34
Primary Lead	1.9	45.5	1.9	33.5	100.00	73.62
Zinc	17.0	178.01	13.7	149.5	80.60	83.28
Fertilisers (000 Tonnes)						
Nitrogenous	563	10964	401	3222	71.23	29.39
Phosphatic	213	3748	53.0	628	24.86	16.75

Source: Public Enterprise Survey 2000-2001, Vol. 1, Department of Public Enterprise, New Delhi, p. 29.

The financial performance of PEs has attracted a tirade of criticism from many quarters. Such critiques see virtue in the financial performance of private enterprises without going into the depth of the structure of profitability and the process through which profits have been arrived at. Table-2 depicts the trend of profitability in PEs which clearly points out to a very high profit before interest and taxes to capital employed(14.7 percent), profit before depreciation, interest and taxes to capital employed(21.0 percent)and even dividend payout (52.8 percent). It is for the ideologues to find out where the counterparts in the private sector stand. So far as the process of computing profits is concerned, the creative accounting has not been the strength of PEs. The private sector has been indulging rampantly in the misuse of the option of selecting the method of depreciation accounting, inventory valuation, treatment of expenses as revenue and capital, declaring dividends from capital and misstating facts. It has become a usual practice to create value for shareholders through mergers and acquisitions which hardly add value to the national economy at the macro level. It is common knowledge that private sector draws heavily

Table-2
Trend of Profitability (Rs. in Crore)

Particulars	91-92	92-93	93-94	94-95	95-96	96-97	97-98	98-99	99-00	00-01
No. of Operating Enterprises	237	239	240	241	239	236	236	235	232	234
Capital Employed	117991	140110	159836	162451	173948	231178	249855	265093	302867	330649
Profit Before Dep. Interest & Tax (PBDIT)	22224	25227	27707	33384	40161	44457	53062	56495	62212	69288
Depreciation	8548	9270	9151	107554	12574	13542	15856	16768	19942	20520
Profit Before Int & Tax (PBIT)	13676	15957	18556	22630	27587	30915	37206	39727	42270	48768
Interest	9673	10881	11901	12862	13966	15537	17990	20025	20233	23802
Profit Before Tax(PBT)	4003	5076	6655	9768	13621	15378	19216	19702	22037	24966
Tax Provisions	1647	1805	2110	2581	4047	5192	5634	6499	7706	9313
Net Profit	2356	3271	4545	7187	9574	10186	13582	13203	14331	156153
Profit of Profit Making PEs	6079	7384	9768	12070	14763	16125	20279	22508	24633	28492

(Contd...)

Loss of Loss Incurring PEs	3723	4113	5223	4883	5188	5939	6697	9305	10302	12839
No. of Profit Making PEs	133	131	121	130	132	129	134	126	126	122
No. of Loss Incurring PEs	102	106	116	109	102	104	100	107	105	111
No. of No Profit/ No Loss PEs	2	2	3	2	5	3	2	2	1	1
Dividend Dividend Tax	687	792	1028	1436	2205	2836	3609	4932	5455	8260
Retained Profit	1669	2479	3517	5751	7369	7089	9509	7734	8085	6551
Financial Ratio (%)										
PBDIT to Capital Employed	18.8	18.0	17.3	20.6	23.1	19.2	21.2	21.3	20.5	21.0
PBIT to Capital Employed	11.6	11.4	11.6	13.9	15.9	13.4	14.9	15.0	14.0	14.7
Dividend Payout	29.2	24.2	22.6	20.0	23.0	27.8	26.6	37.4	38.1	52.8

Source: Public Enterprise Survey 2000-01, Volume 1, Department of Public Enterprises, New Delhi, p.25.

from development financial institutions and organised capital markets. The revolution in the structure of finance visiting PEs has been kept at the bay by the private sector. The protagonists of the private sector should find out as to whether the market based funding has reached the same proportions as that of PEs.

Table-3 presents the resource mobilisation and Plan investment by central PEs.

Table-3

Resources Mobilisation and Plan Investment by Central Public Sector Enterprises

(Rs. in crores)

Year	*Net Internal Resources*	*Extra Budgetary Resources*	*Budgetary Support*	*Plan Outlay*
VIII Plan Period				
1992-93	10081.30	11001.43	3443.66	24526.89
1993-94	9862.03	14743.93	4067.65	28673.61
1994-95	14932.00	13445.53	4379.59	32757.12
1995-96	16726.90	12674.02	3919.46	33320.38
1996-97	13157.81	16901.23	3644.37	33703.41
Total VIII Plan	**64760.54**	**68766.14**	**19454.73**	**152981.41**
1997-98	15111.81	14912.25	3840.56	33864.62
1998-99	19294.95	12280.46	4250.32	35825.73
1999-00	13245.95	17700.37	4528.66	35474.98
2000-01	25046.96	18007.71	4472.09	47526.76

Source: Public Enterprise Survey 2000-01, Volume 1, Department of Public Enterprises, New Delhi, p.90.

The budgetary support has become static. The net internal resources generation registered a whooping increase of about 150 percent and the extra budgetary resources increased by about 65 percent. An analysis of these figures will reveal facts about their access to capital markets – Indian and foreign, widening the instruments base, and increasing their potential to create internal resources through depreciation charge and write-offs.

The productivity growth has emerged as the main strength in PEs which could be leveraged by them to enhance their competitiveness in the global markets. Though the private sector was expected to lead the economy in this direction, it has not been able to achieve much which is borne out by the frustration of the Bombay and Bangalore clubs. Table-4 presents the productivity measures of selected PE units.

Table-4

Productivity Measures of Selected Public Sector Units

Public Sector Unit/ Productivity Measure	*1995-96*	*1996-97*	*1997-98*	*CAGR %*
NALCO				
Value added/employee (Rs. Lakhs)	17.06	15.04	16.95	- .3
Return on Capital (%)	19.24	15.14	15.53	
NTPC				
Value added/employee (Rs. Lakhs)	16.12	17.95	22.88	19.13
Return on Capital (%)	10.39	11.05	12.95	
Bharat Petroleum				
Value added/employee (Rs. Lakhs)	12.64	16.75	12.05	-2.36
Return on Capital (%)	23.42	18.02	24.81	
Hindustan Antibiotics				
Value added/employee (Rs. Lakhs)	0.91	0.70	0.82	-5.07
Return on Capital (%)	- 2.98	-10.18	-11.80	
IDPL				
Value added/employee (Rs. Lakhs)	10.53	-0.16	-0.24	
Return on Capital (-ve capital)				

(Contd.)

Karnataka Antibiotics				
Value added/employee (Rs. Lakhs)	1.94	1.81	2.19	6.25
Return on Capital (%)	17.11	17.00	16.74	
BHEL				
Value added/employee (Rs. Lakhs)	2.80	3.16	3.51	11.96
Return on Capital (%)	21.98	24.07	26.91	
HMT				
Value added/employee (Rs. Lakhs)	1.28	1.75	1.78	17.92
Return on Capital (%)	5.09	15.01	12.45	
Modern Foods				
Value added/employee (Rs. Lakhs)	1.51	1.75	1.42	-3.03
Return on Capital (%)	30.04	27.55	15.06	
NTC				
Value added/employee (Rs. Lakhs)	0.10	0.58	0.51	126
Return on Capital (-ve capital)	NA	NA	NA	NA
CMC				
Value added/employee (Rs. Lakhs)	2.46	2.46	3.01	10.61
Return on Capital (%)	24.30	11.32	14.56	
Air India				
Value added/employee (Rs. Lakhs)	4.42	5.00	7.08	26.56
Return on Capital (%)	-3.06	-3.66	1.25	
Indian Airlines				
Value added/employee (Rs. Lakhs)	4.41	5.40	6.32	19.71
Return on Capital (%)	6.02	8.67	11.58	
SAIL				
Value added/employee (Rs. Lakhs)	2.63	2.55	2.73	1.88
Return on Capital (%)	15.48	9.00	8.11	

Source: Note prepared by IIM Ahmedabad, for the Working Group on Public Sector Undertaking, Department of Public Enterprises, Ministry of Heavy Industries & Public Enterprises, Government of India, New Delhi, p.3.

Table- 5
All India: All States Aggregates

	State Equity to Total Equity	*State Debt Total Debt*	*PBIT as % of Sales*	*Net Profit as % Sales*	*Accumulated losses as % of Capital*	*Net worth as % of Investment*	*Sales as % of Investment*	*Gross Margin as % of Sales*	*Net Profit as % of Total Equity*	*Sales as % Capital Employed*	*Net Worth as % of Investment*	*Accumulated losses as % of Net Worth*	*PBIT as % of Capital Employed*
1990-91	0.724627	0.483282	7.545072	-2.11265	26.2822	13.52262	61.47483	15.1096	-5.65447	82.00194	13.52262	145.7049	6.187106
1991-92	0.705557	0.483755	6.188647	-9.13454	25.34989	15.76769	60.64115	15.99992	-20.5733	80.69753	15.76769	120.8134	4.994086
1992-93	0.673559	0.469659	7.154993	-1.61448	25.10098	17.7244	66.06298	15.91677	-3.76463	88.44172	17.7244	105.7841	6.327999
1993-94	0.715598	0.450518	8.916732	-1.58973	17.11237	19.71616	59.70851	16.25385	-3.29502	56.82943	19.71616	91.19077	5.067328
1994-95	0.742689	0.418431	9.378317	0.40922	23.10026	19.97908	61.29933	15.75246	0.886933	77.3625	19.97908	91.61498	7.2553
1995-96	0.676826	0.438009	8.665135	-0.79507	20.91645	28.84698	68.62148	14.36774	-1.74415	83.60066	28.84698	59.51659	7.24411
1996-97	0.704698	0.423925	8.775705	-2.60756	20.232	28.21755	57.93891	17.20838	-4.55601	70.15143	28.21755	59.21793	6.156283
1997-98	0.70592	0.428032	9.715798	-1.85109	21.70503	27.90449	58.67739	14.99972	-3.23046	72.63134	27.90449	62.83954	7.056715
1998-99	0.732835	0.32453	4.861473	-4.32643	27.51905	30.92823	52.12172	12.3553	-6.52219	67.96206	30.92823	68.23869	3.303957

Source: Public Policy Group Database , Research Division, IPE

Though the performance of CPEs could be benchmarked against the Indian and global enterprises in the private sector, their practices may certainly require the desired toning up. Further, the performance of the SLPEs erode the good work done by CPEs. The SLPEs are heterogeneous enterprises with widely varying investment, output, activity, managerial and financial resources profiles, mostly managed by officers of the Indian Administrative Service. The origins of these enterprises were dominated by political ends. They have utterly lacked business sense and dynamism. Their accountability mechanisms demotivate them to do financially well. Table-5 provides basic data on the various financial performance parameters of these enterprises.

Dissecting PE Policy and Performance

Disinvestment has been the key component of PE policy. The realisations of resources through disinvestment from 1991-92 to 2001-02 have been far lower as shown in Table-6.

Table-6
Disinvestment in Public Sector Undertakings

Year	*Target (Rs. Crore)*	*Achievement (Rs. Crore)*
1991-92	2500	3,038
1992-93	2500	1,913
1993-94	3500	Nil
1994-95	4000	4,843
1995-96	7000	168
1996-97	5000	380
1997-98	4800	910
1998-99	5000	5,371
1999-00	10,000	1,829
2000-01	10,000	1,869
2001-02	12,000	*

Source: Economic Survey 2001-02, Government of India, Ministry of Finance, Economic Division.

Disinvestment Proceeds during 2001-02

Name of PSUs	*Percentage of Equity Disinvested (percent)*	*Proceeds Realised / to be realised (Rs.crore)*
1. HTL Limited	74	55
2. CMC Limited	51	152
3. India Tourism Development Corporation – 9 Hotels	100 in 8 hotels Long-term lease –cum management contract in 1 hotel	181
4. Hotel Corporation of India Limited- 3 Hotels	100	** 243
5. IBP Limited	34	1,154
6. Videsh Sanchar Nigam Limited (Transfer of Cash Reserves)	25	* 3,689
7. State Trading Corporation of India Limited (Transfer of Cash Reserves)	-	* 40
8. Minerals and Metals Trading Corporation of India Limited (Transfer of Cash Reserves)	-	* 60
Total #		5,573

*Decision on withdrawal of reserves taken. Action being taken to implement the decision.

** Proceeds to go to Air India

*** Includes Rs.2,250 crore as dividend /special dividend and tax.

 # Total may not tally because of rounding off

Instead of disinvestment, publicising of PEs, should have been attempted which would have resulted in competition, demonopolisation and mobilisation of resources without changing the organisational attributes. The missing links in disinvestments is gross omission of instituting systems of corporate governance, restructuring PEs, readying them for interface with domestic and international markets, bureaucratisation of disinvestment process, shying away from transparency, and adoption of the method of strategic sale. The valuation process has drawn more controversy than support. The multiple audit and approvals have resulted in less mobilisation of resources and harming the basic culture of enterprise itself. The technicalities such as sales of cross-holdings is yet to have a parallel anywhere in the world. Barring PEs from participating in bidding for the purchase of the shareholdings of another enterprise does not qualify as healthy decision from any parameter. The exclusion of the PE management and workers from the disinvestment process raises questions about the seriousness of the process. Making revenue realisation as the key driver makes a mockery of the whole process of disinvestment. Through IPOs, PEs could have achieved the objective of debureaucratisation and depoliticisation. However, this was not acceptable to the forces in power. This whole chain of action has ultimately painted PEs in black. The 12 months ending June 2002 have seen as many as 24 sell-offs. These ranged from small PEs such as Hindustan Teleprinters, a couple of Hotels of ITDC to big ticket sales like VSNL, IPCL, IBP and CMC. These disinvestments have not created the desired impact as could have happened in case of a handful of few large PEs operating in non-strategic sectors had been divested.

Privatisation

Not content with partial disinvestment the PE policy has been advocating wholesale privatisation. The privatisation of power sector is worth discussing here. The trifurcating of state electricity boards into generation, transmission and distribution entities was supposed to transform power sector in terms of reduction of T&D losses, availability of per capita power, reduction in subsidies and halt in the increase of per unit cost of supply. The Central Electricity Regulatory Commission

(CERC) and the State Electricity Regulatory Commissions were set up to take over the functions of the centre and states respectively. The independent power producers (IPPs) were allowed to come in. the Indian Electricity Act, was reformulated and the Indian Electricity Act 2001 is awaiting comprehensive amendments to pave the way for private participation. The Orissa state electricity reforms were quoted as big success. However the present scenario does not inspire much confidence as the T&D losses continue to be around 18-20 percent and the power tariffs have had a steep increase. The IPPs padded their investments which ought to create a big hole in the pocket of the innocent consumer. Even with the widely publicised success for Orissa's power sector reforms, the T&D losses are said to be around 45 percent.

The privatisation policy is intended to included in its sweep the state road transport corporations. These corporations have been provided un-optimal capital structure, un-economical routes, and have to face considerable onslaught on their autonomy in terms of purchases of inputs, appointment of professionals and acquisition of buses. The root cause of their losses is connected to their onus of fulfilling social obligations. For instance, in Andhra Pradesh, the social obligations cost the Andhra Pradesh State Road Transport Corporation about Rs.250 crore, whereas their net losses having in the range of Rs.150-200crores. The higher incidence of motor vehicle tax as compared to other states and the illicit operations of the private passenger road transport operators, has pushed the Corporation heavy into the red.

The blanket position taken by the government of privatising PEs do not appear to be conducive for the growth of the economy. By examining the MoUs of several PEs, the following PEs appear of strategic importance and thereby disqualify for privatisation. There are number of PEs with dominant market shares such as National Hydro Power Corporation (NHPC), National Thermal Power Corporation (NTPC), North Eastern Electric Power Corporation (NEEPCO),

Table-7
The Effects of Coalition Politics on Public Enterprise Activity

S.No.	*Name of the Govt. Policy Initiative*	*Congress (I) (1991-96)*	*United Front(D) (1996-97)*	*United Front (G) (1997-98)*	*Bharatiya Janata Party (1998-to-date)*
1	Public Enterprise(PE) Portfolio	Select divestment	Reduction of portfolio to a bare minimum	Select divestment	Complete divestment
2	Boards of Directors	Professionali-sation of Boards	Induction of industr-ialists/ general interests	Continuation of domination of bureaucrats	Bigger role to Public Enterprise Selection Board and pruning the role of vigilance agencies in the appointment of directors.
3	Chief Executive Officer	Appointment for 5 years	Toplessness in PEs	Long tenures for CEO	Mixed Policy of uncertain and long tenures
4	Memorandum of Understanding (MOU)	Introduction of MOU as performance monitoring mechanism	Continuation of Congress(I) policy without rewards and punishment	UF(D) policy continued	UF(D) policy continued
5	Disinvestment	Partial disinvestment and announcement of a full-fledged statutory commission on Disinvestment reduced	Majority-stake disinvestment; appointment of Disinvestment Commission with	UF(D) policy continued	Majority-stake disinvestment with Special Purpose Vehicle/ Trusts and preference to internal investors. The

(Contd...)

		the role of Government functionaries and bureaucrats.	executive powers only		Government established Department of Disinvestment to speed up the process of disinvestment.
6	Closure of Sick Units	Closure of continuous cash-loss making PEs	Closure of units approved by the Board for Industrial and Financial Reconstruction (BIFR)	Uncertain about its stand on closure of sick PEs	Hastening the pace of closure of sick units
7	Navaratnas and Miniratnas	No identification of enterprises to be treated on different footing	Identification of Navaratnas (11 PEs) and Miniratnas (97 PEs) subsequently reduced to 45 PEs	Continuation of UF(D) policy without the initiation of relevant measures	Restructuring of Navaratna/Miniratna PE Boards.
8	Government intervention through guidelines	Continue such intervention	Deletion of irrelevant guidelines	892 guidelines reduced to about 130.	UF(G) policy continued
9	Reduction of Budgetary Support	General policy of reduction of budgetary support reduction	Introduction of element of selectivity in the general expenditure being stepped of budgetary support	UF(D) policy continued	UF (D) policy continued while Government up to overcome recession

(Contd...)

10	De-monopolisation	Continuation of monopolisation of PEs in certain sectors	Selective demonopolisation in sectors such as power, telecommunication banking and finance, transport, etc.	UF(D) policy continued	Massive demonopolisation of PEs
11	Globalisation	Economic liberalisation in PEs	Did not take relevant measures for globalisation such as changing of Articles of Association of PEs, amendment of Article 12 of the Indian Constitution, reduction of multiple audits, etc.	Policy of UF(D) continued	Policy of UF(G) continued
12	Internal Restructuring	Commercialisation of PEs and programme to corporatise and privatise PEs were announced but no freedom to purchase goods, hire and fire employees, etc., was extended	Heavy subsidies to consumers of PE goods continued although public enterprise policy was framed in favour of commercialisation and corporatisation	Onslaughts on PEs of UF(D) continued	Onslaughts on PEs of UF(G) continued

Bharat Heavy Electricals Limited (BHEL) and Food Corporation of India (FCI). These cannot be precisely privastised as they do not have their rivals in the private sector. There are a number of PEs discharging social responsibilities in a major way. These include Electricity Trade and Technical Development Corporation (ETTDC), Handicrafts and Handloom Export Corporation (HHEC), Semiconductor Complex Limited, Coal Mining Project Development Institute (CMPDI), Educational Consultants India Limited (EdCIL), Hospital Service Consultancy Service, National Small Industries Corporation (NSIC), Export Credit Guarantee Corporation (ECGC), National Research Development Corporation (NRDC), Artificial Limbs Manufacturing Company of India Limited, National Backward Class Finance and Development Corporation, National Handicapped Finance and Development Corporation, National Minorities Development and Finance Corporation, National SC/ST Development Finance Corporation, National Safari Karmachari Finance Corporation.

It is difficult to privatise even these units unless a mechanism is put in place to discharge their functions.

The impact of coalition politics has acted as a major drag on the performance of PEs. Each coalition in power was ridden with major contradictions about their stand on the various issues and the various aspects of PE policy. The coalition politics has treated PEs as milch cow without caring for their well being (Table-7).

Navartna/Miniratna PEs

The government's initiative of granting more operational autonomy to grand PEs has not produced the desired results, not because, the PEs were wanting in this respect, but for the government's lack of true willingness to divest itself of the controlling power. The Chinese example is worth quoting in this regard. As a part of the new economic policy, China in 1999, has prepared a list of subjects wherein it would not muddle with the working of the non-privatised PEs. The first hand studies point out that the scheme is working very well. Table- 8 points out the limitations of the Navaratna/Miniratna PEs in India.

Table-8
Navaratna/Miniratna Package and Its Impact

Details	*No. of Respondents*			
	Strongly agree	*Agree*	*Neutral*	*Disagree*
a) There is deregulation, depoliticalisation and debureaucratisation	-	3	2	4
b) Decision-making powers vested in various Government agencies has reduced (or altered)	-	5	2	2
c) There is enhanced delegation of powers to the Board now	-	8	-	2
d) Board is given a free hand in taking policy decisions	-	5	2	1
e) There are now transparent and effective systems of decision-making and internal monitoring	-	6	1	1
f) Monitoring the performance of the PE is done primarily by the Board	-	6	1	1
g) Autonomy of the PE has increased	-	4	1	3
h) Accountability of the Management has increased	2	3	2	1
i) Overall performance of the PE has improved	1	5	1	1
j) Employees at all levels are encouraged or actively involved in the areas of quality improvement, productivity, marketing and performance upgradation	2	4	1	1

Source: Database, Public Policy Group, IPE.

Future Scenario

The demystification of the performance of PEs points out very clearly that in the name of sub-optimal performance, various interest groups have tried fishing in the troubled waters. In other words, the institution of a healthy performance system is the need of the hour. The recent management studies suggest the institution of a performance ethic code which survives on performance feedback and consequence management. PEs should become people intensive, financial control driven, operation oriented, opportunity providers, incentive givers and a place humming with values and beliefs. Strong organisations provide a rate of return which is higher by 7 percent to the average rate of return. They should have few layers, transparent, highly aggressive, consistent over time in aspirations. The motivation levers should spawn recognising performance, chances to grow into bigger roles, freedom to shape on work content and autonomy to work on ideas. The navaratna/miniratna system intended to bring a fundamental revolution in the concept of autonomy and accountability turned out to be a fiasco in the absence of the performance ethic framework which was very much within the capability ambit of PEs but was beyond the imagination of the architect of the navaratna/miniratna thought for their being a part of the system which was action oriented.

To Conclude

The period 1991/92 to 2001\02 saw a series of policy measures aimed to dismantle public sector to give fillip to private monopoly and increase the dependence of the Indian economy on global economic powers. An attempt has been made to demystify the existing beliefs about the performance of PEs. Not only that they have done exceedingly well against all odds, but they have even performed better than their counterparts in the private sector. The productivity analysis reveals that the performance of many such units could be benchmarked with the international entities. The government policy of disinvestment, privatisation, and restructuring has created a bias against these enterprises as the various formulations in this regard, are not based on economic reasoning. The impact of coalition politics has destabilised PEs and benefited private enterprise.

Chapter II

Research on Management of Public Enterprises in India

Research on management of public enterprises (PEs) initially began under government initiative, and subsequently private researchers, both individuals and institutions contributed to this kind of research. Various studies conducted on this issue indicate that PE research has undergone radical transformation over a period of time. Its nature, canvas and dimensions have broadened to keep pace with the dynamic settings within which PEs operate. The issues, therefore, range from finance, marketing and business policy to issues on environment and human resource management. However, assessment of research reveals presence of significant gaps in each of these areas. Although, some works have been successful in conceptualising and capturing certain problems associated with PE operations, they did not contribute significantly towards policy making or providing new methodological inputs. The social relevance of such research also has turned out to be limited. We, therefore, feel that the future research thrusts should be so designed as to overcome these pitfalls. We, therefore, recommend that more of collaborative research could be taken up between government agencies/ PEs research scholars / Institutions to make research on management of PEs more relevant and effective.

Introduction

PEs form an important segment of public sector in India. During the last five decades PEs have phenomenally grown in terms of investment and numbers. The rising investment in PEs, with their continuing demand for further investments, and the resource constraints faced by the economy have led to a questioning of their future role. Questions have also been raised as to how far PEs have succeeded in fulfilling the expectations with which they were set up. These questions have been answered in many ways. Various initiatives by the government have set the trend to make PEs more effective and efficient. There are also initiatives of divesting the enterprises under the guidance of Department of Disinvestment (DoD) set up in 1999. There have been wide publications on related issues but most of the writings on the issue have been polemical, apologetic or sometimes downright condemnatory. However, there has been albeit inadequate research on PE performance and problems which has gone without much notice. This is partly due to the fact that research efforts on PEs have been directed towards specific issues based on narrow database, with no attempt to integrate or synthesise such research works.

The objective of this book is basically to consider various aspects of existing research as well as to suggest what should be the future thrusts of management research on PEs. The coverage of the publication is restricted to central and state level PEs. The study covers the period from 1951 to 2002. The source of information consists of published and unpublished literature as well as informal discussions with researchers, experts and policy makers. The classified information available in the form of studies and reports with the central and state level PEs and other organisations also form a part of the book.

Genesis of Research

The genesis of research on management of PEs in India unlike many other countries began under government aegis. PEs were assigned a place of prime importance in the Industrial Policy Resolution (IPR) of 1948. The position continued to remain the same in the IPR of 1956. The policy pronouncements in 1977 however inclined in favour of the private sector enterprises. This was reversed to some extent after 1980. It may be noted that in reality the IPR of 1956 has governed the growth and regulation of industries in India.

Development planning was initiated in the year 1951 with the commencement of the first Five Year Plan. Right from the first Five Year Plan to the present plan period PEs have been assigned the place of pride in our developmental efforts. It is therefore, natural that from time to time attempts have been made by the government to assess the efficacy of these enterprises as instruments of growth and tools of public policy. Consequently we find number of Committees and Commissions being set up by the Government to look into the working of PEs.

In the First Five Year Plan the Government appointed Gorwala Committee and Appleby Committee to enquire into the efficient conduct and operation of PEs. During the Second Five Year Plan, the Krishna Menon Committee was set up by the Congress to sort out the problems of PE-Government interface and several related issues. During the Third Plan period the government set up the Administrative Reforms Commission and one of its Study Groups examined their functioning of PEs and submitted a detailed report containing a plethora of prescription to improve their work. The Congress set up the Pathak Committee in the Fifth Plan period to go into the working of PEs. During the same period, the Economic Administrative Reforms Commission made an in depth study of the problems affecting the performance of PEs. The Seventh Plan period covered an important report covering the different aspects of PE Management, viz., the Arjun Sengupta Committee Report. The Eighth Plan period saw the review of the portfolio of public sector investments with a view to focussing the public sector on strategic, hi-tech, and essential infrastructure and opening other areas selectively to private sector. The Sick Industrial Companies Act, 1985, was amended for enabling referral of sick PEs to BIFR for their revival/rehabilitation or closure. A social security mechanism was also created. A system of MoU was introduced to improve the management of PEs and the concept of Navaratnas and Mini-Ratnas for giving autonomy to PEs was also introduced. The Ninth Plan's focus is on rate of industrial growth, infrastructure building, exports, SSI reservation, flexibility in labour legislation, disinvestment of PEs, regional balance and R&D.

The legislative wing of the government also contributed commendably to the understanding of PE performance and problems. Though, the reports of the legislative committees on PEs cannot be regarded as research pieces, several of them are an in depth examination of the problems of PEs, both specific and general in nature. It would therefore be appropriate to recount their contribution here.

Legislative reports on PEs began from the first Lok Sabha. The Public Accounts Committee (PAC) till the year 1964 submitted about 48 reports to the Indian Parliament. In the year 1964 with the setting up of the Committee on Public Undertakings (COPU), the scope and content of legislative research on PEs tremendously increased. Many of the states followed this by setting up similar committees. By the end of the thirteenth Lok Sabha, COPU submitted around 600 reports on PEs, which is a fast growing area. This is different from academic research in the sense that the purpose of policy research is very sharp and narrowly defined and must have direct utility. In contrast, the academic research does not address itself to specific problems facing the PEs and the Government. The academic research is often of a historical nature. However, we must also add that some of these research works sharply focus on well-defined issues, related to public policy towards PEs and those of which are of interest to PE executives.

International Research

Another interesting trend seen in the current literature on PEs is that some of the International institutions consisting of universities abroad and agencies such as International Monetary Fund and World Bank are researching and analysing the problems pertaining to PEs in India. Their interest, in the management of public sector in India stems from their concern regarding the conditions of repayment of financial assistance given to India, redundancy of surplus manpower in public enterprises, disinvestment etc.

Collaborative Research

An interesting trend observed in the current research on PEs is the interactive and synergic nature of research that is being carried out between institutions both at the national and international development research corporations. Canada heralded the beginning of this era by collaborating with the Indian Institute of Management, Bangalore in 1976 on specific country study, as a part of its comprehensive international research project on PEs. More recently the Commonwealth Secretariat and International Centre for Public Enterprises, Ljubljana collaborated with Bureau of Public Enterprise, Government of India, New Delhi, Indian Institute of Management, Calcutta and Institute of Public Enterprise (IPE), Hyderabad. Another example of such a project is the collaboration between London Business School and IPE under the auspices of the British Council. The two institutions have researched on specific aspects relating to the functioning of PEs and intend to share the experiences to the benefit of their own countries. The Boston Area Group on PEs has also been studying the problems of PEs in India and involving the Indian researchers to make the Indian experience available to them.

Subject Matter

The subject matter of management research on PEs falls into two broad categories. In the first category we can place the research on problems of internal management of PEs, which relate to specific functional areas such as finance, organizational behaviour, production, marketing and business policy. In the second category, researchers dealing with PE environment could be discussed.

Finance

The researchers on finance generally deal with investment, allocation, cash management, profitability and dividend decisions in PEs.

In the area of investment not many studies have come out from the academic centres. The first such study authored by A Besant and C Raj,[277] on PE investment decisions in India came out in the middle of 1970s analysing the practices and problems in this area over a period ending in 1964. The study questioned the cut off rate applied by the Planning Commission in selecting the public sector projects and also methodology for applying the social cost benefit analysis. However, there being a gap between the completion and publication of the study, it lost much of relevance for the policy makers and practising managers. The principles and procedures of public investment choice were streamlined by the central government in the middle seventies. The study however, remained the solitary piece of research on central level public enterprises, without any follow up. But it encouraged researches to examine the nature of investment decision making in the State Level Public Enterprises (SLPEs).

The financing decisions were researched comprehensively by B S Sharma, [323] in his research work on financial planning in the Indian public sector. The study outlined the financing arrangements for PEs in terms of both rupee and foreign finance component. The study discussed the gestation, operation and expansion finance in the context of PEs and suggested the formation of a national bank for financing of PEs. The imbalance in debt-equity ratio has attracted in full measures the attention of the researchers. J. B. Sarkar's thesis analysing the nature and change of the capital structure of the central government companies since1960-61 to 1969-70, brought out these imbalances for a cross section of sector wise PEs. S K Chakraborty,[26] in his monumental research on financial management in PEs also points out the importance of the formulations of capital structure and the role played by the debt equity ratio. A study done by IPE for the Prime Minister's

Economic Advisory Council makes a pointed reference to these imbalances and suggests corrective measures.

The allocation decisions in PEs having a bearing on working capital have been researched intensively. In 1975, a study by R K Mishra[226] on problems of working capital with reference to selected public undertakings in India, presented an integrated theory of working capital management for PEs. The study showed the correlation, an efficient and effective management of working capital has, with maintaining and improving the profitability of PEs. The study noted the absence of a comprehensive policy with regard to the management of cash, receivables and inventory and costs of financing working capital in the PEs. Another study on working capital management in PEs by Vijaya Saradhi [377] points out to the lack of awareness among the PEs about the significance of working capital management.

The problems of working capital management have been discussed at the level of SLPEs in the context of Andhra Pradesh (A.P). A study on working capital management in selected SLPEs of A.P, done by K. Viyyanna Rao, [287] notes the absence of a comprehensive working capital policy in the SLPEs in A.P. The study advocates for the formulation and completion of such a policy.

There has been a spate of studies on the question of pricing in PEs. A number of such studies starting in the early 60s revolved round the question of how public enterprises in monopoly position should price their products with due regard to both social and commercial considerations. Mention may be made in this context of a study done by Geeta Gouri and T. L. Sankar [309] at IPE on pricing of petroleum products, which discusses the equity and distributional objectives and the extent to which these are obtained in the current pricing of petroleum products. In this context government policies on pricing in PEs are set out in the Annual Survey of Public Enterprises prepared by the Bureau of Public Enterprises (BPE). In addition, there exist a number of official committee reports in pricing in PEs like the K.N. Raj Committee on steel prices, Coal Pricing

Revision Committee as well as the reports of the Bureau of Industrial Costs and Prices (BICP). Unfortunately some of these reports are not readily available with the researchers.

Profitability in PEs constitutes the theme of a few doctoral theses. Thus a comprehensive study on the accumulated deficit of PEs by J. Satyanarayana [318] examines the impact of deficits on current profitability of PEs. Another study by Rampershad Sen Gupta presents an indepth analysis of the cost structure and the profit earning capacity of the Public Sector Steel Industry which can be considered as a good medal for conducting similar studies in various other sectors.

A few authors have worked on investment management in public enterprises. Krishnama Chary, [187] in his book on investment management in public enterprises, provides a strong theoretical and conceptual foundation on financial management and each of its activities viz., resource, investment management and working capital management and thoroughly examines the managerial aspects of various sources of financing fixed and current assets.

Prashant Kumar,[269] in his work on financing of public enterprises and public participation, presents an indepth analysis of growth and working of public enterprises. It seeks to discuss in detail the financing of public enterprises in India in relation to public participation.

Budgeting in PEs has been studied both at the Central and State levels. G. P. Keshav and R. K. Mishra have researched on the issues of budgeting in Central PEs and have addressed themselves to "why" and "how" of budgeting. They recommend that budgeting in Central PEs should be made a tool both for planning and control. At the state level, Shankaria looked into the problem of budgeting in different kinds of PEs of Andhra Pradesh. A study done by Nandagopal [239] touches upon the budgeting system and practices that financial discipline was superior in undertakings which had designed and implemented extensive business budgeting systems.

Organisational Behaviour

There have been some studies that compare organisational structure and functioning of PEs with private enterprises, multinationals and enterprises owned by large business houses. The difference in the goals and priorities are as perceived by the top management of the different enterprises and the respective style of functioning have been examined in these studies. The general conclusion drawn in these studies are that the meeting of national priorities is seen as the main goal in PEs and that the style of functioning of the top management is mostly bureaucratic. Authority enjoyed by the top management in the enterprises vis-à-vis the control system in which they are embedded was found to be no different under different ownership categories.

The organisational effectiveness in PEs was studied by B.L.Maheswari [200]. He concludes that PEs totally lack effectiveness, as they do not have clarity of expectations from managers and the nature of their accountability. Th lack of rewards for managerial effectiveness and for reinforcing performance-oriented behaviour has also been noticed.

The study on leadership and managerial styles by Malhotra [202] finds that Craftsman chief executive is not a rarity in PEs as his effectiveness increases with the technical competence and enables him to deal on a professional level with the corporate management. The study points that 'Gamesman' chief executive is yet to emerge in India. The more successful chief executives adopted a decision-making role supported by subordinates, though none seems to go to the extent of allowing complete participation. Paternalistic structure and style of leadership has succeeded in a number of cases. Successful chief executives have tended to spend a great deal of their time in peer interaction. The study by Das and Singh [346] show that bureaucratic style is preponderate in PEs followed by compromising developer and autocratic leaders in that order. Udai Pareek and Rao [259] have examined various issues on organisational goal and efficiency in HRD function. The problems related to man within the organisation such as industrial relations, personnel management, performance appraisal, motivation, workers participation have been in this work. The collection of papers on management of human resources in PEs, by Mishra and Ravishankar [225] indicate that recruitment and selection procedures in PEs have not yet been standardised and the performance appraisal systems and procedures are ad-hoc and deficient and scant attention is being paid to issues of motivation and participatory management in most PEs.

There are many studies on organisational changes and organisational development related to PEs. Bhat's case study [26] on Swaraj Tractors highlights the need for changing the institutional structures to bring about greater commitment of top management. Krishnamurthy has narrated the experience of BHEL during the change. He emphasizes the need for encouraging creativity in bringing about changes in organisations. Prahalad [272] and Kandwala have discussed the organisational changes in the context of "turn-around strategies". The Boards of PEs have been researched extensively, especially their role, composition and size have been studied by a large number of researchers. An edited volume brought out by S.K.Chakraborty discusses different aspects of the Boards of Management of PEs. According to Chakraborty, Boards of PEs should be autonomous and business like in developing strategies, measuring and improving upon the PE performance.

Laxmi Narain,[248] in his work on managerial compensation and motivation in public enterprises, discusses the basic question of managerial motivation which is the basis of efficient management. In his work, he analyses the factors which influence the morale and motivation of PE managers. The work contains a descriptive account of the fringe benefits and a brief comparison of the levels of compensation between public and private enterprise. Laxmi Narain, [241] in his work on Board of Directors of PEs, has also studied indepth the role of boards of PEs with particular focus on the role of the government directors.

Workers participation dimension has also been studied by scholars on public enterprise. Laxmi Narain,[246] in his book on worker's participation in PEs", discusses the status of workers participation in India, West Germany and Yugoslavia. The findings of the macro level survey on worker's participation in management throw light upon the attitude of top management, constraints of participative management, conviction and attitude of trade unions, effect of worker's participation in management, multiplicity and politicisation of unions and creating an environment to make worker's participation in management succeed. The survey findings also highlight the mechanism and implementation of worker's participation with particular reference to participation at Board level and in PEs. A micro-level survey has been conducted through a case study on worker's participation in the Electronics Corporation of India (ECIL).

Production

The production function in PEs includes designing and engineering, production planning and control, materials management, maintenance and quality control. Of these, only materials management has been studied extensively by researchers. The committee on Public Undertakings highlighted the importance of materials management in PEs in a report submitted in 1967. The Administrative Reforms Commission and Mohd. Fazal Committee as also the expert study groups set up by the BPE to look into the performance of PEs has highlighted the importance of this area. The capacity utilisation in PEs is another topic, which has attracted some attention. Almost all the studies point out the role of external factors in the way of full capacity utilisation in PEs. However, inadequate attention has been paid to the role of internal factors in the literature. M P Shrivastva, [334] in his work, deals with the capacity utilisation and cost of production in PEs wherein he analyses the existing scenario in PEs. Khan [185] studied the productivity dynamics in PEs throwing light on application of emerging concepts such as total factor productivity in PEs.

Singh & Bhattacharya [331] discuss some crucial aspects of management in public enterprises. It covers vital aspects such as financial management of public sector undertakings, the operation of cooperatives, turnaround strategies for sick enterprises, the system of incentive and discipline in these units and the role of labour in both effective management and optimal productivity. Bishwa Nath [333] studies the theoretical and practical aspects of production in public enterprises.

Marketing

Marketing includes planning, organisation of marketing, sales forecasting, pricing, distribution and promotion of products. Among the studies, J. D. Singh's [343] research on Marketing Planning practices of PEs in India based study of 30 enterprises deserve a special attention. The study showed that even though the PEs were gradually becoming market oriented, their marketing planning function had not reached a high level of sophistication. It was further noted that the enterprises producing industrial goods performed their marketing planning function in a more systematic manner than the ones dealing in consumer goods. In conclusion the study observed that given the gradual transition of Indian markets from one of sellers to that of buyers and given the growing size of PEs, they cannot afford to neglect the systematisation of their marketing planning efforts for long.

Business Policy/Strategic Management

The environment in which the PEs operate and their interface with the Government have been studied in depth by well known experts like Murthy, Praxy Fernandez, Patil, Omprakash, Chakraborty, Sankar, Dholakia and Laxmi Narain. A summary of these studies tells that PE-government boundary conditions are difficult to define and consequently PE executives find it difficult to define and consequently PE executives find it difficult to manage their external environment to their advantage. However, it is agreed by all that there is considerable scope for reduction in controls imposed by the Government, Parliament and Comptroller and Auditor General. This has been supported by K.R.S. Murthy [237] in his study on strategic management of PEs compared Indian experience with those of other countries and points out the possibility of PEs gradually growing to a state of mature independence.

Studies on Corporate Planning are conspicuous by their absence. In this area IPE has, in collaboration with BPE, completed a research project on Corporate Planning in PEs. This study by K.S. Bhat notes that while there is an urgent need to do corporate planning in PEs, many PEs needs to be educated in this regard. Prajapathi Trivedi, [362] in his book which was a critique of PE policy, analysed various aspects of PE policy. He had discussed at length the various issues relating to performance evaluation of PEs and a meaningful discussion on the comparative performance of public and private enterprises.

The political dimension has been studied by Laxmi Narain in his work on PEs in India which is a study of public relations and annual reports, [249] and is based on a pioneering study undertaken by the author on a topic, which hitherto had till then received little or no attention. The book presents the result of an intensive study of the annual reports of PEs in India. The study covers 45 government companies and a dozen public corporations together with a departmental enterprise in the form of Indian Railways. The book discusses broadly the issue of public relations of public enterprises and deals with the annual reports as an important aspect of their public relations. The author brings out through a very close scrutiny shortcomings and defects of annual reports. The book makes numerous suggestions for the improvement of annual reports presented by PEs.

The performance evaluation system has been a complex problem and eluded an acceptable solution. There have been both explicable and inexplicable reasons responsible for this phenomenon. Among explicable reasons to mention a few, multiplicity of conflicting objectives, non-uniformity in lines of business activity, nature, age and product range of PEs have been the main factors. Other reasons include the socio-economic philosophy and divergence of interests between shareholders.

Though, the views on performance evaluation, both at the national and enterprise level, have differed sharply in the past, they have now come to agree on the viewpoint that profitability of these enterprises can be taken as the main indicator for the performance evaluation. For example, the UN publications, ARC report, Arjun Sengupta Committee Report as also the CPU and ICPE reports have explored this point. However, among all studies, that by Dholakia can be considered as a path breaking work on this thorny issue. Dholakia suggests total factor productivity approach to measure the performance of PEs.

Performance Evaluation/ Accountability

The issue of autonomy and accountability of PEs has been studied by various experts. A pioneering work by Laxmi Narain & B S Murthy, [250] on PE and fundamental rights, discusses a new dimension of public accountability of PEs. The book examines the impact of Supreme Court decisions by which autonomous government corporations and companies are treated as "State" as defined in Article 12 of the Indian Constitution and are thus subject to the writ jurisdiction of the courts for enforcement of fundamental rights against them. The book presents many facets of the theory and implications of extending the writ jurisdiction to the autonomous public enterprise in their day to day functioning.

Laxmi Narain, [242] in his book on autonomy of PEs, contains basic perspective of autonomy and the various facets of loss of autonomy. It also provides the private sector dimension of accountability. The book contains papers giving a way out of the problem of lack / inadequacy of autonomy. The problems of SLPEs have also been discussed.

Purushotham, P. W, [273] in his book on organisation and management of PEs, deals with the various aspects relating to public enterprise management, nationalsiation of road transport, administrative structure of transport corporation, government control and public accountability.

The system of performance evaluation in PEs has been studied by various experts. Prajapati Trivedi, [363] in his pioneering work on performance evaluation of public enterprises has exhaustively studied the working of the system of MoU in PEs. He also makes a comparative study of the system in other countries like Korea, Pakistan, Africa etc. The system of performance evaluation in PEs has been studied by R K Mishra, P Geeta, & B Navin,[230] in their study on memorandum of understanding in PEs in India, wherein, the authors have made an indepth study of the working of the MoU system in India.

Privatisation

Geeta, Gouri, [86] in her edited volume on privatisation and PE and the Asia-Pacific experience, presents a compilation of a series of reports, case investigations of actual privatisation that had taken place in the region and discussion of papers on a number of issues.

V.V. Ramanadham,[285] in his work on PE privatisation, brings in thought provoking discussion on development, and the role of United Nations with which he was associated for 25 years offering advice to developing countries on PE and privatisation. He analyses uniquely the current trends in privatisation in this volume. R K Mishra, [232] & K S Bhat, in their recent publication on privatisation and the Indo-UK experience, have made a comparative study of the process in the two countries. R K Mishra & B Navin,[226] in their recent publication have made an indepth study on the restructuring of SLPEs in Madhya Pradesh.

Gaps in Research

The survey of management research on PEs shows that over the years both volume and depth of research have increased. But the impact of these studies on public policy towards PEs and the management of PEs seem to be marginal. The management research in general seeks to conceptualise the actual happenings or experiences in managing enterprises, so as to formulate general theories on management or provide insight, which could be used in other enterprises for improving their performance. Such research mainly benefits the practising managers, students of management or academics in management. The management research on PEs on the other hand, concerns also the policy makers in government. Unfortunately, existing research on PEs, with a few exceptions, have shown inadequate appreciation of the difference between management research on PEs management research in general. The research studies fall into the following six categories:

Descriptive compilations, historical narration.

General evaluation studies of individual enterprises.

Case studies: These are different from general evaluation studies (category 2). These attempt to make an in-depth analysis of the factors that led to a particular incident, decision, or happening in the enterprises.

Comparative evaluation of a specific function in management (like HRD or Corporate Planning) in a few selected enterprises. The focus of such research is to identify best industry norms or practices and to derive relative weight of various factors, which determine the efficiency, or effectiveness of a particular function.

Survey of the whole PE system with reference to a particular issue at hand, say profitability or productivity.

Political Economy of PEs

For the policy makers, operating in a field charged with politics, the research which looks upon PEs issues purely from profit maximisation or productivity increase is not of much use. The management research on PEs (in the author's opinion) has not so far developed a framework for analysing PE issues in their total environmental context. In fact there are very few research studies from management institutes and universities that deal with the political economy of PEs.

For the general public, with some concern about PE

investment and return, the existing body of research has not provided answers to simple questions. A few of these are cited:

PEs do not show acceptable rate of return on investment, as they have social objectives to fulfill. How many research studies have attempted to analyse the nature and extent of social objectives and their impact on different aspects of management in quantitative terms.

Over-manning is often cited as a cause for the erosion of profits in the public enterprise. There are not many studies which analyse wage cost of the PEs in comparison with the wage cost in similar industries in private sector and identify the extent to which excess labours has contributed to the profit or loss of the enterprise.

Questions on reorganising the structure of the enterprise came up as a major issue with the Kumaramangalam thesis on Holding company. The concept has been interpreted in different ways by different scholars and government agencies. Since the formation of SAIL and Coal India Limited, there have been several adjustments in the relative responsibility of the subsidiary, holding company and the government ministry. On separate considerations, Fertilizer Corporation of India was split into several units. Attempts to split LIC have been stalled not on the findings of any research study. The proposed merger of Air India and Indian Airlines has not been analysed from the managerial efficiency point of view.

Technocrats Vs generalist refers to an old controversial issue. The experience of over 500 PEs for 30 years is available for analysing to seek answers on the nature of technological knowledge and experience needs to make the best top executives in different categories of PEs.

One can keep on adding to the list. But the illustrative list is adequate to bring out the need for relevance in research.

So far as methodological contribution is concerned, the trend in PE research is not encouraging. The researchers, in general, have not had recourse to advanced research tools and depended mostly on elementary statistical and mathematical approaches. In most of these researchers, sampling has been done without thought and therefore generated basis.

The information from secondary sources, mainly published literature has been used extensively. The questionnaire approach has been resorted to in collecting primary data and information. Excepting the policy research, and in certain cases, because of linkages with the policy makers, researchers in general could not have access to classified information, in the possession of various governmental bodies and organisations. Finally many of the researchers have taken a narrow and isolated view of their research problems. In this research therefore the interdisciplinary approach is yet to find its roots.

Future Thrust

Usually in the discussion of this issue, the problem of access to data is raised. While it is true that government agencies are reluctant to part with data and information on their internal decision making, it is also true that with some lapses of time, more data are generally available regarding public enterprises than their private counterparts.

A major hurdle to sustained research efforts on relevant issues is lack of a proper perspective of the issues on which the government agencies would like to have research contributions. Usually the demand for studies, analytical reviews and suggestions on issues spring up suddenly with the setting up of a Committee or Commission by the Government. But such Committee's and Commissions have six months to one years time to finalise their report and in turn can give two to three months time only for any scholar or institution to provide the study required by them. With a disorganised database and the scholar's lack of familiarity with the systems and procedures of the particular PE or government agency, such studies tend to be more descriptive than analytical.

A possible solution to this problem has been discussed in the Planning Commission Research Committee and at the ministerial level. The identification of a research agenda for each Ministry and groups of PEs for a medium term say five years and selecting some particular academic or institution to take up the studies on issues identified could be an improvement over the present situation. Each issue could be entrusted to more than one institution also. The access to information from government records could be arranged on a mutually agreed basis. Some progress was made on these lines in the Ministry on Industrial Development a year ago, but the efforts appear to have been bogged down.

There is also need to organise a Data Bank on PEs and Information Centre. Besides the 200 PEs managed by the Central government, there are over 1000 PEs in the State government and an additional 500 joint ventures promoted by them. All these companies do publish their annual accounts though some of them may be delayed by several years. The available data has to be kept at a central place and relating to the companies in the same product market can be analysed. There are a number of reports commissioned by different departments of government both at the centre and state on the working of certain aspects of the PEs operating under their aegis. Research on PEs has been handicapped for want of access to this data. It may be pointed out here that as a part of its effort to promote research on PEs, IPE has set up a computer based data bank and information centre on PEs. Such efforts could be taken up by other institutions also. Extensively availability of data in this way will also help the researcher to respond quickly to government departments for their views on different issues relating to PEs.

There is also need to study the consequences of disinvestment and privatistaion. The issue of redundancy of labour in PEs and Voluntary Retirement Schemes offered by various PEs could be closely studied. There is an urgent need to look into the issue of social safety net in public enterprises and retraining of workers and upgrading their skills.

Conclusion

As already indicated the volume and depth of management research on PEs is growing. But considering the size of PEs and the complexity of problems, which they encounter, there is still need to increase these research efforts. While doing so, we should ensure that research is directed to relevant areas and is based on most up to date and complete data. To do this research institutions should come together and join hands with government departments and other agencies.

BIBLIOGRAPHY

Abdul, Aziz (ed.), *Management Problems of State Public Undertakings*, Printwell Publishers, Jaipur, 1990.

Adiseshaiah, M.A, (ed.), *The Why, What and Whither of the Public Sector Enterprise*, Lancer, New Delhi, 1985.

Agarwal, G.C, *Public Sector with Special Reference to Steel Industry in India*, Allahabad University, 1968.

Agarwal, M K, *Human Resource Development in Public Sector Undertakings: A case study of Life Insurance Corporation of India*, Sarup & Sons, New Delhi, 1995.

Ahmed, Z U, *Financial Profitability and Losses in Public Enterprises of Developing Countries*, International Centre for Public Enterprise in Developing Countries, Ljubljana, 1982.

Ahmed, Z U, (ed.) *Pricing Policy and Investment Criteria in Public Enterprises*, International Centre for Public Enterprise in Developing Countries, Lijubljana, 1982.

Ambwani, U, *Public Enterprises in India's Economic Development*, Allahabad University, 1968. (D.Litt.)

Anand, Rao B, The Present State of Corporate Planning in Public Sector, *Lok Udyog* 11 (10) Jan. 1978, 25-31.

Anand, Rao C R, *Public Enterprise and Parliamentary Committees*, Osmania University, Hyderabad, 1979. (Ph.D. Thesis)

Appleby, P H, *Re-examination of India's Administrative System with Special Reference to Administration of Government's Industrial and Commercial Enterprises*, Manager of Publications, New Delhi, 1956.

Asian Centre for Development Administration, Approaches to the Public Enterprise Policy in Asia on Investment, Prices and Returns Criteria – Proceedings of the Papers Presented at the Asian Think-Tank meeting held at Kualalumpur, 1-3 Sept., Asian

Centre for Development Administration, Kualalumpur, 1976.

Committee on Public Undertakings. *Role and Achievements of Public Undertakings*, Dispur, Assam Legislative Assembly, Committee on Public Undertaking, Report No.1 1975.

Ayyar, J M, The Growth of Public Sector Techno-Economic Contribution by the Soviet Union-Soviet Financial Management Techniques for Performance Evaluation. *Lok Udyog*, 19(1), April 1985, 25-27.

Balmohan, Das V, et al, Delegation of Authority in Public and Private Sector Enterprises, *IPE Journal*, Hyderabad, Vol. no.3, 1983, pp.83-86.

Bansal, M P, *Human Resource Development in Public Enterprises*, RBSA Publishers, Jaipur, 1991.

Batra, G S, *Leading Issues in Public Enterprises: Control and Accountability*, Anmol Publications, New Delhi, 1993.

Basak, A K, Management and Performance of Public Enterprises in Developing Countries: The Need for Further Research, *Lok Udyog*, 9(3), 1975, pp. 9-25

Basu, P.K, *Managerial Civil Service in Asia*. Asian Centre for Development Administration, Kualalampur, 1976.

Basu, P.K, & Nove, A, (ed.), *Public Enterprise Policy on Investment Pricing and Returns*, Asian and Pacific Development Administration Centre, Kuala Lampur, 1979.

Basu, P.K, *Public Enterprises: Policy, Performance and Professionalisation*, Allied Publishers, New Delhi, 1982.

Batra G S and Narinder Kaur, *Privatisation of Public Enterprises Emerging Dimensions*, Anmol Publications, New Delhi, 1995.

Bharadwaj, S B L, *Research Project on Managerial Appraisal*, Report 1-Managerial Appraisal Practices in Public Enterprises, Bureau of Public Enterprises, New Delhi, 1971, (mimeographed)

Bharadwaj, S B L, *Managerial Appraisal Practices in Public Enterprises*, Administrative Staff College of India, Hyderabad, 1971.

Bharadwaj, S B L, *Research Project on Managerial Appraisal*, Report 2-Managerial Appraisal Practices in Public Enterprises, Bureau of Public Enterprises, New Delhi, 1971, (mimeographed)

Bhargava, N K, *Financial Structure of Public Enterprises*, R B S A Publications, Jaipur, 1991

Bhatt, S C L, *Design of Information System of Industrial Financing Institution of a State*, Gujarat University, 1977 (Ph.D. Thesis)

Bhatt, V V, Decision-Making in the Public Sector: A Case Study of Swaraj Tractor in Bhat V V (ed.) *Development Perspectives*, Pergamon, Oxford, 1980.

Bhatt, V.V, Decision Making in the Public Sector: A Case Study of Swaraj Tractor, *Economic and Political Weekly*, 1978, 13(21), M 30-45.

Bhattacharya, B, Economic Benefits of Public Research and Development, *Lok Udyog*, 8 (9 & 10), Dec. 1974- Jan.1975, 51-54.

Bhattacharya, C D, *Public Sector Enterprises in India*, Kitab Mahal, Allahabad, 1990.

Bhattacharya, S. K, Management Reporting System in Public Undertakings, *Economic and Political Weekly*, 31st May 1969. M 43-54.

Bokhari, R H., Strategic Financial Planning in Public Enterprises in Developing Countries: The Capital Structure Issue, *Public Enterprise*, 6(4), 1986.

Boysob, R, (ed.), *Goodbye to Nationalisation:* A Symposium on the Economic, Political and Social Failure of the Publicly Controlled Industries and the Need to Return them to a Competitive Framework, Churchill Press, Enfield, Middlesex, 1971.

Bureaucrats in Business: The Economics and Politics of Government Ownership, Oxford University Publications, Oxford, 1995.

Chacko, T. I, Influence of Size, Ownership and Industry on; Organisational Structure and Practices in a Developing Country, *Indian Management*, 1976, 9 (4), 31-42.

Carter, S, Marketing in Less Developed Countries – Time for Dedicated Marketing Systems – Not Adaptive Transfer, *Public Enterprise*, 6(2) 1986.

Chakraborty, S K, Restructuring the Debt/Equity Ratio of Public Enterprise – Methodological Note, *Lok Udyog*, 13(4) July 1979, 43-48.

Chakraborty, S.K, *Board of Directors*, All India Management Association, New Delhi, 1985.

Chakraborty, S. K, *Financial Management and Control*, Macmillan Publications, New Delhi, 1981.

Chandra, Sekhara Rao, K and Madhavilatha, K, *Financial Management in Public Sector Enterprises*, Discovery Publishing House, New Delhi, 1991.

Chatterjee, N N, *Performance Appraisal Systems in Public Enterprises*, SCOPE, New Delhi, 1978.

Chatterjee, P, Productivity Audit in Public Enterprises, *Lok Udyog*, 9(4) July 1975, pp.31-42.

Chattopadhyay, P, Importance of Performance Audit in Public Undertaking, *Capital*, 25 Feb. 1971, pp.339-340.

Chattopadhyay, P, Improving the Management of Public Sector Enterprises through Performance Audit, *Capital*, 12 Aug. 1971, p. 310.

Chattopadhyay, P., Quality Audit in Public Sector, *Mainstream*, 1 Dec. 1973.

Chattopadhyay, P, *A Study in Some Aspects of Public Enterprises in India Since Independence*, (Ph.D. Thesis), Delhi University, 1965.

Chauhan, A B, *Organisation and Working of Public Enterprises in Gujarat*, (Ph.D. Thesis), Sardar Patel University, 1974.

Chaudhuri, S, Management of Technological Innovation: Evidence from a Case Study, *Lok Udyog*, 19 (10), 1986, pp.3-10.

Chawla, S K, Managerial Problems of Public Sector Undertakings, *Defence Management*, 8 (1-2), 1981, pp. 52-60.

Chida, A R, *Accountability of Public Sector Enterprises in Tamil Nadu*, Madras University, 1981. (Ph.D. Thesis)

Commonwealth Secretariat, National Policies and Programmes for Public Enterprise Management Training: Report of a Meeting of Senior Officials, 5-7 November 1979, the Secretariat, London, 1980.

Commonwealth Secretariat, *Management of the Privatisation Process: A Guide to Policy Making and Implementation*, Commonwealth Secretariat, London, 1994.

Commonwealth Secretariat, *Performance Evaluation of Public Enterprises:* Report of a Seminar Organised by the Commonwealth Secretariat and the Institute of Development Management – Botswana, Lesotho, Swaziland, Goborone held at Botswana on 3-7 April 1978, the Secretariat, London, 1978.

Commonwealth Secretariat, *Issues in Public Enterprise Development*, Commonwealth Secretariat, London, 1978.

Commonwealth Secretariat, *The Role and Management of Public Enterprises*, Commonwealth Secretariat, London, 1977.

Coopers & Lybrand, Deloitte, *Privatisation its Place in Public Enterprise Reform*, Springfield, London, 1991.

Correa, C M, The Legal Nature and Effects of Performance Guarantees in Transfer of Technology Transactions, *Public Enterprise*, 4(4) 1984, 5-14.

Crokett, Joan, Nuallain, Colm & Wettenhall, Roger (ed.), *Public Enterprise Boards: What They Are And What They Do*, Report From An International Study, International Association of Schools and Institutes of Administration, Hong Kong, 1994.

Curwen, P, *Public Enterprise: A Modern Approach*, Wheatsheef Books, Sussex, 1986.

Datt, Ruddar (ed.), *Privatization: Bane or Panacea*, Pragati Publications, New Delhi, 1993.

Dave, Ganpat Lal, *Financial Management in Public Enterprises*, Vidya Prakashan, Jodhpur, 1991.

De, N R, Approach to Research Methodology on Employee Motivation in Public Enterprises, *Manpower Journal*, 12(2) July-Sept. 1976, 40-60.

Desai, S R, Transactional Analysis: A New Way to Managerial Effectiveness, *Lok Udyog*, 14(7) October 1980, 5-10.

Deshpande, V S, *State Enterprise and the Law*, Documentation Centre for Corporate and Business Policy Research, New Delhi, 1981.

Dhankar, Raj S, (ed.), *Managing Public Sector Undertakings Finance*, Westvill Publishing House, New Delhi, 1995.

Dholekia, Bakul H, *The Changing Efficiency of Public Enterprises in India*, Samaiya, Bombay, 1980.

Doraiswamy, P K, Public Enterprise Autonomy: An Advocacy of the Legislature's Point of View, *Public Enterprise*, 3(4) 1983, 9-16.

Dube, R, *State Financial Corporations in India: A Critical Study*, Indore University, 1968 (Ph.D. Thesis).

Dutt, R C, & Nigam, R K, (ed.), *Towards Commanding Heights*, Standing Conference of Public Enterprises, New Delhi, 1975.

Dutt, R C, Management of State Enterprises: The Kumaramangalam Model, *Lok Udyog*, 7(4) July 1973, 5-10.

Dutt, R C. State Enterprises in a Developing Country: The Indian Experience 1950-90, Abhinav Publications, New Delhi, 1990.

Eastern Region Public Enterprise Group, Report of the Expert Committee on Public Enterprises on General and Important, Issues Relating to Public Sector Management and Performance, Calcutta, 1990.

El– Namaki, M S S, A Strategic Planning Model for Public Enterprises in Developing Countries, *Public Enterprise*, 4(4) 1984, 15-26.

International Centre for Public Enterprises in Developing Countries, *Essays on Relations Between Governments and Public Enterprises*, ICPE, Ljubljana, 1985. 248p.

Fernandes, P, Management Culture, Changing Public Policies and Management, *Public Enterprise*, 1(1), 1980, 11-17.

Fernandes, P, Management Culture, Changing Public Policies and Management, *Public Enterprise*, 1(1), 1980, 11-17.

Fernandes, P, "OPTIMA" (Optional Performance through Internal Management Action), An ICPE approach to self-reliant public enterprise management, *Public Enterprise*, 2(2) 1981, 5-12.

Fernandes, P, Pricing Fallacies and Fantasies: A Search, *State Enterprise*, 1(1) Jan-Mar. 1982, 26-40.

Fernandes, P, *Promise and Performance: A Search for a Credible System of Evaluating the "Efficiency" of Public Enterprises*, Standing Conference of Public Enterprises, New Delhi, 1982.

Fernandes, P, & Sicherl, P, (ed.), *Seeing The Personality of Public Enterprises – An Enquiry into the Concept, Definition and Classification of Public Enterprises*, International Centre for Public Enterprises in Developing Countries, Ljubljana, 1981.

Fitzerald, E V K, *Public Sector Investment Planning for Developing Countries*, Macmillan Publications, New Delhi, 1978.

Fligler, C, *Multinational Public Corporations*, International Bank in Reconstruction and Development (IBRD), Washington, 1967.

Fubara, B A, *Business Policy in Government-Owned Companies in LDCs: The Nigerian Experience*, University of Strathclyde, Glasgow, 1982. (Ph.D. Thesis)

Fubara, B A, Negative Profitability Performance of Public Enterprises in Developing Countries: A Business Policy Anatomy, *Public Enterprise*, 4(3) 1984, 61-72.

Ganguly, B, *Productive Efficiency of Public Enterprises in a Developing Economy-With Special Reference to India,* Magadh University, 1977. (D Lit.).

Garg, Subhash & Handa, Sunil (ed.), *Privatization of Public Enterprises in India: Nature, Problems and Prospects,* Arihant Publishers, Jaipur, 1991.

Gedam, Ratnakar, Public Sector Management: Performance and Efficiency, Deep & Deep, New Delhi, 1995.

George, P V, & Deenadavain, P D, *Overview of PE Sector in India: A Preliminary Report,* IIM, Bangalore, 1976.

Geeta, Gouri (ed.), *Privatisation and Public Enterprise: The Asia-Pacific Experience,* Oxford & IBH Publishing Co. Pvt. Ltd., New Delhi, 1991.

Ghosh, Asit K & Prem, Kumar (ed.), *Public Enterprises Management,* Anmol Publications, New Delhi, 1991.

Ghai, Y (ed.), *Law in the Political Economy of Public Enterprise: African Perspectives,* Scandinavian Institute of African Studies, International Legal Centre, Uppsala, 1977.

Girish, Nandan, *The Role of Hindustan Steel Ltd.,* in the Development of Iron and Steel Industry in India, Bihar University. (Ph.D. Thesis)

Gorwala, A D, *Report of the Efficient Conduct of State Enterprises,* Planning Commission, New Delhi, 1951.

Govindarajan, P S, Corporate Planning in Public Enterprises, Perspectives and Problems, *Lok Udyog,* 14 (3) June 1980, 7-13.

Gupta, A. K, Public Sector Needs Tough Decision-Making, *Eastern Economist,* 19 October 1979, 819-21.

Gupta, C B, Corporate Planning in Public Enterprises, *State Enterprise,* 3 (1) Jan-Mar. 1984.

Gupta, K L, *Research and Development in Public Enterprises,* Indus, New Delhi, 1994.

Gupta, K R, (ed.), *Organisation and Management of Public Enterprises,* Atlantic, New Delhi, 1978, 2 v.

Gupta, K R, (ed.), *Pricing in Public Enterprises,* Atlantic, New Delhi, 1978.

Gupta, L C, *Corporate Management and Accountability Towards a Joint Sector,* Macmillan Publications, New Delhi, 1974.

Gupta, N B, Management Development and All That: The Public Sector Concept, *Lok Udyog*, 9(6) Sept. 1975, 21-26.

Gupta, R.K, *Managerial Motivation in Public Enterprises*, Agra University, 1978. (D Lit).

Gupta, S, *The Iron and Steel Industry in India: A Study of Some Aspects of Productivity*, University of Rajasthan, 1977. (Ph.D. Thesis)

Guru, D D, *Public Enterprise*, Amrita Prakashan, Bombay, 1990.

Hafeezuddin, *Extensive Development as a Means of Higher Productivity in Public Enterprises in India with Reference to Iron and Steel Industries*, Aligarh. 1969. (Ph.D. Thesis)

Halachmi, A, *Innovating in the Public Sector: The Case for Action Research and Training, Management in Government*, 12(4), Jan-Mar. 1981.

Hamilton, R E, Damodar Valley Corporation: India's Experiment with the TVA (Tenessee Valley Authority) Model, *Indian Journal of Public Administration*, 15(1) Jan-Mar. 1969, 86-109.

Hanson, A H, *Managerial Problems in Public Enterprise*, Asia Publishing House, Bombay, 1962.

Hanson, A H, *Parliamentary and Public Ownership*. London. Cassell, 1961.

Hanson, A H, *Public Enterprise: A Study of its Organization and Management in Various Countries*, International Institute of Administrative Sciences, Brussels, 1955.

Hanson, A H, *Public Enterprise and Economic Development*, Routledge, London, 1959.

Hanumanulu, V V, *The Organisation and Management of Public Enterprises in India*, Allahabad University, 1965 (D Lit).

Hanumantha, Rao N, *Industrial Relations in Public Enterprises*, Printwell Publishers, Jaipur, 1990.

Harlow, C, *Innovation and Productivity Under Nationalisation: The First Thirty Years*, London, 1977.

Hassan, E E, Marketing Research for Public and Non-Profit Organisations, *Public Enterprise*, 4(4) 1984, 39-52.

Huang, J C, *Transfer of Public Enterprise to Private Ownership: An Experience in the Republic of China*, U N Seminar on Organisation and Administration of PEs, August, Taiwan, 1966.

Iglesias, G U, Sushil, Chandra & Salazar M., Jr. (ed.), *Training Public Enterprise Managers*, Asian and Pacific Development

Administration Centre, 1980, Kuala Lampur, 753.

Inderjit, Singh, *Management Perspectives: Problems of Management in Public Undertakings and Public Administration in India*, Sagar Publications, New Delhi, 1971.

India Administrative Reforms Commission, (Chairman: K Hanumanthaiya) Report on Public Sector Undertakings, Manager of Publications, New Delhi, 1969.

India Administrative Reforms Commission, (Chairman: Ravindra Verma) Report on Public Sector Undertakings, Manager of Publications, New Delhi, 1969.

India Bureau of Public Enterprises, Government the Policy for Management of Public Enterprises, Vol. l-General Management and Financial Management, Standing Conference of Public Enterprises, New Delhi, 1976.

India. Bureau of Public Enterprises, Government Policy for the Management of Public Enterprises, Vol.2 – Construction Management and Production and Materials Management, Standing Conference of Public Enterprises, New Delhi, 1976.

India. Bureau of Public Enterprises, Production, Structuring and Technology: A Study of Japanese Experience and its Applicability to India, The Bureau, New Delhi, 1978.

India. Bureau of Public Enterprises, Public Enterprises Survey: Annual Report on the Working of Industrial and Commercial Undertakings of the Central Government, Controller of Publications, New Delhi, 2 v.

India. Bureau of Public Enterprises, Information and Research Division: Report of the Study Team on Design Organisations in Selected Public Undertakings, The Bureau, New Delhi, 1974.

India. Bureau of Public Enterprises, Report of the Working Group on Management Information System, The Bureau, New Delhi, 1975.

India. Bureau of Public Enterprises, Report of the Working Group (Chairman: Dr.S.Varadarajan) on Research and Development in Public Sector Enterprises, the Bureau, New Delhi, 1977 (mimeographed).

India. Bureau of Public Enterprises, Towards Higher Productivity: Report of Seminar on Higher Productivity in Public Sector Production Enterprises, Sept 12, 1975, Vigyan Bhavan, Standing Conference of Public Enterprises, New Delhi, 1976.

India. Economic Administrative Reforms Commission, Report of the

Economic Administrative Reforms Commission on Government and Public Enterprises, Bureau of Public Enterprises, New Delhi, 1985.

India. Lok Sabha, 3. Committee on Public Undertakings, Management and Administration of Public undertakings: Planning of Projects, Lok Sabha Secretariat, New Delhi, 1965. (Report No. 13)

India. Lok Sabha, 3. Committee on Public Undertakings, Materials Management in Public Undertakings, Lok Sabha Secretariat, New Delhi, 1967. (Report No. 40)

India. Lok Sabha, 3. Committee on Public Undertakings, Planning, Management and Administration of Kerala State Government Companies, Lok Sabha Secretariat, New Delhi, 1966 (Report No.27)

India. Lok Sabha, 4. Committee on Public Undertakings, Action taken-Contained in the 40th Report (3rd Lok Sabha) of the CPU – Materials Management in Public Undertakings, Lok Sabha Secretariat, New Delhi, 1969, (Report No.38)

India. Lok Sabha, 4. Committee on Public Undertakings, Action taken-on the Recommendations Contained in the 52nd Report of the Estimates Committee (3rd Lok Sabha) on Personnel Policies of Public Undertakings, Lok sabha Secretariat, New Delhi, 1969, (Report No.50)

India. Lok Sabha, 4. Committee on Public Undertakings, Financial Management in Public Undertakings, Lok Sabha Secretariat, New Delhi, 1968, (Report No.15).

India. Lok Sabha, 4. Committee on Public Undertakings, Public Relations and Publicity in Public Undertakings, Lok Sabha Secretariat, New Delhi, 1969. (Report No. 47)

India. Lok Sabha, 4. Committee on Public Undertakings, Production Management in Public Undertakings, Lok Sabha Secretariat, New Delhi, 1970. (Report No. 67)

India. Lok Sabha, 5. Committee on Public Undertakings, Foreign Collaboration in Public Undertakings, Lok Sabha Secretariat, New Delhi, 1976. (Report No. 89)

India. Lok Sabha, 5. Committee on Public Undertakings, Personnel Policies and Labour Management Relations in Public Undertakings, Lok Sabha Secretariat, New Delhi, 1972. (Report No. 17)

India. Lok Sabha, 5. Committee on Public Undertakings, Role and

Achievements of Public Undertakings, Lok Sabha Secretariat, New Delhi, 1973. (Report No.40).

India. Lok Sabha, 5. Committee on Public Undertakings, Action taken ... on the recommendations contained in paragraph 3.58 of the 40th Report of the COPU (5th Lok Sabha), Lok Sabha Secretariat, New Delhi, 1974. (Report No. 46).

India. Lok Sabha, 6. Committee on Public Undertakings, Action taken ... contained in the 89th Report of the CPU (5th Lok Sabha) on foreign collaboration in public undertakings, Lok Sabha Secretariat, New Delhi, 1979.

India. Lok Sabha, 6. Committee on Public Undertakings, Appointment of Auditors in Government Companies, Lok Sabha Secretariat, New Delhi, 1979.

India. Lok Sabha, 6. Committee on Public Undertakings, Delays in Commencement of Production/Business, under utilisation of Capacity and related matters, Lok Sabha Secretariat, New Delhi, 1979. (Report No. 28).

India. Lok Sabha, 6. Committee on Public Undertakings, Structure of Boards of Management of Public Undertakings and other allied matters, Lok Sabha Secretariat, New Delhi, 1979. (Report No.20)

India. Lok Sabha, 7. Committee on Public Undertakings, Action taken .... Recommendations contained in the 20th Report of the CPU (6th Lok Sabha), Lok Sabha Secretariat, New Delhi, 1969. (Report No.8)

India. Lok Sabha, 7. Committee on Public Undertakings, Action taken .. recommendations contained in the 28th Report of the CPU (6th Lok Sabha) on Delays in Commencement of Production/ Business, Underutilisation of Capacity and Related Matters, Lok Sabha Secretariat, New Delhi, 1981. (Report No. 10).

India. Lok Sabha, 1. Estimates Committee, Organisation and Administration of Nationalised Industrial Undertakings, New Delhi, 1955. (Report No. 16).

India. Lok Sabha, 2. Estimates Committee, Action taken by Government on the 16th Report (1st Lok Sabha) on the Organisation and Administration of Nationalised Industrial Undertakings. New Delhi, 1958. (Report No. 19).

India. Lok Sabha, 3. Estimates Committee, Personnel Policies of Public Undertakings, Lok Sabha Secretariat, New Delhi, 1964. (Report No. 52).

India. Lok Sabha, 2. Estimates Committee, Preparation of Budget Estimates of Public Undertakings and Presentation of their Annual Reports and Accounts to Parliament, Lok Sabha Secretariat, New Delhi, 1960. (Report No. 73)

India. Lok Sabha, 3. Estimates Committee, Action taken... contained in the 73rd Report (2nd Lok Sabha) of Estimates Committee on Preparation of Budget Estimates of Public Undertakings and Presentation of their Annual Reports and Accounts to Parliament, Lok Sabha Secretariat, New Delhi, 1962. (Report No.9)

India. Lok Sabha, 2. Estimates Committee, Public undertakings – Forms and Organisation, Lok Sabha Secretariat, New Delhi, 1960. (Report No. 80).

India, Lok Sabha, 3 Estimates Committee, Action taken... contained in the 80th Report (2nd Lok Sabha) of Estimates Committee on public undertakings-Forms and Organisation, Lok Sabha Secretariat, New Delhi, 1964. (Report No. 56).

India, Ministry of Home Affairs, Department of Personnel and Administrative Reforms, Report of the Standing Group of Management of Public Enterprises in the States, New Delhi, 1979.

India. Ministry of Finance, Department of Economic Affairs, Administered Price Policy: A Discussion Paper, New Delhi, 1986.

India. Planning Commission, Committee on Plan Projects, Feasibility Studies for Public Sector Projects, New Delhi, 1966.

India. Planning Commission, Committee on Plan Projects, Management Planning in Public Enterprises, New Delhi, 1965.

India. Planning Commission, Guidelines for the Preparation of Feasibility Reports for Industrial Projects, Controller of publications, New Delhi, 1975.

India. Planning Commission, Committee on Plan Projects, Seminar on Materials Management, Aug. 8-19, 1962: Summary of proceedings. New Delhi, 1963.

India. Statistical Institute: Industrial Management Research Unit for Planning, Organisation and Management of Public Enterprises: Symposium, ISI, Bangalore, 1956.

Indra Kumar & James, Biji, Public Sector Enterprises in India, Commonwealth Publishers, New Delhi, 1990.

International Development Research Centre, Public Enterprises in the

Economic Development of Sri Lanka, Colombo, National Institute of Management, 1976.

International Legal Centre, Law and Public Enterprise in Asia, Praeger, New York, 1975.

Iqbal, Narain, The Management of Public Enterprises: A Study of Some Aspects in the Context of the Scientific Pattern, Indian Journal of Public Administration, 4(3) July-Sept. 1958, 302-318.

Iyer, R. P, Sector Corporations: Some Organisational Experience in India, Public Enterprise, Vol. V(2), Feb. 1985, pp. 139-53.

Jagdish, Prakash, Industrial and Parliamentary Control over Public Enterprises in India, Allahabad University, 1975. (D Lit).

Jagdish, Prakash, Public Enterprises in India: A Study in Controls, Thinker's Library, Allahabad, 1980.

Jain, R K, Management of State Enterprises in India: A Study of the Organisation and Management of Public Sector Enterprises in Indian Setting, Manaktalas, Bombay, 1967.

James, J, Public Enterprise, Technology and Employment in Less Developed Countries, Public Enterprise, 4(2) 1983, 37-50.

Janiszewski, H., & Fernandes, P, What Price Technology? Public Enterprise, 1 (4) 1981, 23-41.

Jenkins Glenn P, An Operational Approach to the Performance of Public Sector Enterprises, Harvard Institute of Development (HIDD). 1978 (Discussion paper No. 47).

Jogendera, Prasad, A Study of the Impact of Management Development Programmes in Selected Public Sector Undertakings in India, University of Delhi. 1977. (Ph.D. Thesis).

Jones, L P, (ed.), Public Enterprises in Less Developed Countries, Cambridge University Press, Cambridge, 1982.

Joshi, B, Economics of Transfer of Technology in the Public Sector: A Study of Indian Drugs and Pharmaceuticals Limited, Lucknow University, 1977. (Ph.D. Thesis).

Kabra K N, "Role of Public Sector in Introducing Technological Innovations in the third world" in Sapru, R K (ed.) Management of Public Sector Enterprises in India, Vol. 1, Ashish Publishing House, New Delhi, 1987, 169-176.

Karma, M R., & Shamsunder, K, Introduction of Management by Objective in a large Iron Ore Project, *Lok Udyog*, 8 (9 & 10), Dec. 1974/Jan. 1975, 9-12.

Kapoor, M C, & Singh, J D, Market Planning in Public Enterprises, Lok Udyog, 10 (12) March 1977, 17-21.

Kar, N C, Liquidity Management in Public Enterprises in India, Discovery, New Delhi, 1993.

Kathpalia, Ravi (Ed.). International Conference on Financial Management and Accountability in the Public Sector: Strategies for Managing Change, February 7-11, Oxford & IBH, New Delhi, 1994.

Kaura, M N, Performance Budgeting System in Government Organisations, Lok Udyog, 18 (2) May 1984, 15-24.

Keshave, G P, Readings in the Operational Problems of PEs, S Chand & Co., Delhi, 1970.

Keyser, W, & Windle, R, (Eds.), Public enterprises in the European Economic Community, Sijthoff & Noordhoott, Netherlands, 1978.

Khandwalla, P N, Strategies for – Turning Around Complex Sick Organisations, Vikalpa, 1981, 6, 143-146.

Khan, A Q. Productivity Dynamics in Public Enterprises, Vohra Publishers and Distributors, Allahabad, 1991.

Khan, A Q. Efficiency Profile of Public Enterprises in India, Vohra Publishers & Distributors, Allahabad, 1990.

Khera, S S, Government in Business, National Publishers, New Delhi, 1977.

Khera, S S, Management and Control in Public Enterprises, Asia Publishing House, Bombay, 1964.

Kolekar, B D, Human Resources Development: A Study of Selected Public Undertakings in Maharashtra and Goa, Northern Book Centre, New Delhi, 1993.

Krishnama, Chary P, Investment Management in Public Enterprises, Printwell Publishers, Jaipur, 1990.

Krishna, Kumar, A comparative study of general management function between private sector, public sector and multinational subsidiary companies in India, Indian Institute of Management, Ahmedabad, 1979. (Ph.D. Thesis).

Krishnamachary, T R, Accountability of Public Undertakings: A study, Bureau of Parliamentary Studies and Training, Lok Sabha Secretariat, New Delhi, 1980.

Krishnamurthy, V, Management and Organisational Change: The BHEL Experience, Vikalpa, 1977, 2(2), 113-139.

Kumar, L, Pricing and Performance Evaluation in Public Enterprises, *Public Enterprise*, 1 (2) 1980, 46-53.

Kumar, P, & Bhatia, B S, "Strategic Management in the Public Sector: Some Issues" in Sapru, R K (Ed.). Management of Public Sector Enterprises in India, Vol. 1, Ashish Publishing House, New Delhi, 1987. 242-48.

Kusuma, N, Management Control System in Public Enterprises, Printwell Publishers, Jaipur, 1990.

Lakhera, M L, Capital Formation in the Public Sector with Special Reference to Manufacturing and Mining, Agra University, 1962-66. (Ph.D. Thesis).

Lalamani, Prasad, Upward communication within the management hierarchy: A Case Study of Public Sector Enterprise, Banaras Hindu University, 1070-75. (Ph.D. Thesis).

Lal, Krishna, Legislative Process in India, Deep & Deep Publications, New Delhi, 1992.

Long, F, Corporate Planning, Technology and the Role of Public Enterprises in Promoting Technological Self-reliance in Developing Countries, Public Enterprise, 3(4) 1983, 17-28.

Mahajan, Y S, Development of Backward Areas: Role of Public Sector, *Lok Udyog*, 19 (3) June 1985, 3-16.

Maheshwari, B L, Managerial Effectiveness in Public Enterprises, in T L Sankar (ed.), *Leading Issues in Public Enterprise Management*, National Publishers, Bombay, 1983, 67-76.

Maheshwari, B L, Review of Research in Organisational Behaviour in Public Enterprises in Sankar, T. L, et al (ed.), *Public Enterprises in India*, National Publications, Bombay, 1983, 51-100.

Malhotra, A K, Leadership Styles in Indian Public Sector, Indian Management 1979, 18 (12), 2-6.

Mallon, R D, Public Enterprises: Pricing Policies, State Enterprise, 2 (1) Jan-Mar. 1983, 1-18.

Mane, S N, Pricing Policy for Public Sector Enterprises: Retrospect and Prospects, Lok Udyog, 19 (7) Oct. 1085, 41-51.

Maniatis, G C, Managerial Autonomy Vs. State Control in PE: Fact and Antifact, Annals of Public and Cooperative Economy, 39(4) 1968, 513-30.

Marglin, S A, Public Investment Criteria: Cost- Benefit Analysis for Planned Economic Growth, George Allen & Unwin, London, 1967.

Mascarenhas, R C, Autonomy in the Management of Public Enterprises in India, (Ph.D. Thesis), Delhi University, 1970.

Mascarenhas, R C, The Bureau of Public Enterprises in India, Revere Internationale des sciences Administration, 34(3) 1968, 246-64.

Mathur, B P, Financial Administration and Control of Public Enterprises in India with Special Reference to State Enterprises of Uttar Pradesh, University of Allahabad, 1969. (Ph.D. Thesis).

Mathur, B P, Public Enterprises in Perspective, Orient Longman, New Delhi, 1973.

Mathur, B L (ed.), Leading Issues in Public Enterprise Administration, Arihant Publishers, Jaipur, 1992.

Mathur, N D, Price Policy in Public Enterprises, National Publishing House, Jaipur, 1990.

Mathur, B L, (Ed.), Privatisation of Public Sector, RBSA Publications, Jaipur, 1992.

Matzner, E, Technological and Institutional Innovation, Annals of Public and Co-operative Economy, 56 (No.1-2) Jan-June 1985, 71-80.

Mazzolini, R, Government Controlled Enterprise: International Strategic and Policy Decisions, Wiley Eastern Publications, New York, 1979.

Meena, D D, Corporate Reporting Practices in Public Enterprises, ESS Publications, New Delhi, 1995.

Menon, T M C, & Jha, P S, Management of Public Enterprises in Developing Asian Countries: A Guide, Asian and Pacific Development Centre, Kuala Lumpur, 1980.

Minhas, Anil; Singh, Amrik; Chumber, Gurbax Ram & Chanana, Sanjeev, Financial Committees at State Level, Deep & Deep Publications, New Delhi, 1990.

Mir, A E, The Evaluation of Public Enterprise Performance: Crucial Issues, Public Enterprise, 2(3), 1982, 49-62.

Mishra, R K, Budgeting in Public Enterprises, Management in Government, 14(4), Jan-Mar 1983, 400-411.

Mishra, R K, & Ravishankar S, (Eds.), Current Perspectives in Public Enterprise Management, Ajanta Publications, New Delhi, 1985.

Mishra, R K, & Ravishankar S, (Eds.), Dynamics of Public Enterprise Management, Ajanta Publications, New Delhi, 1985.

Mishra, R K, & Ravishankar S, (Eds.), Management of Human Resources in Public Enterprises, Vision, New Delhi, 1985.

Mishra, R.K & Navin, B, Restructuring of State Level Public Enterprises, Anmol Publications, New Delhi, 2002.

Mishra, R K, Management of Cash in Public Enterprises, Eastern Economist, 17 Sept. 1976, 568-575.

Mishra, R K, Problems of Working Capital with Reference to Select Public Undertakings in India, Rajasthan University, 1972. (Ph.D. Thesis)

Mishra, R K and Bhat, K S., *Commercial Public Enterprise Management*. Jaipur, 1996.

Mishra, R. K, Geeta, P & Navin, B, *Memorandum of Understanding in Public Enterprises in India*, Vikas Publishing House, New Delhi, 2002.

Mishra, R. K, Geeta, P & Navin, B, *Recent Trends in Public Enterprise Management*, Anmol Publications Pvt. Ltd., New Delhi, 2002.

Mishra, R.K, Bhat, K. S, *Privatisation- The Indo-UK Experience*, Vikas Publishing, New Delhi, 2002.

Mishra, S, *Role of Public Sector in the Industrial Development in India*, Lalit Narayan Mithila University, 1976. (Ph.D. Thesis)

Mittal, D K, *Price Policy for Public Enterprises in Indian Plans*, Delhi University, 1977. (Ph.D. Thesis)

Mohanty, R P, Mechanics of Technology Transfer for Developing Countries, *Lok Udyog*, 19 (6) Sept. 1985, 21-29.

Murthy, K R S, Control Systems in Public Enterprises; T L Sankar et al (ed.), *Public Enterprises in India: The Focus on Research*, Himalaya Publishers, Bombay, 1983, 378-396.

Murthy, K R S, Strategic Management in PEs – A Framework for Analysis: T L Sankar et al. (ed.), *Leadership Issues in PE Management*, Himalaya, Bombay, 382-428.

Nakra, D S., Financial Management in Public Undertakings, *Lok Udyog*, 5(3) June 1971, 245-255.

Nandagopal, R, *Budgeting in State Government Enterprises of Tamil Nadu*, University of Madras, 1985. (Ph.D. Thesis).

Narain, Laxmi, *Principles and Practice of Public Enterprise Management*, S. Chand & Company, New Delhi, 1998.

Narain, Laxmi, *Boards of Directors of Public Enterprises-A Study*, SCOPE Publications, New Delhi, 1990.

Narain, Laxmi, (Ed.), *Autonomy of Public Enterprise*, Standing Conference of Public Enterprises, New Delhi, 1982.

Narain, Laxmi, Making Public Enterprises an Effective Instrument of State Policy, *Lok Udyog*, 18(3) June 1984, 35-4[illegible].

Narain, Laxmi, Managing Public Enterprise: Reflection on three Decades of Indian Experience, *Public Enterprise*, 1 (3) 1981, 23-37.

Narain, Laxmi, *The Establishment of the Fertilizer Corporation of India*, Indian Institute of Public Administration, New Delhi, 1967 (Mimeo).

Narain, Laxmi, *Worker's Participation in Public Enterprises*, Himalaya Publishing House, Bombay, 1984.

Narain, Laxmi, *Organisation Structure in Large Public Enterprises*, Ajanta Publications, New Delhi, 1981.

Narain, Laxmi, *Managerial Compensation and Motivation in Public Enterprises*, Oxford & IBH Publishing Co., New Delhi, 1973.

Narain, Laxmi, *Public Enterprise in India- A Study of Public Relations and Annual Reports*, S. Chand & Company, New Delhi, 1967.

Narain, Laxmi & Murthy, B S, (ed.), *Public Enterprise and Fundamental Rights*, N. M. Tripathi, Bombay, 1984.

Nath, N C B, Public Enterprise as an Intervention Mechanism, *Public Enterprise*, 6 (2) 1986, 95-106.

Nath, N C B, A Presentation on the Holding Company Concept, Indian Institute of Management, Ahmedabad, 1986.

National Economic Development Office, *A Study of U K Nationalised Industries*, HMSO, London, 1976.

Nayar, Baldev Raj, *Political Economy of India's Public Sector: Policy and Performance*, Popular Prakashan, Bombay, 1990.

Nigam, R K, Changing Horizon: Public Sector, *Lok Udyog*, 3 (7), 1970.

Nigam, R K, Concept of Efficiency Audit and its Application to Public Enterprises, *Lok Udyog*, 2 (10), Jan. 1968, 11-15.

Nigam, R K, (Ed.) *Management of Public Sector in India*, Vora, Bombay, 1971.

Nigam, R K, Management Practices Contribute to Productivity, *Industrial Times*, 31 Jan. 1977, 6-8.

Nigam, R K, (Ed.), *National Aspirations and Public Sector, Standing Conference of Public Enterprises*, New Delhi, 1976.

Nigam, R K, New Financial Discipline for Public Undertakings for Improving their Performance, *Lok Udyog*, 3 (7) Nov. 1969, 907-15.

Nigam, R K, *Personnel Management in Public Undertakings – A Study Based on the Chief State Enterprises of Uttar Pradesh*, Agra University, 1970. (D Lit.).

Nigam, R K, Public Sector's March Towards Commanding Heights, *Lok Udyog*, 9 (10) Jan. 1956, 5-14.

Nigam, Raj K (Ed.), *Policy Reference for Public Sector Enterprises.* New Delhi, DC Publications, 1993.

Nigam, R K, *Social Justice Through Public Sector*, Communication Centre-India, New Delhi, 1976.

Nigam, R K, Tasks Before the Public Sector. Indian Finance, 4 Oct. 1975, 278; 11Oct. 1975, 296-297, *Lok Udyog*, 9 (6) Sept. 1975, 1-5.

Palas, Sengupta, R, *Social Performance of Public Enterprises: An Indian Perspective*, Kanishka Publishers, New Delhi, 1993.

Panandiker Pai, V A, & Sud, A, *Public Sector as an Instrument of Development—A Survey of Agriculture*, Education and Health Sectors 1950-1975, Centre for Policy Research, New Delhi, 1978.

Parameswaran, N, Cash Management in Public Sector Undertakings, *Lok Udyog*, 12 (9) August 1978, 15-18.

Paranjape, H K, *The Flight of Technical Personnel in Public Undertakings*, Indian Institute of Public Administration, New Delhi, 1964.

Pareek, Udai, Human Resource Development in Public Enterprise, in T L Sankar (ed.), *Leading Issues in Public Enterprise Management*, Himalaya Publication, New Delhi, 1985.

Pareek Udai & Rao, T V, *Designing and Managing Human Resource Systems*, Oxford & IBH, New Delhi, 1981.

Patil, S M, & Nigam, R K, *Public Enterprise Management: Constraints and Autonomy*, Documentation Centre for Corporate and Business Policy Research, New Delhi, 1981.

Personnel Management in Public Enterprises, *Indian Journal of Commerce*, 19 (4) Oct-Dec 1966, 373-381.

Phatak, A, Governmental Interference and Management Problems of Public Sector Firms, *Annals of Public and Co-operative Economy*, 40 (3) Sept 1969, 337-51.

Pillai P M, Foreign Collaboration in Public Sector, *Economic and Political Weekly*, 13 (21) 27 May 1978, M 48-55.

Pleskovic, B, & Trevino, G, *The Use of a Social Accounting Matrix Framework for Public Sector Analysis: The Case Study of Mexico*, International Centre for Public Enterprises in Developing Countries, Ljubljana, 1985

Pozen, R C, *Legal Choices For State Enterprises in the Third World*, New York, 1976.

Prahalad, D K, & Thomas, P L, Turnaround Strategy: Lessons from HPF's Experience, *Vikalpa*, 1977, 2(2), 99-111.

Prakash M S, Technological Change and Manpower Planning in the Public Sector Undertaking-A Theoretical Framework, *Manpower Journal*, 10 (1) April-June 1974, 7-34

Prakash, Jagdish, *Privatisation of Public Enterprises in India*, Himalaya Publishing House, Bombay, 1992.

Prashant Kumar, "Financing of Public Enterprises and Public Participation", in Scott , Maurice & Lal, Deepak (Eds.). *Public Policy and Economic development: Essays in Honour of Ian Little*, 1990.

Public Enterprise in the National Economy-Summary of the Deliberations held at the National Convention of Public Enterprises held at New Delhi, 13-14 April 1976, Standing Conference of Public Enterprises, New Delhi, 1976.

Purushotham, P. W. *Organisation and Management of Public Enterprises*, Kanishka Publishing House, New Delhi, 1992.

Rao, K V, *Management of Working Capital in Public Enterprises*, Deep & Deep Publications, New Delhi, 1990.

Raja, Ram & Bhure Lal, *Controlling Public Sector Sickness*, Siddharth Publications, New Delhi, 1994.

Raj, Besant C, *Public Enterprise Investment Decisions in India: A Managerial Analysis*, Macmillan, New Delhi, 1978.

Raja, S T, Middle and Higher Management Personnel in Public Sector,

Indian Journal of Public Administration, New Delhi, 11 (1) Jan-Mar 1965, 19-25.

Rajadhyaksha, V G, Certain Key Effectiveness Variables: Organisation Size, Structure, Selection of Top Leaders and Management Development, *Yojana*, New Delhi, 16 Nov 1978, 5-8.

Rajeshwar, Rao K, *Working Capital Problems of Public Enterprises in India With Special Reference to Selected Undertakings*, Kakatiya University, 1980. (Ph.D. Thesis).

Ram, B P, Chanravanshi, A N, & Sharma, P K, Twenty Eight Years of Project Activities and Management in Bhilai Steel Plant, *Lok Udyog*, 18 (7) Oct 1984, 19-31.

Ramanadham, V V, *Pricing Labour and Efficiency in the Public Sector-Proceedings of the First Seminar on Public Enterprise*, Osmania University, Department of Commerce, Hyderabad, 1962.

Ramanadham V V, *Pricing and Investment in Public Enterprises*, Oxford & IBH, New Delhi, 1974.

Ramanadham, V V, *Economics of Public Enterprise*, Routledge, London, 1991.

Ramanadham, V V, *Reflections on Public Enterprise and Privatisation*, Vikas Publishing, New Delhi, 1996.

Ram, Prakash, *Management of Inventories in Selected Public Undertakings of Central Government*, Delhi University, 1978. (Ph.D. Thesis).

Ram, Reddy G, (ed.) *Government and Public Enterprise: Essays in Honour of Prof. V V Ramanadham*, Frank Cess, London & N M Tripati, Bombay, 1983.

Ramulu, D, *Capital Structure Planning in Public Enterprises*, Anmol Publications, New Delhi, 1995.

Rao, K L K, & Tagat, R G, Management of Imported Technology in Public Sector Enterprises: A Strategy for Internalisation, *Public Enterprise*, 6 (1) 1985, 27-40.

Rao, Viyyanna, Problems of Working Capital Management in Selected Public Enterprises in Andhra Pradesh – Nagarjuna University, 1983 (Ph.D. Thesis).

Report of Economic Administration Reforms Commission on Government and PEs (I-UV(m)) New Delhi, 1985.

Report of the Committee to Review Policy for Public Enterprises, New Delhi, 1984 (Chairman: Arjun Sengupta).

Report of the Action Committee on Public Enterprises (Pathak Committee), New Delhi, 1971.

Research Report on Corporate Planning in Public Enterprises in India, K S Bhat, Hyderabad, 1986.

Report of the Study Team of the Administrative Reforms Commission on Public Sector Undertakings, Government of India, New Delhi, 1966.

Report of the Expert Committee on Public Enterprises (Mohd. Fazal Committee), Government of India, New Delhi, 1982.

Report of the Committee on Parliamentary Supervision over State Undertakings (V K Krishna Menon Committee), New Delhi, 1951.

Sadique A S H K, *Public Enterprise in Asia: Studies on Coordination and Control*, Kuala Lumpur, Asian Centre for Development Administration, 1976.

Saraf, Vinay Kumar (ed.), *Evaluation of Public Enterprises*, Anmol Publications, New Delhi, 1991.

Sahani, B S, Public Sectors in Less Developed Countries: Development Goals and Efficiency, *Annals of Public and Cooperative Economy*, 54 (3), September 1983, 325-335.

Sankar, T L, (and others) (eds.), *Management of Research and Development in Public Sector*, Himalaya Publications, Bombay, 1986.

Sankar, T L, Mishra, R K & Nandagopal, R, Valuation of Equity Shares: Approaches for Public Enterprises, *IPE Journal*, Hyderabad, 1992.

Sankar, T L, Mishra, R K & Ravishankar, S, (eds.), *Public Enterprises in India: The Focus on Researches*, Himalaya Publications, New Delhi, 1983.

Sankar, T L, Mishra, R.K & Nandagopal, R, (ed.) *PE Managers in Nineties Role*, Tasks, Responsibilities. Printwell Publishers, Jaipur, 1992.

Standing Conference of Public Enterprises. Reports/ Recommendations of Various Committees on Public Enterprises, SCOPE Publications, New Delhi, 1990.

Sengupta, N K, *Unshackling of Indian Industry: Towards Competitiveness through Deregulation*, Vision, New Delhi, 1992.

Sankar, T L, Mishra, R K, Ravishankar, S, (eds.), *Leading Issues in Public Enterprise Management*, Himalaya Publications, Bombay, 1985.

Sankar, T L, (and others), *Public Enterprise Policy in India and U.K in 1980s*, Himalaya Publications, Bombay, 1987.

Sankar, T L, & Geeta Gouri, Pricing on Petroleum Products, *IPE Journal*, Hyderabad, 1985.

Sapru, R K, (Ed.), *Management of Public Sector Enterprises in India*, Ashish Publishing, New Delhi, 1987. 2 v.

Sapru, R K, *Managing Projects and Public Enterprises*, Sterling Publications, New Delhi, , 1998

Sarma, M S, & Rajeshwar, Rao K, Management Information System Policy in Public Enterprise: A Case Study of Rashtriya Chemicals & Fertilizers Ltd., *Lok Udyog*, 19 (2) May 1985, 49-58.

Sarabhai, V A., *Control and Management of Public Sector Enterprises*, Administrative Staff College of India, Hyderabad, 1970.

Sastry, K S, Performance Evaluation of Public Enterprises: An Approach, *Lok Udyog*, 19 (12) March 1986, 3-14.

Sastry, K S & Dhameja, Nand, *Performance Evaluation of Public Enterprises*, Manas Publications, New Delhi, 1993.

Satendra Kumar, Management of Production Functions in Some of the State Enterprises of Gujarat, South Gujarat University, 1972. (Ph.D. Thesis).

Satyanand, Singh, Profitability Measurement in Public Enterprises, Jabalpur University, 1975. (Ph.D. Thesis).

Satyanarayana, J, & Sarma, K R K, Capacity Utilisation in Public Enterprises in India, *Indian Journal of Commerce*, 32 (1) March 1979, 9-21.

Schloss, H H, Productivity in Public Enterprise, *Annals of Public and Cooperative Economy*, 41 (4) Oct-Dec 1970, 317-323.

Sengupta, R, *Public Sector Steel Pricing in India*, JNU, New Delhi, 1981 (Ph.D. Thesis).

Sankaraiah, A, *Budgeting in State Undertakings of Andhra Pradesh*, Kakatiya University, 1980. (Ph.D. Thesis).

Sharma, Arvind K, *Grammar of Public Enterprise*, Uppal Publishing House, New Delhi, 1991.

Sharma, B S, *Financial Planning in the Indian Public Sector: A Management Approach*, Vikas Publishing House, New Delhi, 1974.

Sharma, D D, MIS in Public Sector Undertakings: Need for Further Research, *Productivity*, New Delhi, 2 (3) Oct-Dec 1980, 23-31.

Sharma, G D, *Working of State Enterprises in Rajasthan*, Sterling Publications, New Delhi, 1975.

Sharma, T R, *Management of State Industrial Undertakings in India*, Agra University, 1959. (P h. D. Thesis).

Sharma, L, Scientific Inventory Control in Public Sector Industries, *AICC Economic Review*, 15 Oct. 1965, 35-37 & 42.

Singh, M K & Bhattacharya, A, (eds.), *Management of Public Enterprises*, Discovery Publishing House, New Delhi, 1990.

Singh, Mohinder, *Some Aspects of Public Enterprises in India: A Plea for Reforms*, Uppal, New Delhi, 1993.

Singh, Bishwa Nath, *Public Enterprise in Theory and Practice*, Deep & Deep Publications, New Delhi, 1991.

Shrivastava, M P, *Capacity Utilisation and Cost of Production: A Study of Public Enterprises*, Deep & Deep Publications, New Delhi, 1992.

Shrivastava, M P. *Parliamentary Accountability and Supervision over Public Enterprises*, Deep & Deep Publications, New Delhi, 1992.

Sunil Mani, Biotechnology Research in India: An Exploration into it's Implication for Indian Public Sector Enterprises, *IPE Journal*, Hyderabad, 1990.

Sunil Mani, *Foreign Technology in Public Enterprises*, Oxford & IBH Publishing Co. Pvt. Ltd., New Delhi, 1992.

Shiva Ramu S, *Approaches to Evaluation of Public Enterprises*, Indian Institute of Management, Bangalore, 1978.

Shereenivasan, N P, *Investment Criteria in Industrial Commercial Undertakings of the Government of Tamil Nadu*, University of Madras, 1981. (Ph.D. Thesis).

Shukla, Mata Badal, *Profitability Management in Public Enterprises*, Tiwary Publications, New Delhi, 1991.

Shrivastava, J P, *Labour, Productivity and Incentives in Public Sector: Bhilai Steel Plant – A case study*. Rajasthan University, 1971. (Ph.D. Thesis).

Siddique, A A, *Role of Public Enterprises in Mobilising the Resources for Economic Development*, Aligarh Muslim University, 1979, (Ph.D. Thesis).

Singh, J D, *Marketing Planning– A Comparative Study of Public and Private Sectors in India*, University of Delhi, 1979. (Ph.D. Thesis).

Shukla, P R & Chowdhry, Roy K (eds.), *Public Sector in India: Role, Problems and Prospects*, Akashdeep, New Delhi, 1992.

Singh, P, & Das, G S, Managerial Style of Indian Managers: A Profile, *ASCI Journal of Management*, Hyderabad, 1977, 7 (1), 1-11.s

Som, Singh S P & Nath, Surendra, *Workers' Participation in Public Enterprises*, Deep & Deep Publications, New Delhi, 1992.

Srinivasan, C V, *Corporate Planning in the Public Sector, Management in Government*, 17 (4), Jan-Mar 1986, 288-302.

Srivastava, M, *A Study of Steel Industry in the Public Sector With Special Reference to Hindustan Steel Limited*, Lucknow University, 1973. (Ph.D. Thesis).

Srivastava, V K L, *Price Policy for Public Undertakings With Special Reference to India*, Banaras Hindu University, 1979. (Ph.D. Thesis).

Stefani, G, The Productivity of Public Enterprises, *Annals of Public and Co-operative Economy*, 44 (1) Jan-Mar 173, 13-58.

Subbaramaiah, S, *Economics of Public Enterprises in India with Special Reference to Mysore: Case Study of Eleven Public Enterprises of Mysore State*, University of Mysore, 1956-59 (Ph.D. Thesis).

Subba, Rao G, Practical Approaches Toward Higher Productivity, *Lok Udyog*, 19 (94) July 1985, 23-33.

Sundaram, S, Technological Problems of Public Sector, *Financial Express*, 28 Nov. 1972, 4.

Sudarshan, R, *Accounting Control in Public Enterprises*, Printwell Publishers, Jaipur, 1990.

Sukumaran, S., *Budgeting in Selected Private and Public Undertakings (A Case Study of Kerala)*, Commonwealth Publishers, New Delhi, 1992.

Swamy, K, *Financial Performance of Manufacturing State Level Public Enterprises*, Delta Publishing House, New Delhi, 1994.

Tamarkar, B, *The Management Structure of Bhilai Steel Project*, Jabalpur University, 1970. (Ph.D. Thesis).

Thavaraj, M J K, Performance Budgeting for Public Enterprises in Nigam R S., (ed.). *Issues in Public Enterprises*, Pragathi, New Delhi, 1980, 67-71.

Towards Higher Productivity – Report of Seminar on Higher Productivity in Public Sector Production Enterprises, Standing Conference on Public Enterprise, New Delhi, 1976.

Tripathy, B N, *Public Corporation as a Form of Organisation for the public Enterprises in India*, Ranchi University, 1964 (Ph.D. Thesis).

Trivedi, Prajapati, Effect of Public Ownership on Working Capital Management, *Public Enterprise*, 6 (3) 1986, 195-206.

Trivedi, Prajapati S, *Critique of Public Enterprise Policy*, International Management Publishers, New Delhi, 1992.

Trivedi, Prajapathi, *Memorandum of Understanding: An Approach to Improving Public Enterprises Performance*, International Management Publishers, New Delhi, 1990.

Turk, I, Accounting Information Needed in Assessing the Efficiency of the Public Enterprise, *Public Enterprise*, 1 (2) 1980, 7-17.

United Nations, Department of Economic and Social Affairs, Financing of Public Enterprises in Developing Countries: Co-ordination, Form and Sources, United Nations, New York, 1976.

United Nations, Department of Economic and Social Affairs, Measures for Improving Performance of Public Enterprise in Developing Countries, United Nations, New York, 1973.

United Nations, Department of Economic and Social Affairs, *Organisation, Management and Supervision of Public Enterprises in Developing Countries*, United Nations, New York, 1974.

United Nations, Department of Economic and Social Affairs, *Public Industrial Management in Asia and the Far East: A Selection from the Material* Prepared for a U N Seminar held in New Delhi in December, 1959, United Nations, New York, 1960.

United Nations, *Report of the Seminar on Management of Public Industrial Enterprises in the ECAFE Region Bangkok*, UN, Economic Commission for Asia and the Far East.

Vaid Raizada,V K and Rana, M R, *Public Enterprises in India*. New Delhi, Anmol Publications Pvt. Ltd., New Delhi, 1990.

Vathsala, S, & Krishna, Kumar, Top Executive Pay Parity, *Lok Udyog*, 1979, 13 (3), 19-29.

Venkaiah, V, Impact of Public Enterprise on Rural Development: A Case Study of Nizam Sugar Factor, *Institute of Public Enterprise Journal*, Hyderabad, 6 (1) Jan-March 1983, 18-33.

Venkatachalam, G, & Dakshinamurthy, D, Performance of Public Enterprises in India: Impact of Heavy External Finance, *Public Enterprise*, 6 (2) 1986, 147-156.

Venugopal, Reddy Y, *Public Enterprise Reform and Privatisation*, Himalaya Publishing House, Bombay, 1992.

Venugopal, Reddy Y, Koteswara, Rao T, & Mishra, R K, (ed.), Public Enterprises: Towards a White Paper, *IPE Journal*, Hyderabad, 1990.

Vijaya, P. Saradhi, *Working Capital Management in PEs*, ICPE, Ljubljana, 1982.

Wahi, S P, Management of Public Sector Enterprises. *Towards Continuing Education*, 2 (8) Nov. 1980, 327-9.

Wettenhall, Roger & Nuallain, Colm O (Eds.), International Institute of Administrative Sciences, *Public Enterprise Performance Evaluation: Seven Country Studies*. (Internationalisation of Public Enterprise—Performance Evaluation) Brussels, 1990.

Workshop on Public Sector, Organised by IPE for Economic Advisory Council at New Delhi, September 1986.

Chapter III

Performance Evaluation of Public Enterprises in India

Public Enterprises (PEs) have been assigned a place of prime importance in the planned economic development of India, through a series of five-year plans seeking to achieve a socialistic pattern of society. It is vital that they function effectively and efficiently in order to ensure the success of this effort in economic planning. The central purpose of this paper is to evaluate the efficacy of the performance evaluation system for Indian PEs and to suggest how educational and training programmes for PE board members, executives and "external governors" may be improved to secure better performance evaluation in the future.

Nature of Public Enterprise Activity

PEs operate at three levels in India, central, state and municipal. The central PEs are engaged in agriculture, mining, manufacturing, construction, energy, transport and communications, trading, finance, defence production, defence service, printing and publishing, forest conservation and development, and dairy development and milk supply. State-level enterprises (SLPEs) operate in agro-industries, mining and mineral development, manufacturing, industrial development, small industries promotion, road transport, export promotion, electricity generation and supply, warehousing, development finance, dairy and milk supply, forest conservation and development, printing and publishing, river transport, commodity trading and fisheries development. Municipal enterprises are engaged in the fields of transport, electricity and milk supply, but they are insignificant in terms of investment and the state governments have taken over many such enterprises.

There has been little systematic effort to collect data on these enterprises, either for research purposes or to provide assistance in the formulation of public policy. Excluding the municipal enterprises, the overall investment in PEs is in the vicinity of Rs 274114 crores. The ratio of investment in the central PEs and SLPEs is in the order of 7:3.

The dominance of PEs in core industries and certain service sectors indicates that they control the commanding heights of the economy and provide sinews for its growth. Having said this, it will be useful to note here that in recent years there have been some deviations from the established philosophy for the public sector. Many PEs have been set up in the consumer goods industry, while the public sector's share of in the core industries has declined somewhat. Nevertheless, the performance of PEs continues to be very critical for the efficient conduct of the entire Indian economy.

Though the number of PEs and investment therein have grown phenomenally over the four decades since independence, ten units in the central sector and another 40 enterprises generating power and engaged in road transport business in the different states of the Indian Union controlled more than 50 per cent of the total investment in PEs in 2000-2001. In the central sector, the top ten enterprises in terms of investment operated in these industries: oil, petroleum, food grains, power generation, steel, gas and telecom. Appendix 1 provides investment details about these top ten enterprises. At the state level, the power boards and the road transport corporations are the leading enterprises with over 80 per cent of the total investment in the SLPEs.

PEs in India variously take the form of statutory corporations, government companies, cooperative enterprises and departmental undertakings. Government policy has been to set them up in the statutory corporation form. But this has not found favour in practice. Appendix 2 shows that out of 1118 identified central (239) and state (879) PEs, 943 or 84 per cent have been incorporated as government companies. This form of organisation is enormously popular as it offers government flexibility in setting up an enterprise and provides the requisite degree of commercial freedom for the management. The statutory corporations and cooperative enterprises come next in popularity to the government company form. Though we do not have data about the departmental form, the available evidence suggests that as far as possible it is being discarded in favour of the other forms.

Interface Relationships

Over the years a very comprehensive system of interface has emerged spelling out the relationship between the government and PEs and detailing the devices to act as elements of the translating mechanism. The system takes care of the constitutional and legal requirements on the one hand, and the needs of the government as owner on the other. The interface relationship is exhibited in the diagram1.

The departmental enterprises have no autonomy and are completely controlled by the creating governments. The partial exceptions here are the railway, postal services and telecommunications boards of the government of India which are semi-autonomous organisations set up to facilitate quick decision-making. For all the other enterprises, the provisions regarding accountability to the central apparatus of public administration are specified in the parliamentary / state legislative procedures and in documents of incorporation of PEs. Four major constituents of the PE interface environment are now considered.

Network of Relations between the Focal Organisations and the Enabling System

Diagram 1

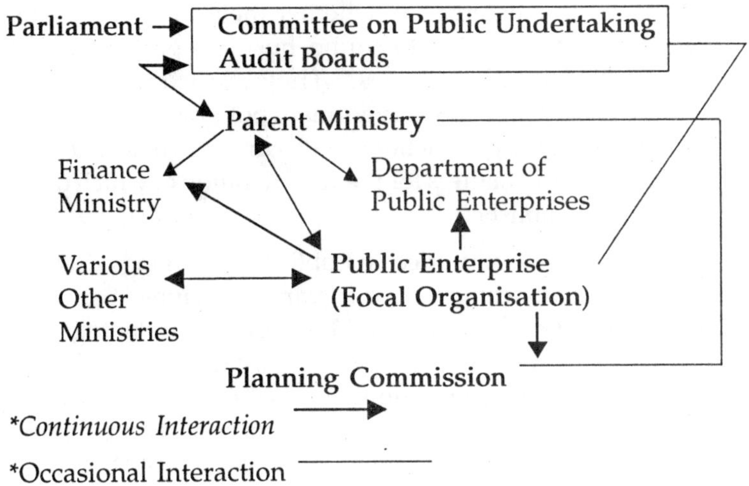

Accountability to Parliament / State Legislatures

The public control through parliament is very extensive and probing. It is exercised through questions; short discussions including the formal half-an-hour discussion; calling attention to matters of urgent public importance and short debates on such matters; budget discussions; and debates on public corporation statutes and amendments thereto. Besides, the establishment of a full-fledged Committee on Public Undertakings (COPU) by the parliament and many state legislatures has provided a permanent tool for ongoing assessment, control and monitoring of PE performance.

The public control of PEs in principle is restricted to the policy aspects of their functioning; day-to-day management decisions are exempted from this control. But it is very difficult in practice to draw a line between the two and instances are not lacking where detailed interventions have been made on the ground of public interest. The Committees on Public

Undertakings examine the reports and accounts of PEs, and those of the Comptroller and Auditor General of India (CAG) on PEs; and they study, in the context of autonomy and efficiency of these enterprises, whether their affairs are being managed in accordance with sound business principles and prudent commercial practices. They are excluded from examining matters of major government policy as distinct from business or commercial functions of PEs, matters of day-to-day administration, and matters for the consideration of which other machinery is established.

The role of the Committee on Public Undertakings (COPU) has been especially commended in various forums. Set up in 1964, this committee has examined 114 public undertakings and undertaken visits to 1005 undertakings/ establishments/ units for on the spot study. The committee has presented 497 reports so far. Of these, 248 are the original reports and 249 are reports on action taken by government on earlier reports of the committee[3]. The committee brings out three kinds of studies: "horizontal" reports, reports on individual PEs and "action-taken" reports. Horizontal reporting occurs once a year, when the committee takes up an important element of the functioning of PEs, collects relevant information from as many PEs as possible, and studies the different dimensions of the problem in detail. The reports on individual enterprises presents a plethora of information on the various aspects of their working and offers recommendations for improving performance. As the selection of PEs is mostly done on leads provided by the CAG in his audit reports, the report on an individual enterprise is often restricted to the problem(s) raised by the CAG. To ascertain the extent to which recommendations have been implemented, the committee brings out within the time-lag of from one to two years action-taken reports which highlight rejected recommendations. The committee has made recommendations about project appraisal, forms of organisations, functional aspects, corporate planning, public accountability, international operations, productivity, public image, R & D, technology management etc., and about two-thirds have been accepted by the government.

Though public control is often assumed to be the strongest device for monitoring PE performance, it has not turned out to be so in practice because of certain serious limitations. The parliament / state legislatures are constrained by dearth of time from initiating full fledged debates and by lack of technical competence from probing PE working. In addition, instances are not lacking where parliamentary opportunities have been used to question day-to-day matters and not the policy aspects. The permanent Committees on Public Undertakings have only partially remedied this situation. Lack of required competence to develop deep into efficiency issues and inability to cover all PEs even once in five years have been the principal deficiencies of these committees.

Relationship with the Government

There is a very close and constant interaction of PEs with government. This manifests itself in the form of advice, persuasion, simple communication, directions issued by the government formally, and its views conveyed to PEs on several matters informally. The minister, the secretary of the administrative ministry and the PE chief comprise the triumvirate for overseeing, controlling and managing a PE. A close, continuous and meaningful liaison among the triumvirate is essential for fast change of persons in the three positions.

Controls exercised by government itself are of the following kinds:

Prior approval: On a number of matters board decisions can only be taken after obtaining the approval of the government. These include capital expenditure and replacement beyond a specific limit, variations in capital expenditure beyond a certain percentage, appointment of persons above a specific salary range, reappointment / appointment of persons who have attained the age of superannuation, formation of a subsidiary company, agreement involving foreign collaboration, borrowing, investment and distribution of profits, making of rules governing the conditions of service of employees, provident fund and creation of reserves and special funds.

Power to issue directions: Ministers can issue directives of two kinds-general and specific. The general directives are applicable to all PEs whereas the specific directive relates to a specific enterprise. The power to issue such directives is conferred in the articles of association in the case of the statutory corporations. The cooperative enterprises are bound by the provisions contained in the cooperative law which permits the issuance of such directives. For all kinds of PEs directions can be issued on policy matters and in the public interest on any aspect of their operations. In the case of government companies, directives can be issued to cover a wider area of operations. The directives have to be issued in writing. In practice, these directive powers have been sparingly used. However, the practice of giving informal directives is very common.

Circulars and Office Orders: The government-PE interaction frequently takes place through the circulars and office orders issued by official agencies. These circulars and office orders, though mere advice in nature, are extremely effective in that, informally, implementation by PEs is obligatory. The nodal agencies, viz. The Bureau of Public Enterprises (BPE) at the centre and similar bureau/cells in different states, have hardly left any operational or policy matters, which has not been, covered by these circulars and office orders.

Board Appointments: All board-level appointments are made by government. The super-cession of the boards is also within the jurisdiction of government; and tenures of board members have been very short.

Reports, Returns and Meetings: The government receives a number of reports and returns and holds review meetings to keep itself in touch with the activities of PEs. These processes allow it to render its advice to improve general management and various operational practices and leave hardly any major activity untouched.

Power of Investigation: Where maladministration or malpractice is suggested, the government can refer the matter to the specialised agencies. In the case of central enterprises, the Central Bureau of Investigation and the Central Vigilance Commission investigated by their anti-corruption bureaus. Some state governments have set up ombudsman-type bodies. Both central PEs and SLPEs have registered numerous cases with these bodies, in order to gain redress against supposedly corrupt officials.

The government-PE interface is regulated by a sprawling government machinery which includes, at both the central and state levels, the administrative ministry in each case, the finance ministry, the department/bureau of public enterprises or public enterprise cell, other ministries and ad hoc committees. These are discussed very briefly below:

Administrative Ministry: Each PE has to be under the control of one or other ministry. There is a tendency to refer matters of small significance to the administrative ministry. On the other hand, the administrative ministry tries to usurp all decision-making powers of the PEs by impinging on its autonomy to decide upon many issues on its own.

Finance Ministry: From project-approval stage and its implementation to day-to-day management and expansion, the finance ministry has its say. Its representative frequently finds a berth on the PE board to ensure that the necessary financial discipline is maintained.

Department of Public Enterprises (DPE): This department was set up by the central government in 1985 to deal with PE issues and oversee the working of the Bureau of Public Enterprises. The department also acts as the administrative ministry for PEs under its control.

Department of Public Enterprises/Public Enterprise Cells: On the lines of the DPE at the centre, many states have set up bureaus/cells to monitor the performance of PEs. The organisational arrangements vary greatly.

Other Ministries and Departments: PEs usually have to interact with home, labour, energy, and transport and environment ministries to sort out issues pertaining to security, recruitment, availability of energy, adequate transport facilities, and expansion and maintenance of projects. The Planning Commission at the centre and state planning boards have to be approached for clearance of projects, and account has to be rendered to them for performance in terms of the internal generation of resources. The Public Investment Board has to be approached by central PEs for the clearance of projects ranging between Rs10 crores to Rs. 200 crores. SLPEs normally have to approach state-level investment committees to seek clearance of projects exceeding $4 millions (Rs. 50 lakhs).

Accountability through Audit

The CAG is empowered to audit PEs under Article 151 of the Indian Constitution, primarily because money for investment are advanced to PEs from the Consolidated Fund of India. The CAG's audit comes into the picture in another way too. PEs have to present their annual audited statements to the legislature either under the Companies Act or under the specific acts of their incorporation. Starting from selection of the statutory auditors, CAG has the power to direct the manner in which the audit should be done and also the authority to conduct supplementary audits for the government companies. For the statutory corporation, the audit process is conducted in the same way as in the case of the government accounts.

The CAG can also conduct efficiency and performance audits. The efficiency audit goes into wisdom, faithfulness and economy of expenditure. The performance audit questions the necessity of the expenditure itself and the overall pay-off. The CAG has set up an audit board comprising five to six official and non-official members who have industrial and professional experience. Each year five or six PEs are reviewed in detail.

In sum, the CAG audit is the third-tier audit for PEs, additional to internal and financial audits. Private enterprises have only the internal and financial audits.

Accountability through Annual Reports

Whether central or state, PEs have to bring out annual

reports on their financial and physical operations over a stipulated period in conformity with formats indicated in the governing statutes. These reports are presented to the parliament/state legislatures, but no time-limit has been prescribed for this purpose. They are expected to contain information on

- the state of PE affairs
- the amounts of reserve created and dividends declared
- any changes in the nature of the business
- changes in the accounting methods
- a summary of financial results
- important changes in the price-policy
- staff welfare activities
- new projects and expansion
- increases in paid-up capital and long-term loans
- general order-book position
- main events which have influenced production and profitability
- outlook for the future
- achievement in import substitutions
- production capacities and
- targets, levels of production and factors affecting production levels, utilisation of principal implement of production, etc.

These reports, which are prepared with a long time-lag, are not analytical in nature. They do not incorporate inter-firm comparison. Nor does parliament find time to discuss them.

Overview of Performance Evaluation System

In this section, the major instruments or techniques used to evaluate the performance of PEs are identified, the development of the techniques over the years is traced, and the machinery for performance assessment indicated.

Techniques

Financial and economic techniques have been used for performance evaluation of PEs in India. Of the two, financial techniques have been resorted to more intensively and have acquired general acceptance because of legal stipulations and their easy application.

Financial Techniques: In evaluating agencies and monitoring organisations, administrative ministries use financial techniques to assess financial health, including profit-earning potential of PEs. Ratio analysis, funds-flow, common-size analysis and inter-firm comparison are the widely used financial techniques. A host of financial ratios are calculated to evaluate the liquidity, leverage, turnover and profitability status of PEs. The Return on Investment (ROI) ratio is calculated as the key ratio. Appendix 3 gives the list of various financial ratios computed for performance evaluation of PEs. The basic objective of this ratio analysis is to present the overall picture of the financial health of these enterprises and provide clues to good or indifferent financial performance.

The fund-low analysis indicates the PE performance in respect to sources and application of funds. It points to the composition of funds and assets build-up, and the changes in the two annually. Managerial decisions about asset investment and about raising finance through different sources and their effectiveness in terms of profit generation are evaluated by this technique. The common-size technique helps in reducing the different items of expenses as a percentage of total income and presents trends relating the different components to expenses over a time-period, thereby revealing the operational efficiency. The inter-firm comparison is conducted by PEs for their different units and for PEs vis-à-vis their counterparts in the private sector.

Economic Techniques: The Planning Commission at the centre is mainly interested in these techniques as, through their application, it assesses the resource-generation capacity of PEs in order to find out how much can be obtained from them for financing the national plans. They include quantification of surplus generation, computation of input-output relationships, calculation of quality of project management expressed in terms of time-and cost-overruns, and the position of international operations.

The surplus generated by PEs is quantified to assess the ability of a PE to contribute to the exchequer for the growth of the economy as a whole. The input-output relationship is computed in monetary terms to find out how PEs have been using the economic resources allocated to them.

Since sound project management is very vital for growth and sustenance of the economy, the time-and cost-overruns in PEs are studied to assess performance in this area. Similarly, since effective international operations will reduce external dependence and thereby contain the foreign exchange drain, PE performance is evaluated on these counts also.

Development of Techniques and Agencies Involved in Performance Evaluation

As already noted, the parliamentary / state legislature COPU, administrative ministries, BPE and C&AG are the prominent agencies evaluating the performance of PEs. Further discussion in this sub-section will be restricted to PEs of the central government.

COPU was set up in 1964. In its reports on individual undertakings it mostly discusses their overall working and suggests measures for better performance. It studies the functioning of PEs in relation to their objectives in order to develop committee placed the emphasis on aspects such as business performance, finance and accounts, utilisation of plant and machinery and organisational and staff matters (COPU 1965). The emphasis subsequently shifted in the 1970s to matters such as: demand projections, diversification, contribution made by the PE to the development of the industry, machine and labour utilisation, sales management, materials management and inventory control, financial matters and organisation (COPU 1973a, b). During 1980s and 1990's, the committee has strengthened its appraisal of PEs by concentration on the quality of corporate planning, organisation development, marketing management, production management, management information system, productivity, management by objectives, costing systems and composition of costs.

In the early years, while analysing the working of PEs, the committee used percentages and growth-rate techniques. But over a period of time it extended these tools to common-size analysis and inter-firm comparisons. In the 1980s the performance evaluation has been made more rigorous in that the committee has added marginal costing, standard costing, inventory management, internal audit and productivity-accounting tools to its performance evaluation kit.

As noted earlier, the committee brings out each year a horizontal report on a PE topic of vital significance to the nation. The first such report was published in 1965. The ratio, inter-firm comparison and the other techniques have been proficiently applied to arrive at useful conclusions. To cite an illustration, the committee's report on *Materials Management in Public Enterprises* (COPU 1967) gave an indication of an excessive build-up of inventory in relation to sales/output and of the scope for possible economies for PEs. This analysis was carried further to locate the extent and nature of stockpiling in the different components of inventory. The study was extended to identify the causes of over-stocking and the extent to which PEs were aware of materials management techniques. Finally, an agenda for reform in the materials management techniques, but it also compared the position prevailing in Indian PEs with private sector enterprises in India and abroad.

In their third report, the Estimates Committee had recommended to the government that, in addition to the individual annual reports each enterprise laid on the table of the house every year, a separate comprehensive report should be submitted to the parliament indicating government's total appraisal of the working of PEs (Estimates Committee 1964). The first such report was prepared by the Cabinet Secretariat for the year 1960-61 and brought out in 1961. The report presented a microscopic view in the form of summary statements of industrial undertakings incomplete and not in full operation; and commercial, financial, general development and miscellaneous undertakings. These statements included summarised balance sheets and data on net profit and number of people employed. The report also contained details about the constitution, capital structure, financial working, production operations and employment of the various PEs (Cabinet Secretariat 1962).

After creation of BPE in 1965, preparation of this report was passed to its hands. It revised the format and divided the report into two parts: text and annexures. The text of the first report contained information on the performance of undertakings under construction, Hindustan Steel Ltd (a major PE), promotion and developmental undertakings, and financial institutions. In addition, information was provided on internal resources, sales production and exports, working capital and inventory employment, and undertakings with central government investment without direct responsibility for management. Based on the new accounts were prepared in respect of each category and their performance in aggregate was reviewed. In addition, the performance of each undertaking was also reviewed, and a brief write-up giving its progress was included in the report (BPE 1966).

Since then, the form and contents of the Annual Report have undergone many changes. The latest (1986-87) is divided in to three volumes. Volume 1 presents a macro-appraisal of the performance of PEs in terms of broad physical and financial performance. The analysis includes the contribution made by these enterprises towards the attainment of the multi-dimensional objectives for which they were set up. This is done in three parts: the first includes overview and performance appraisal of operating enterprises; the second contains group-wise performance of PEs; the third comprises details about PEs with respect to growth and pattern of investment, generation of internal resources, pricing policy, productivity, international operations, managerial personnel policy and human resources development, wage policies, industrial relations, cost control and internal audit, socio-economic and welfare measures, and extent to which balanced regional development is promoted. Volume II presents an analysis of the performance of these units in different sectoral groups, disaggregated further into individual enterprises. It also contains a narrative on their performance. Volume III is divided into two parts. The first contains a comparative analysis for three years consisting of the resources and utilisation of funds, working results and year-wise inventories together with accounting and management ratios in respect of individual enterprises. The second contains the summarised profit and loss account and balance sheet for each individual enterprise for three years (DPE 2000-2001).

The performance evaluation techniques of DPE have undergone a complete transformation. Instead of restricting the measurement to financial aspects, especially profitability, the physical aspects of evaluation have also been accorded due importance. In fact this DPE report now makes an attempt to measure the national, economic, social and financial contribution of PEs.

The CAG's performance evaluation of PEs is based on a different approach and the techniques employed to assess the performance have not changed much over the last three-and-a-half decades. Between 1951 and 1969 the CAG's consolidated report on PEs was divided into two parts. In Part I, an overview of the working (financial and physical) including investment, break-up of investment, turnover, value of production, capacity utilisation, productivity etc., of PEs was provided in the overview; the performance of government companies and statutory corporations was shown separately. In Part II, the working of about 15-20 enterprises was discussed in detail. The individual units also included those undertakings against whom special audit para existed connected to some bad business practice (e.g. CAG 1968). After the constitution of Audit Boards, the approach has changed radically. Now the CAG in his Union Government (Commercial) Report provides a general view of the working results of the government companies, deemed government companies and corporations. The results of the comprehensive appraisal of the selected undertakings conducted by the Audit Boards are published in separate volumes. In 1986 (CAG 1987a) the CAG brought out in all eight reports including the one providing general review. The CAG undertakes a sort of efficiency-cum-propriety audit in the reports on individual undertakings. The general review of PEs, as a matter of fact, is in many respects a summary of Volume I of the DPE report. It concentrates mostly on investment net profit/return on capital employed, return on paid-up capital, return on net worth, financial relief, township maintenance and value of production. The reports on individual companies touch upon the general and functional aspects, productive performance, diversification, machine utilisation, working system and analysis of costs, pricing, financial position and working results etc.

But the techniques applied are elementary, and the CAG's macro-performance evaluation of PEs does not offer much. However its evaluation of individual enterprises is enlightening, although the number covered is very small. But the scope of CAG's audit extends also to SLPEs. In each state, through his functionary known as Accountant General, he gets a report on the SLPEs; these reports are separately published (e.g. CAG 1987b). The CAG also conducts performance reviews of departmental PEs of the central government. This review of the techniques of performance evaluation and accomplishment of agencies involved therein points out that the whole exercise suffers from the absence of novelty and lack of innovation.

Efficacy of Performance Evaluation System

This section probes the measuring techniques used by the various agencies identified, the methods for reporting outcome of various exercises, the way the government and other central agencies respond to the messages they receive, the general impact on PEs themselves, the extent to which comments have come on the whole evaluation process and the suggestions that have emerged for the improvement of that process.

Measuring Techniques

Studies looking into the measuring techniques for performance evaluation have indicated that they have mostly failed to take into consideration the multi-dimensional objectives of PEs. PEs, as is self-evident, are characterised by "public" and "enterprise" dimensions. The measuring techniques in vogue attempts to evaluate either of the two dimensions or to that extent fail to present a composite view of PE performance. The stakeholders in PE are not interested in either of the two components alone, and need to be distinguished from the stakeholders of a joint stock company in the private sector who are interested only in the maximisation of the present value of their stock. The information needs of the former group are different as they would like to know about the quality of products, efficiency in the use of inputs, input-output relationship, capacity utilization, unit-cost reduction, the consequences of giving effect to directions from the government, diversification, expansion and modernisation, total factor productivity, internal accruals, international competitiveness, organisational cohesion, human resources development, and linkage with the other components of the economy. As noted earlier, the present instruments over-emphasise financial evaluation and assessment of some physical aspects of operations, viz., capacity utilization and inventory.

Methods for Reporting

The prominent instruments of performance evaluation include COPU and DPE (and state equivalents), the administrative ministry and the C&AG.

COPUs present their reports to the parliament or the state

legislature, with copies going to the concerned PEs. The DPE at the centre, and similar establishments at state level, bring out annual reports on the working of PEs under their control which are presented to the parliament and the state legislative assemblies. The central DPE presents its report along with the budget papers in the budget session of the parliament, which assists parliamentarians in gathering knowledge about the various aspects of the functioning of PEs.

At the level of the states-excepting kerala (DPE-Kerala 1988)-it has not been possible to follow the centre in this practice. The administrative ministries review PE performance with the help of appraisal and quarterly performance review meetings with their chief executives. The CAG assesses performance by conducting the test-check supplementary and performance audits. The repots on test-check and supplementary audit are included in the annual reports published by PEs. In the case of the central enterprises, however, performance audit is conducted and the findings reported and published separately. These reports are tabled prior to publication in the parliament/ state legislature.

Responding Mechanism

COPU reports-central and state-are sent to the concerned administrative ministries and the nodal agencies (DPE and its state equivalents) for follow-up. These nodal agencies play a major role in responding to the reports. They process the recommendations and issue office memorandums to the concerned ministries requesting them to write to all PEs under their control to give effect to the recommendations and to explain the reasons if certain recommendations cannot be implemented by them. These interventions have been mostly welcomed (Narain 1988).

The DPE/state level bureaus tender advice on various issues of common interest through circulars to PEs via their administrative ministries. Though these circulars contain "mere advices", in effect they have to be implemented. Both at central and state levels these circulars have been resented by PE executives, who feel that many of them curtail managerial authority (Patel 1987).

As discussed earlier, the administrative ministries have wide-ranging powers relating to the regulation and control of PEs. Their orders have to be given effect by PEs. Any disobedience may lead to punitive action against the whole board, one or more members of the board, or the managing director. CAG's reports draw attention of the parliament/state legislatures and PEs through their administrative ministries to any defaults: implementation of recommendations is thus virtually mandatory.

Impact on PE Performance

Appendix 4 provides data on the performance of the central PEs. We do not have as much detailed data on the performance of SLPEs. However, data on assets, profits and losses in SLPEs are given in Appendix 5. Data relating to the capacity utilisation of the central PEs are given in Appendix 6. About 30 per cent of central PEs were using less than 50 per cent of the installed capacity in 1986-87. The position of SLPEs noted that the rate of capacity utilization was below 25 per cent in the majority of states, and that the profitability rate was negative in all states (Capoor 1979).

Despite a sprawling machinery for performance evaluation and its presence for a very long period, why is it that PE performance has been dismal all these years? Why has the existing framework proved ineffective? The answer could be found in deficiencies in the role played by CAG, administrative ministries and the nodal agencies. They have followed the fault-finding approach and taken a one-sided view of performance which did not have any place for involvement of PEs in the process. The negative pull in the entire exercise was so forceful that it overshadowed the constructive approach of COPU and similar committees in the other states.

The CAG's audit is based on the "para" approach wherein irregularities are often blown out of proportion, with no effort to help a PE overcome the deficiencies. This has resulted in hampering initiative and creativity. The administrative ministries and the nodal agencies have acted no less irresponsibly. The performance evaluation process followed by these agencies has promoted dependence, indecision and rigidity. To cite an example, even wage revisions and bonus-payment decisions have got to be approved by the nodal agencies, who take much time in working through such issues. There have been instances when a nodal agency indecision has led to strikes in PEs resulting in colossal production loss and unveiling the incapacity of the top management of the enterprises to handle the situation. Another instance pertains to ridiculously short tenures of board members and chief executives which have promoted a "tourist culture" in PEs. But the combined effect of all such pitfalls has been much worse, in that excessive doses of intervention by government have impended the growth of a distinctive PE culture, with the result that personnel in these enterprises do not have the sense of belonging to their employing organisations.

The parliamentary/state legislature Committees on Public Undertakings have been an exception to this trend. Thus recommendations made by COPU regarding performance evaluation indicators, elimination of performance retarding factors, and exploitation of performance-improving factors have contributed significantly to a smooth functioning of the PE system. Why is it that the impact of COPU on the PE performance evaluation system has been positive? An important reason for this outcome could be that, in formulating recommendations, the committee invites the views of both the controlling ministries and the PE and thus takes a balanced view of the situation-which is greatly appreciated by the PEs.

Views and Suggestions on Evaluation Process

Academics, official commissions and committees, PE managers and some free-standing institutions have commented upon and made suggestions for reforming the performance evaluation system.

Ramanadham (1988), Prakash (1971), Murthy (1983), Narain (1988,p.245), Shivaramu (1978), Sankar (1981) and Dholakia (1980) have viewed performance evaluation as a unified system and observed that prevailing methods do not follow this holistic approach. They argue for the development of suitable instruments to enable the installation of the unified system. They believe that, while profitability, capacity utilisation, internal generation of resources, machine down time, and provision of employment to weaker sections of the society can be good indicators to reveal partial performance, the unified system of performance evaluation needs to be based on a negotiated settlement between the government and PEs specifying government's expectations of PEs and detailing also the steps government must take to make the realising of such expectations possible. Ramanadham (1974) and Sankar (19897a, p.14) have gone a step further in suggesting the setting up of a PE Commission which could judge the performance of PEs and suggest improvements in an unbiased manner. Murthy (1983, pp.381-96) offers a slightly modified approach by imposing the "stage-of-operation", condition which implies that the unified performance evaluation model could be operative only during the third stage of operation of an enterprise where economic considerations override political considerations. According to Murthy, in the second stage of operation economic considerations balance the political, and in the first stage the latter override the former.

Official commissions and committees going into the issue of performance evaluation include importantly the Administrative Reforms Commission, Economic Administration Reforms Commission, Prime Minister's Economic Advisory Committee, the Arjun Sengupta Committee and the working group involved in the preparation of the White paper on PSEs.

The Administrative Reforms Commission rejected the popular approach of discussing macro-PE performance. It suggested evaluating performance of a public enterprise in terms of the success achieved by management in the following spheres and in the order indicated below:

a. furthering of the non-commercial objectives of the enterprise as specified by the government;

b. furthering of the commercial objectives of the enterprise and maximisation of profits subject to (a) and within the constraints of government directives;

c. improvement in the quality of products and services; and

d. economy and efficiency in the use of resources (men, money and materials)(ARC 1966)

The Economic Administration Reforms Commission did not approve of the Administrative Reforms Commission's view. It suggested that performance criteria may be defined simply as the quantifiable expression of the objectives of an enterprise and that such criteria should be specified in terms of an enterprise and that such criteria should be specified in terms of quantity, quality, cost and time-frame for objective evaluation (EARC 1985). The Arjun Sengupta Committee submitted its report to the *Prime Minister on Review of Policy for Public Enterprises* on December 31,1984. It observed that, while the public enterprises were to be judged by their "total results", the monitoring and evaluation system of the government had not been adequate. While recognising that PEs pursue multiple objectives simultaneously and that a single measure of performance is difficult to specify, the committee felt that there were certain objectives which were common and could form the basis for general performance criteria. It recommended the following four criteria:

1. Financial Performance
2. Productivity and Cost Reduction
3. Technical Dynamism
4. Effectiveness of Project Implementation

A major structural reform suggested by the Arjun Sengupta Committee to facilitate performance evaluation and strengthen the system is the creation of a holding company and introduction of the system of Memorandum of Understanding (MoU) (Sengupta 1984).

The Economic Advisory Committee to the Prime Minister in its report on public undertakings submitted in May 1987 divided the whole spectrum of central PEs into competitive and non-competitive enterprises. It noted that 78 out of 207 enterprises were competitive and suggested that their performance be judged in the same way as that of their counterparts in the private sector. For the 80 enterprises operating in a non-competitive environment, the committee suggested close vigil by the government. The other 49 were "sick" private sector firms taken over by the government and they needed to be treated differently from the other categories of PEs (EAC 1987, p.24).

The Government of India is finalising its first ever White paper on the public sector. The government has been actively considering providing a charter for PEs and asking each enterprise to submit an annual self-appraisal (socio-economic plus financial, with reference to this charter). Further, the government proposes to strengthen the MoU system by making it clear to both PEs and the administrative ministries that the essence of the system is not merely to assign tasks and set targets for PEs but also for the administrative ministries concerned to bind themselves to discharging certain obligations such as price approvals, payments of subsidies at agreed levels (where aplicable), investment approvals, procedural clearances, where called for, etc. with the least possible delay (DPE 1987, p.24).

Patil, Krishnamurthy and Wahi have been outstanding PE chiefs in India and Fernandes, Basu and Sankar have exhibited a tremendous understanding of the PE systems: their concern for developing appropriate performance evaluation systems has made a great impact in policy-making circles.

The Institute of Public Enterprise (IPE), Boston Area Public Enterprise (BAPEG), Asian Pacific Development Administration Centre (APDC) and the World Bank are some free standing institutions which have done considerable work on performance evaluation.

Conclusions

To sum up, PEs constitute an important segment of the public sector in India and their performance is highly critical to the success of the Indian economy.

Since PEs control the commanding heights of the economy and the government has reendorsed their role (*Business Standard* 1986), these enterprises need to perform to the best satisfaction of their stakeholders. Two problems are faced in resolving this issue of the satisfactory performance of PEs: first, what could be the technique for measuring it? And second, what could be done to minimise the excessive external controls on these enterprises to enable them to function as business enterprises? This study has revealed that the total performance of PEs cannot be measured in terms of physical and financial indicators alone. The unified approach to performance evaluation could be a good solution for this ticklish issue, as it implies a composite evaluation. The Public Enterprise performance Index has been suggested to operationalise the concept of composite performance evaluation in Indian PEs. We have suggested the distancing out of PEs from the government and the other external governors such as the CAG and the parliament/state legislatures through (i) strengthening the MoU and holding-company reforms and (ii) creating conditions favourable for passing on enterpreneurial functions to these enterprises.

These reforms in PE management could be facilitated by management education and training programmes directed to achieve perceptional, attitudinal and skill transformation in the external governors, PE board members and PE executives. Such programmes should relate particularly to the performance evaluation issue.

Appendix 1

Investment in Top Ten Public Enterprises

Sl. No.	*Name of Enterprise*	*Investment*
1.	National Thermal Power Corporation	17617.27
2.	Housing and Urban Development Corporation	15875.99
3.	Steel Authority of India Limited	14502.93
4.	Indian Railway Finance Corporation Limited	13021.11
5.	Coal India Limited	11405.37
6.	Power Grid Corporation of India Limited	10726.02
7.	Power Finance Corporation	10347.59
8.	National Hydroelectric Power Corporation Limited	10312.70
9.	Rural Electrification Corporation Limited	10133.77
10.	Nuclear Power Corporation	9642.98
	Total	**123585.73**

Source: Public Enterprise Survey, 2000-2001, Vol.1, Government of India, New Delhi, 2001, p.21.

Appendix 2

Forms of Organisation of PEs in India

Sl. No	*State/Central*	*Total No. of PEs*	*Statutory Corpo-rations*	*Govt. Comp-anies*	*Coop. Societies*
1.	A.P	54	6	40	8
2.	Assam	44	6	34	4
3.	Bihar	49	20	29	–
4.	Gujarat	60	20	35	5
5.	Haryana	24	6	11	7
6.	Himachal Pradesh	20	1	19	–

(Contd...)

7.	Jamu & Kashmir	14	–	14	–
8.	Karnataka	56	2	41	13
9.	Kerala	96	10	86	–
10.	Madhya Pradesh	33	1	32	–
11.	Maharashtra	68	2	61	5
12.	Orissa	33	5	28	–
13.	Punjab	25	4	21	–
14.	Rajasthan	33	4	15	14
15.	Tamilnadu	65	6	59	–
16.	Uttar Pradesh	66	1	65	–
17.	West Bengal	45	4	44	1
18.	Arunachal Pradesh	4	--	4	–
19.	Chandigarh	28	--	28	–
20.	Goa	11	2	9	–
21.	Manipur	12	--	12	–
22.	Meghalaya	13	3	10	–
23.	Mizoram	2	1	1	–
24.	Nagaland	12	3	9	–
25.	Tripura	12	1	11	–
	Total	879	108	714	57
	(ii) Central	239	10	229	–
	Grand Total:	1118	118	943	57

Source: Public Enterprise Survey, 2000-2001, Vol.1, Government of India, New Delhi, 2001.

Appendix 3

Financial Ratios

1. Value of Production: Capital Employed (%)
2. Cost of Production (Rs. in Lakhs)

(Contd...)

3. Materials Content: Cost of Production (%)
4. Man Power Cost: Cost of Production (%)
5. Value Added (Rs. in Lakhs)
6. Value added: Capital Employed (%)
7. Cost of Sales (Rs. in Lakhs)
8. Cost of Sales: Net Sales (%)
9. Net Sales: Capital Employed (%)
10. Net Sales: Current Assets (%)
11. Average Capital Employed per Employee (in Rs.)
12. Average monthly emoluments per Employees (in Rs.)
13. Value of Production per man Month (in Rs.)
14. Value added per man month (in Rs.)
15. Average monthly sales per employee (in Rs.)
16. Finished Goods: Net sales (%)
17. Work-in-progress: Cost of Production (%)
18. Finished Goods inventory (as no.of days of sales)
19. Raw Material inventory (as no. of days consumption)
20. Work-in-progress inventory (as no.of days cost production)
21. Sundry Debtors (Expressed as no. of days of sales)
22. Gross Margin: Capital Employed (%)
23. Gross Profit: Capital Employed (%)
24. Gross Profit:Net Sales (%)
25. Profit before Tax: Net
26. Worth (%)
27. Net Profit: Paid-up Capital (%)
28. R & D Expenditure: Net Sales (%)
29. Gross Margin (Rs. in Lakhs)
30. Gross Profit (Rs. in Lakhs).

Source: Public Enterprise Survey, 2000-2001, Vol.1, Government of India, New Delhi, 2001.

Appendix 4
Trend of Profitability

(Rs. in Crore)

Particulars	*91-92*	*92-93*	*93-94*	*94-95*	*95-96*	*96-97*	*97-98*	*98-99*	*99-00*	*00-01*
No. of Operating Enterprises	237	239	240	241	239	236	236	235	232	234
Capital Employed	117991	140110	159836	162451	173948	231178	249855	265093	302867	330649
Profit Before Dep. Interest & Tax (PBDIT)	22224	25227	27707	33384	40161	44457	53062	56495	62212	69288
Depreciation	8548	9270	9151	107554	12574	13542	15856	16768	19942	20520
Profit Before Int & Tax (PBIT)	13676	15957	18556	22630	27587	30915	37206	39727	42270	48768
Interest	9673	10881	11901	12862	13966	15537	17990	20025	20233	23802
Profit Before Tax(PBT)	4003	5076	6655	9768	13621	15378	19216	19702	22037	24966
Tax Provisions	1647	1805	2110	2581	4047	5192	5634	6499	7706	9313
Net Profit	2356	3271	4545	7187	9574	10186	13582	13203	14331	156153
Profit of Profit Making PEs	6079	7384	9768	12070	14763	16125	20279	22508	24633	28492
Loss of Loss Incurring PEs	3723	4113	5223	4883	5188	5939	6697	9305	10302	12839

(Contd...)

No. of Profit Making PEs	133	131	121	130	132	129	134	126	126	122
No. of Loss Incurring PEs	102	106	116	109	102	104	100	107	105	111
No. of No Profit/ No Loss PEs	2	2	3	2	5	3	2	2	1	1
Dividend	687	792	1028	1436	2205	2836	3609	4932	5455	8260
Dividend Tax Retained Profit	1669	2479	3517	5751	7369	7089	9509	7734	3085	6551
Financial Ratio (%)										
PBDIT to Capital Employed	18.8	18.0	17.3	20.6	23.1	19.2	21.2	21.3	20.5	21.0
PBIT to Capital Employed	11.6	11.4	11.6	13.9	15.9	13.4	14.9	15.0	14.0	14.7
Dividend Payout	29.2	24.2	22.6	20.0	23.0	27.8	26.6	37.4	38.1	52.8

Source: Public Enterprise Survey 2000-01, Volume 1, Department of Public Enterprises, New Delhi, p.25

Appendix 5

Distribution of Number, Total Assets, Sales/Turnover and Profit before Tax of Public Enterprises

(Rs.crores)

State	*No.*	*Assets*	*Sales/Turnover*	*Profit before Tax*
Andhra Pradesh	35	562.0	522.1	(-) 51.0
Assam	24	73.7	39.8	(-) 0.3
Bihar	25	215.3	119.8	(-) 36.4
Gujarat	32	178.1	276.9	7.9
Haryana	11	168.1	72.1	(-) 2.6
Himachal Pradesh	12	36.0	61.9	0.1
Jammu & Kashmir	13	78.6	44.6	3.9
Karnataka	48	297.1	598.2	(-)29.8
Kerala	68	111.6	413.0	(-) 19.9
Madhya Pradesh	23	15.9	83.5	1.9
Maharashtra	45	315.0	304.9	(-) 5.3
Nagaland	2	4.2	2.3	(-) 0.3
Orissa	37	199.2	207.4	0.8
Punjab	8	4.9	1.8	--
Rajasthan	13	164.9	79.4	(-) 2.6
Tamilnadu	59	1054.4	1157.4	17.5
Uttar Pradesh	78	617.2	522.7	(-)36.7
West Bengal	33	197.8	901.0	(-) 34.4
Chandigarh	29	299.8	119.1	(-) 2.9
Delhi	5	15.8	95.0	0.2
Goa, Damanu & Diu	8	21.1	9.8	1.2
Manipur	6	4.4	0.6	--
Meghalaya	7	23.4	7.8	(-) 0.4
Pondicherry	3	10.3	1.1	--
Tripura	6	16.3	6.2	(-) 5.2
Arunachal Pradesh	1	--	--	--

(Contd...)

Mizoram	1	1.5	---	--
Andaman & Nicobar Islands	--	–	—	–
Total	632	7054.4	5733.2	(-) 200.8
State Electricity Boards	19	13918.0	6670.3	(-) 1545.2
State Road Transport Corpns	9	1703.4	1532.9	118.8
Total	660	22675.8	13936.4	(-) 1627.2

India, Planning Commission, Annual Report , 2000.

Appendix 6

Capacity Utilization in Public Enterprises

	Capacity Utilisaton	2000-2001	1999-2000	1998-1999
A	Units reporting capaicity utilisation exceeding 75%	144	133	119
B	Units reporting capacity utlisation between 50 and 75%	33	30	46
C	Units reporting capacity utilisation less than 50%	59	65	69
	Total	236	228	234

Source: Public Enterprise Survey, 2000-2001, Vol.1, Government of India, New Delhi, 2001, p.31.

Chapter IV

Annotated Bibliography

The vast literature on PE performance evaluation has been collected and brought out in a volume by the authors in the present study.

1. On Performance Evaluation Philosophy & Policy Issues

Ali El Mir, The Evaluation of Public Enterprises Performance: Some Critical Issues, International Centre for Public Enterprise Quarterly, Ljubljana, Vol.2, 1982, p-49.

There has hardly been any international, regional or national seminar dealing with public enterprise management in developing countries which did not stress the need for developing some evaluation procedure to asses public enterprise performance. For example, a recent event organized by this center, although in a rather specific area of training management in public enterprise, laid particular emphasis on performance evaluation as a prerequisite for sound manpower planning and development assessment of training needs and training implementation. The discussions were with reference to: how to evaluate the performance of public enterprise management? How to design indicators for such evaluation? What are the relevant aspects of such an evaluation? How to go about introducing sound evaluation system? These are only some of the basic questions that need to be examined in the framework of Herculean task.

Some of the problems in evaluation relate to:

- Changes are needed in large doses
- Changes are needed with utmost urgency.
- Internal adjustments are inadequate to adapt changes in external environment.
- The environment is changing at a rapid pace: Who, what, when, and how aspect of evaluation needs consideration.

In this context it should be noted that:

- Evaluation is too serious a matter to be left to accountant.
- Evaluation should be thoroughly systematic and continuous.
- The sole aim of evaluation should be improved management ways and means should be sought to minimize threats to the validation of evaluation.

Another important aspect of evaluation is the distinction made between summative and formative forms of evaluation. Summative evaluation assumes that the treatment has been properly implanted and is thus concerned how effective the programme is in attaining its objective. Formative evaluation takes place during the planning and implementation stages of a programme with the aim of contributing to better design and proper implementation. It may turn out to be that as far as 1) summative evaluation of some sort is a necessary prerequisite for formative evaluation. 2) Formative evaluation is desirable form of evaluation 3) there can be no general model of evaluation approach to public enterprises 4) evaluation may have to be molded into problem solving approach.

Problem arises in attempts to link basic goals to performance evaluation in public enterprises in developing countries because the concept of goals has yet to be well defined. A number of goal setting models have been 1) Bargaining model. 2) Problem solving model 3) Coalition model.

Bakul, Dholakia H, The Changing Efficiency of Public Enterprises in India, Somaiya Publications, Bombay, 1980

Different economic systems world over have experimented various organization instruments for solving their problem. Of all such instruments PE is the most debated, totally inescapable and widely used. India has also gone the PE way to meet the challenge of poverty and endure socialistic pattern of society. How far it has progressed in this direction, is a matter which needs to be researched intensively to make PE yield the desired results. While there has been a spate of studies on efficiency evaluation and PE's in India, they have not been able to shed much light on the phenomenon mainly because of an adequate and inconsistent perception of the problem. It is in this context that Dholakia's study has come as a bold relief and created opportunity to make a realistic assessment of the performance of PE. At the outset, Dholakia, rejects the sole use of profit criterion. The study concentrates on the quantitative analysis of the major source of growth of net output originally in the PEs in India mainly with the purpose of:

- Quantifying the importance of various factors in the observed growth of net output from PE
- Comparing the sources of output growth in general and the contribution of the changing total factor productivity in particular in PE and private enterprises in Indian economy mainly to asses the performance of the former in relation to the later.

In sum, Dholakia's study highlights the application of new approach for an objective assessment of the performance of PEs. This would surely be of great use to the policy makers and the system involved in appraising the performance of PEs and for studying efficient use of scarce resource in the public and private sector.

Basu, P K, Structural Changes in Human Relationship between Manager and Worker, SCOPE, New Delhi, 1983, p- 42-46.

The Public sector is paying adequate attention to quality of life of people through the provision of social amenities like housing, school, hospital, recreational facilities for the worker as well by providing facilities for continuous education and training. The Directive Principle's of State Policy incorporated in the contribution by that all states shall take steps to ensure the participation of worker in the Management of Industry. However there are number of Historical and Social factors which affect the effective workers participation in management & Industry. These can be overcome by attitudinal changes.

Bhat, V.V, Public Enterprise Sector and Development Lessons From International Experience, International Centre for Public Enterprise Quarterly, Ljubljana, Vol. 12, No. 3, July-September, 1987.

Improving the performance of public enterprise sector is critical for continued development, since it already accounts for a large share in domestic capital formation, industrial investment and output in most developing countries. Unlike in the past net reserve inflow into less developed countries will cease if not reverse because of interest payments and debt repayment. International experience shows that for public enterprise to perform an effective and efficient instrument of development certain preconditions have to be fulfilled. Dr. Bhat describes in this "perspective like what there are and what decision making and learning mechanism have to be institutionalized in the political and administrative apparatus to meet the challenge of continued development in the difficult environment ahead.

Bladimir Kreacic & Philip Marsh, Public Enterprise in Developing Countries- Structure, Performance and Culture, International Centre for Public Enterprise Quarterly, Ljubljana, August 1985, Vol.5 No.4.

It is argued that organizational structure in public enterprises in developing countries is rarely used to aid performance and is often not congruent with indigenous culture. The contingency approach is suggested with comment on the relevance of environment, size, technology, life cycle, internal efficiency and culture. Organization structure is a means of allocating, declaring and putting limits to the power of people at work. It provides a framework for operation and people, which facilitates performance responsibility and appraisal.

It is a vehicle for control mechanism and it contributes substantially to orderliness. The purpose of this paper is to explore the ways in which public enterprise end up with the structures, to discuss organization theory pertinent to public enterprises and to emphasise that structure can be planned and intelligently modified so as to make powerful contribution. Organization structure has to be contingent on several major influences sometimes to accommodate those influences sometimes to cope up with them.

Impact of Environment

Three dimensions of environment- dynamism, complexity and threat- effects the type of structure and effective organization will develop. Where the enterprise environment is fluid or turbulent the structure needs to be congruent. With that in order to adapt rapid changing political matters in consistent are fluid market demand high rate of technical innovation in the industry, requires corresponding internal fluidity. Where stability is usual- in political impact and market demand where technological advance is occasional congruent structures are appropriate. An organizations environment will be complex if its product range is wide or technologically advanced, its market diverse, its customers multiple, its value subject to influence from conflicting vested interests. On the other hand, simplicity weather in products, number of buyers, and suppliers and technology generates no pressure towards decentralization. Decision-making can be more easily routinized and communication is less complex. So its process can be relatively straightforward. Where the internal integrity of an organ and its managerial autonomy is under question outside the more powerful agencies it is likely to encourage that organization to centralize its power to cope with that question which it will perceive as a threat.

Institutionalized Norms

For instance, following a public scandal government may suddenly require all public enterprises to have anti-corruption departments reporting to the chief executives. As well as in the structural change there will be a new major new variable in power dynamics and structurally reinforced suspicion on the integrity of the staff.

Size and Structure

Size in relation to organizational structures, fail to produce any meaningful correlation. Subsequent researches tying size to technology identified that in small firms technology will be critical to structure while in large organizations the impact of technology is to be felt at the operational level. Technology is one of the variables which has been extensively researched as it seems that it is one of the factors which has an almost dominant position in determining structures of organizations. The more routine the workflow is the more centralized and formalized structure is required and vice-versa. The more non-routine the workflow is the more determined, informal, organic structure is required for organization to be effective. The smaller the organization, the larger is the influence of technology on the organization structure. The following are also dealt in this paper, internal efficiency and appropriate structures. The real value of capable structural design is in the internal functioning of the organization.

Some public enterprises do not have formal organizational structure at all. In the same environment a variety of structures can be found in successful public enterprises. Organizational Structure is not determined by any single factor. External control by government is by far the single most frequently mentioned grievance of public enterprise management.

It was observed that many public enterprises have centralized structure because they are public, rather than because their activities suggest such a structure or rather they regard government externalities. Different technologies require different structures. Structural changes may occur from external pressure increased control, approaching election, changing of political parties.

A major observation is that organizational structures are rarely seen as means of enhancing realization of enterprise strategy, attainment of objectives, or unimpeded flow of work.

Serious difficulties with the implementation of various managerial approaches and techniques in developing countries are explained in the vast majority of cases by the low level of development.

Changes in structure should follow effort concentrated on classification of objectives, formulation of strategies. Structural changes initiated by regulatory changes will usually be experienced by manager as an external constraint rather than as a contribution towards better performance. Change in size of organization can be usefully viewed as opportunity for deep thinking structural design of whole enterprise. In enterprise with a significant manufacturing and processing activity, the associated technologies is a measure towards a particular and appropriate design. The above proposition is likely to apply when such initiatives are rooted in systematic and regular analysis.

Christopher, K. J, Evaluation of Training – A Few Considerations and An Experience, ISTD Journal, New Delhi, 2(3-4), 1972, p-91-101.

It is argued on the basis of experience, that it is possible to evaluate changed behaviour of participant in their work situation both in qualitative and quantitative terms. A summary of such an evaluation carved out at a certain training institute in Hyderabad is reported. This evaluation is from the participants from the superior peer and subordinates. The author feels that given proper attention evaluation studies can be designed by an independent organisation.

De, R Nitish, Organizational Energy-A Diagnostic Exercise, in edited vol. of Sankar, T. L, Mishra, R. K, & Ravishankar, S, Leading Issues in Public Enterprise Management, Himalaya Publication, Bombay, 1985, p-15.

Nitish De discusses the vital problem of organizational analysis in public enterprises and suggests various approaches to organizational analysis. The author has studied five public sector organizations and one private sector firm. He concludes that, I) The higher the age, the more the energy generating activities ii) The higher the position, the greater the authority and more discretionary the contents of the job. iii) The shorter the length of the service, the greater is the energy draining activity and iv) Energy cost is higher in work activities within the department/division/function.

Dholakia, B.H., Curriculum Development for Evaluating Public Enterprise Performance: Special Issues and Problems, IPE Journal, Hyderabad, April-June, 1982, p. 54-64.

This paper observes that the basic purpose behind performance evaluation of a corporate enterprise is to provide proper timely signals to managers of the enterprise clearly indicating the right track. The author suggested strategies for implementing the training curricula on performance evaluation. He suggested the methods regarding development of training materials, like compiling a detailed bibliography of the relevant books for the different aspects of curricular on programme evaluation. He has given the measures for developing trainers as under; 1) to begin discipline oriented as well as functional area-based programmes may be organized. 2) to depute the prospective trainers in appropriate organization and 3) to organize a workshop which would enable the trainers to learn a variety of approaches to improve the effectiveness of classroom teaching.

Geeta Gouri, Transnational Corporations and Public Enterprises In India, in (ed.) Vol. of Sankar, T. L, Mishra, R. K, & Ravishankar, S, Leading Issues in Public Enterprise Management, Himalaya Publication, Bombay, 1985, p. 25).

Geeta Gouri in her paper argues that most of the collaborations with the transnational corporations have been technical in nature. An overview of the case studies presented by the author indicates that the public enterprises and the Government of India have not utilized their bargaining powers to the fullest extent.

Goel, Amit, Draft on Revamping PSUs: Government Identifies 58 Sick Units, Economic Times, 20 November 1993, p- 22.

Referring to the draft on revamping PSUs, the author explains that the loss in the sick public sector units is due to government's take over of such units to protect employment. Goel also points that from about 131 profit making public enterprises, there is a scope in increasing their performance in 84 enterprises and government can gain an additional Rs. 5000 crore without any further investment. Goel also feels that the main cause of sickness relates to over-employment and outdated technology.

Goyal, D V, Evaluation as a Positive Activity, State Enterprises, SCOPE, New Delhi, July- September 1983, p. 287-292.

Considering the growing importance of public enterprises in entire world economy whether it is committed to free market, controlled-socialists or some kind of mixture the need for performance evaluation can hardly be over emphasized. The fact that the public enterprises are subject to a wide variety of scrutiny is in the view of the wider social impact of their performance. It is necessary to develop objective criteria for evaluation so that subjective individual and ideological considerations may not interfere with evolution and growth of their endeavour for management of human welfare.

Khandwala, Pradeep N., Excellent Management in Public Sector (cases and models), Vision Books, New Delhi, 1990, p. 522.

The book probes into the determinates of their performance through a thorough study of four Indian engineering enterprises leading to very significant insights for achieving excellence in the Management of Public Enterprise. The book is in several parts. Part A reviews the public sector in India, the structure of control over public enterprises, including the goals of the ministry to which these four enterprises were attached. It survey's the various studies on public sector management and develops a list of hypothesis case studies, constitute part B through E. Part E summarises the major findings, spotlighting the key determinants in their performance and growth. Based on rigorous and very comprehensive research effort-including study of annual financial reports and other internal records interviews with a number of executives in each enterprise, and information secured through questionnaires completed by a number of top, senior, middle level executives in each enterprise. The book uses a different perspective than most studies of PEs, approaching them as it does from the perspective of organization theory. The findings have very significant implications for excellent management in the public sector. It also offers a wealth of data about performance of public sector.

Khandwala, P. N, Some Lessons for Management of Public Enterprises, Vikalpa, Ahmedabad, 7(4), October- December 1982, p- 311-326.

Based on intensive case studies of four equipment manufacturing enterprises in the Indian public sector, the author has developed a model of appropriate management for public enterprises to turn around from sickness, effective management of diversification, regulating ministry management of the PE ministry, interface and the assessment of the investment proposal of PEs. A number of implications of the study are also stated.

Kidwai, Waris, K & Sahai, Baldeo, Dynamics of Management of Public Enterprises, (ed.), SCOPE, New Delhi. 1989.

This edition by Kidwai and Sahai, has seasoned managers heading huge public sector enterprises, candidly discuss their experiences in running their industries. The difficulties faced by the industry in interacting with some of the ancient laws of the land on one hand, and ensuring smooth labour relations on the other have been amply explained.

The papers deal with areas of socio-economic environment, organizational problems, and management issues, upgradation of technology and international experiences are discussed.

Latha Jishnu, Legal Reforms Must for Efficient PSU Working, Economic Times, Mumbai, 2 August 1992, p. 7.

In this article the author advises the government that as shares of PSUs come up for listing, it should prepare itself for the scrutiny of the investors, who will be interested in their record of productivity, profitability, generation of internal resources etc. The author says that the first round of disinvestment has done nothing to improve the efficiency of PSUs except in raisin some money for the exchanges. The author says that in the past decade, the ratio of net profit to capital employed has shown a barely perceptible rise, although the investment increased by as much as 80,000 crore. And the author suggested that to correct this, a total reorientation towards a market economy is required, without the traditional cost advantages such undertakings have enjoyed in the past. According to the author, experts have suggested that the 4 sections of the Company's Act that governs the functioning of such undertakings should be scrapped i.e.; the articles of association have to be changed to take away from the government the power by veto (the idea is that state enterprises should function as board managed companies on an equal footing with the others to provide the competitive spur to better performance. The author concludes the article by saying that the Bombay Stock Exchange has already notified those undertakings where partial disinvestment has taken place of the need to change these dated regulations.

Lakshmipathy. V, Operative Perception on Performance Appraisal in Public Enterprise. IPE Journal, Hyderabad, July-September 1983, p-17-37.

In view of increasing enrollment of labour force in public enterprises and the wage bills assuming significant proportions, the performance appraisal of employees is essential. In this paper Dr. Laxmipathy presents the findings of a study of employee perception on the administration of performance appraisal in a large public enterprise. The study reveals that more than 50% of the respondents did not posses knowledge of their job description, 40% perceived their work load as too much or inadequate. It is also found that the superior subordinate relationship is also not conducive for organizational growth.

Leonard Sithebe, Commonwealth Secretariat, Performance of Public Enterprise (Report of a seminar organized on the Commonwealth Secretariat), Management by Botswana, Lesotho 3-7 April 1978, p-63-73.

The comments, which follow on the performance of public

enterprise, are made from the standpoint of developing countries with mixed economies. In looking into the performance of public enterprise one has to look into the basic requirement for their establishment and principle objective they were set up to achieve.

a) Stimulation of economic growth through this position of infrastructure b) to assume national control of major sector of the economy c) to make investment in important sector of the economy d) to pursue political and social policy through direct government intervention in the economy e) to support economic recovery in times of crisis.

In theory therefore monitoring and evaluation of public enterprises should not be difficult exercise provided they are objective and clear. Often public enterprises are not set up with clear goals. They are sometimes set up to achieve conflicting objective, which really makes difficulty in assessing the performance evaluation. One of the reasons for this is that public enterprises are created by the government intended to look at the problems from political and social point and not from economic point of view. This makes their evaluation a difficult task.

Criteria

In recent years World Bank and UN agencies who are now channeling their aid programmes to developing countries through public enterprises, insist on the use of economic method to evaluate the performance of public enterprise.

Policies and Objectives

It is necessary to test and evaluate performance against the underlying objectives and policies of an enterprise. A periodic review of policies and objectives are also necessary in the light of changing objectives.

Government Control

Government controls certain aspects in public enterprises, which might influence the performance.

Organization Control

In many cases the government when creating a public enterprise frame the legal statues, aims and objectives of the enterprises. These are approved by the parliament and enacted as law. The advantage in public enterprise will be under close scrutiny of government and the disadvantage is that they talk flexibility.

Project Control

In some countries government planning ministries play an important role in evaluation of new projects to be executed by PE. Government sometimes go further and require that its approval be sought for each major stage in project.

Financial Control

It is most powerful tool that government is drawing at their disposal to see weather the PE is doing well or not. The manner and extent to which government effects their control however have a considerable impact on the performance of public enterprises.

Accounting and auditing: PE are subject to close scrutiny and audit is a form of control by government through the appointed agencies like CAG.

It is felt that public enterprise need to make economic analysis of their prospects and programme both before and during implementation in order to carry out their proper role both in the proper use of limited financial resources at their disposal and as development agencies. One of the problems is that technical expertise in economic analysis in developing countries is hard to come by. Scarcity of qualified and experienced professionals with a sensitivity and understanding of each developing country is not only confined to public enterprises but also private sector. Another problem is that management of enterprise may not feel the need for economic analysis because in their programme they are obliged to accept the economic decision of government. Enterprise are always faced with many demand on this limited financial resources. By subjectivity each of the project to an economic analysis they are in a position to put them in order of priority from an economic stand point and may reject project which show negative returns. It is however, necessary to establish very clear criteria for economic appraisal of projects. The government confidence in such criteria should be obtained properly.

Financial Requirements

Most enterprises think in terms of profitability. The assessment of performance of the enterprise in this case need to take into consideration the attendant social and development benefits in addition to normal test of benefit compared with costs.

Mahaeshwari, B L, Managerial Effectiveness in Public Enterprises, in edited Vol. of Sankar, T. L, Mishra, R. K, & Ravishankar, S. Leading Issues in Public Enterprise Management, Himalaya Publication, Bombay, 1985, p-20.

B.L Maheshwari, draws attention towards the managerial effectiveness in the public enterprises in India and says that it is at its lowest ebb in the public enterprises. He observes that action has to be taken from the side of the managers of the public enterprises and the government also should be working on creating a positive atmosphere. There is a problem of low pay package to the employees and lack of recognition at the managerial levels of the enterprise. All these factors indicate a need for toning up the performance of public enterprises.

Mathur, B.L., Public Enterprises: Policy and Performance, Jaipur, Arihant Publishers, 1988, p-248.

This volume identifies and analyseses the various key issues confronting the PEs for better performance. It brings together the thoughts of eminent experts on the policy and performance of PEs. The major focus is on the policy issues, government PEs interaction, planning and control, financial management, capacity utilisation, personnel management and industrial relations etc. The papers in this volume are authored by eminent management experts from India and abroad.

Mishra, R. K., Performance Evaluation of Public Enterprises in India, Institute of Public Enterprise Journal, Hyderabad, October-December, 1981, p- 88.

Public enterprises have been assigned a place of prime importance in the planned economic development in India. The success of planned economic effort rests a great deal on the effective and efficient functioning of PEs. It is therefore vital to ensure that PE produces the desired result continuously to help accelerate the process of bringing about the socio-economic transformation for the emancipation of the masses in the country. The central purpose of this paper is to evaluate the efficiency of the performance evaluation system in the PEs in India and suggest how educational and training programmes for PE board members, executives and "external governors" may be improved to secure better performance evaluation in the future. A comprehensive introduction to the nature of PE activity prepare this central theme in order to understand the need for the performance evaluation and explain in detail the context of governing. The major finding and issues arising there of have been summed up in the concluding section of this paper. The following are discussed in this paper 1) Nature of activity 2) rationale 3) typicality's 4) forms 5) interface 6) accountability to parliament 7) relationship with government 8) accountability through audit 9) an overview of performance evaluation system.

Mishra R.K. and Nandagopal, R. Public Enterprises — Performance in North Eastern Region, Economic Times, Mumbai, July 27, 1989.

This paper sums up the performance of public enterprises in the North-Eastern region and provides a first hand account of their operational problems. The paper reveals lack of coordination as the principal problem in this area. The paper suggests a plethora of management development programmes for the top executives in the SPLEs of North-East.

Nag, A, Public Enterprises Performance Evaluation, Economic Times, Mumbai, August 8 1986, p-7.

An established fact about PEs in India, is their low profitability. Profitability may be conceived as either surplus generation or as the ratio of gross or net profit to sales or turnover or in the broader sense, return on investment. The object of this paper, is to discuss the phenomenon of low profitability of PEs in India and in the world at large and to focus on issues which are critical to understanding of the state of profitability and in general and performance evaluation of PEs in particular.

Nagaraj, R., Macroeconomic Impact of Public Sector Enterprises– Some Further Evidence, EPW, Mumbai, 27(3, 4), 1993, p. 105-109.

Public enterprises in general are the targets for criticism from all quarters. The arguments against them range from causing fiscal imbalances to widespread inefficiencies in the non-farm sector. This note attempts to empirically scrutinise the status and answer a) if the deficit of public sector enterprises increased over the years b) if the financial burden of the non-departmental, non-financial enterprises on the budget increased over the years and c) if the internal resource generation of non-departmental and non-financial enterprises is lower than that of the private corporate sector in recent years and d) if the observed improvement in resource generation in the 80s is entirely due to increases in administered prices. Short methodology has been used for tracing the macroeconomic impact of PEs in India. The findings indicate an insignificant increase in the overall deficits of PEs. The study rejects the hypothesis that the observed improvement in resource generation in the 80s is entirely on account of increase in administered prices and attributes it to better capacity utilisation or operation performance of these enterprises. The findings question the implicit premise of the current policy reforms heading towards diluting public ownership.

Nageshwara Rao, Role and Achievement of Public Enterprises, Vora Publications, Allahabad, 1985, p. 340.

The present study seeks to make a detailed, comprehensive and systematic analysis of all the manufacturing units of the central government operating in Uttar Pradesh. The study divided into six parts, makes a synthesis of micro and macro position. On the basis of unpublished and published information of concerned units the constraints in the working of these units have been pinpointed and valuable suggestions have been offered for the concerned units and policy makers. The study has examined in detail the contribution of these units in improving the economic and social life of the state of Uttar Pradesh. The suggestions are of relevance as much to the public sector undertakings of the central government operating in Uttar Pradesh as also to the PEs operating in other states of our country.

Nayar, B.R., Political Economy of India's Public Sector (Policy and Performance), Popular Prakashan, Mumbai, 1990, p. 323.

This book is divided into five parts. Part one discusses theory and methodology relating to the study of public sector performance. It examines the subject in a broad context so as not to overlook such national goals as are often claimed to mark out the distinctive character of the public sector. Part two looks at the interaction of the public sector and economic policy. Since such interaction has been estimated at length in India's mixed economy in so far as the Nehru and Indira Gandhi periods are concerned it is particularly concerned with Rajiv's period in office from 1984-89. Parts three and four, constitute the empirical case studies in which the performance of public sector, in the steel and aluminum industries is analysed. Through out the analysis, a comparison is made with comparable firms in the private sector. Part five provides a summary of the study.

Om Prakash, Public Sector Performance Evaluation in Sankar T. L, Mishra R.K, Ravishankar S. (ed.) Leading Issues of Public Enterprise Management, Himalaya, Bombay 1985

This paper suggests that the conflict between accountability and autonomy can be resolved by spelling out the relevant criteria for performance evaluation. The author observes that vagueness in objectives may be a major constraint on the judicious evaluation of a public undertaking performance so also may be the situation in which public sector programme are announced without taking into account or revealing the full implications of the lost revenue relationship. The author suggests quantitative and qualitative evaluation should ensure a balance between the autonomy and accountability of PEs. According to him quantitative evaluation should include such parameters as financial resources utilization, physical resource utilization, human resource utilization, market/product development, diversification. The qualitative aspects include customer satisfaction, employee satisfaction, and the level of public satisfaction and acquisition of latest technology, R & D. Environmental / social / organizational changes and the pattern of economic growth. A major problem with regard to performance is operationalisation. The author has taken due care of this problem and suggests that there is need for working out wide range of productivity, profitability, growth and other positive indices for PEs. We may then expect higher and higher output per man, net value added per employee, capital formation and the like. On the other hand we have to consider negative indices also. This one may look for lower and lower breakage / scrap percentage, failure cost, proportion / no. of man-days lost, absenteeism, idle time, no. of accidents. Between the two extremes there may be a no. of ratio's which may be high or low. In this category may fall the inventory turnover ratio, liquidity, labour turnover ratio.

Paxy Fernandes, Promise and Performance: A Study for Creditable System of Evaluating the Efficiency of Public Enterprise, SCOPE, New Delhi, 1982, p-112.

The book is a commendable effort at deciphering and detecting the complex and vital problems at evaluating PE performance. The author with his vast knowledge and experience has analyzed the difficult problems with such clarity and understanding. In this analysis he has kept in mind the basic dimension of the problem namely, multidimensionality of PE goals and the need to counter multidimensional instruments of performance evaluation. Evaluation of PE performance is and would continue to be a controversial matter. As the PEs are clear about their overriding objectives the problem becomes more complex. Mutually conflicting objectives is a common phenomenon in many countries. The author mentioned issues such as 1) what is rationale and the purpose of the enterprise 2) who is expected to pay for the cost of its goods and services are often not faced fairly and squarely. The author tries to show the difficulty and subjectivity of the problem 3) potential profitability 4) other firms in the same field of endeavour.

Praxy Fernandes, Optima- An ICPE Approach to Self-Reliant Public Enterprise Management, International Centre for Public Enterprise Quarterly, Ljubljana, Vol. 2, No. 2, 1981.

The word Optima by itself conveys unmistakable connotation of the quest of excellence. Optima is an acronym for optimal performance. This is a significant and meaningful phrase embedded within which lies two vital ideas. 1) The idea of seeking performance improvement. 2) Seeking such performance improvement through self-reliance. Optima identifies the following factors for effectiveness, viz., self-realization, harmonization, directionalization, creativity, environmentalization and humanization.

Optima has attempted to outline the factors which envelop the environment and public enterprise and it has evolved a concept described as PEPPER which is an acronym for six parameters.

1. Pluralistic and multidimensional objectives.
2. Environmental factors.
3. Public opinion.
4. Propriety
5. External control.
6. Relationship and inter-linkages.

The instruments in the package of Optima include Corporate Planning, Inter-linkages planning, Organized system of performance evaluation, Organizational Restructuring, the development of Problem Solving and Self -Reliance.

Public Enterprise Management Strategies for Success, Commonwealth Secretariat, London, September 1987.

In 1986 the Management Development Division of the Commonwealth Secretariat initiated a project to study the cause of successful public enterprise and profits of successful enterprise chief executives. In pursuance of this a roundtable was held in June 1987 in Cyprus.

The primary objectives of roundtable, the first in a series was to discuss case studies of successful enterprises and also find out from successful chief executive the ingredients of successful management- despite the increasing importance of PE and expanding role in the social and economic development of developing countries, there is a growing concern about their performance levels. Government's are finding it increasingly difficult to maintain subsidies for loss making enterprises and are searching for innovative ways of improving their performance.

Various national and international bodies, through different interventions like workshops, studies, etc are assisting governments to identify strategies processes and procedures which might help to upgrade the performance.

The Round Table was involved in the following:

- Identifying managerial innovation, which contribute to success of individual PE.
- Translating these lessons of success into appropriate national and organizational performance improvement strategies.
- Developing appropriate roundtable strategies.
- Developing top management based on successful indigenous management. The first conference discussed the strategies and tactics, which contributed to success in the PE performance.

This publication described in nutshell the following strategies:

- Strategies for managing the interface between the enterprise and government.
- Influencing government policy environment.
- Establishing clear agreed objectives.
- Securing government support: policy package.
- Maintaining government enterprise relationship.

Several important factors under different categories as listed below were identified that need attention for promoting a relationship or mutuality between an enterprise or government:

- Chief executive and chairman.
- Involvement in strategic planning.

- Information sharing.
- Exchange of personnel.
- MoU supervisory control and coordination.
- Role of supervisory ministry.
- Role of other agencies.
- Role of boards.
- Parameters for performance evaluation.

Strategic Internal Management

- Financial restructuring.
- Managing redundancies.
- Diversification.
- Market orientation.
- Export markets.
- Technology absorption.
- Ancillarization.
- Competition
- In search of excellence.
- Leadership.

Implementation of strategies

- Communication.
- Action.
- Human resource development.

Raghavaiah, Y, Public Enterprises in The Third World Countries-An Emerging Scene, in edited Vol. of Sankar, T. L, Mishra , R. K, & Ravishankar, S. Leading Issues in Public Enterprise Management, Himalaya Publication, Bombay, 1985, p-8.

Y. Raghavaiah examines the role of public enterprises in the third world countries in his paper. He noted that the origin and growth of the public enterprises in the third world are conditioned by a completely different set of forces and circumstances in contrast to those in Western experience. While the public enterprise in the West reflect the dynamics of social and economic reality, this is not so in developing countries. The author is of the opinion that the philosophy of the public enterprise in developing countries is different from that of those in the developed countries. The expansion of public sector in the developing countries has mainly emphasized the development administration.

Ramanadham, V. V, The Control of Public Enterprises in India, Asia Publishing House, New Delhi, 1964, pp. 304.

This study is the result of a research project sponsored by the Research Programmes Committee of the Planning Commission. Its value arises from the fact that the success of the public sector in this country depends on the efficacy of public sector exercised over it without affecting its efficiency. It is a highly comprehensive and analytical study on the subject of control of public enterprises in India, based on an extensive collection of data from the public enterprises all over the country and on discussions with persons concerned with their working or control.

Ramanadham, V. V, (ed.), Public Enterprise: Studies in Organisational Structure, Frank Cass, London, 1986, pp-292.

This volume contains papers on select public enterprises in different countries, developed and developing, written by the respective top executives, besides an opening analytical review and a chapter on the Yugoslav enterprise by the editor. The broad theme of each paper is to bring out the major features of the organisation of the public enterprise concerned. Questions relating to the constitution of the enterprise, the board, the social and commercial functions, dealings with consumers, and control relationships with government are examined. The organisational structures within the enterprise are particularly highlighted.

Ramanadham, V. V, (ed.), Public Enterprise and the Developing World, Select Book Service Syndicate, New Delhi, 1984, pp.234.

This book focuses on the working of public enterprises in developing countries. In many Third World countries the development status was so low that first efforts towards change involved them in heavy costs that were analogous to the overheads of national economic development. A significant proportion of these devolved on public enterprises, which happened to be the vehicle of development strategy.

This book reviews the experience of a wide range of developing countries and illustrates how each country has been able to use public enterprises in different ways to solve their own problems. At the same time, certain common concessions have led to public enterprises being used in very similar ways in different parts of the third world.

Ramanadham, V. V, (ed.), The Nature of Public Enterprise, Croom Helm, London & Sydney, 1984, pp.300.

The work is a profound analytical study on public enterprises in the light of global experiences. The author explores systematically and lucidly the contrast existing between conceptual essence and actual public enterprise, and introduces worthwhile suggestions to narrow gap and sets out policies under which utility of public enterprises are likely to be maximum to the nation.

Ramanadham, V. V, Public Enterprises in Britain, Frank Cass & Company Ltd., London, 1959, pp-200.

The author has observed at first hand the working of public enterprises in Britain. He has coupled objectivity with an acute sense of economic perception and has produced a clear and ordered study of the workings of nationalisation in industry. This book does not contain an argument on whether nationalization is desirable or not. On the assumption that there is nationalization, an attempt is made to discuss certain important problems raised by it in the fields of management, pricing, resource allocation and public control.

This book attempts to present a norm towards which the public corporation as an institution in the field of industrial organisation should strive if its basic objectives are to be achieved most satisfactorily.

Samarapungava, S., Conceptual Review of Public Enterprises, Lok Udyog, 18(4), July 1984, p. 23-26.

In this article the author elucidates the need and importance of public enterprise for the development of our economy at a faster rate. He explains the contribution of public sector enterprises to the growth rate and the production during the first four years of sixth plan. Later he explains the problems in measuring their performances and the problems for their better performance. He classifies the industries as two, one as manufacturing and other as service organisations. He feels that issues relating to the performance can be made common and sustained management the public sector can improve its efficiency.

Saidayya, Y, Public Sector- Promises Programmes, Performances And Prospects, Modern Management, New Delhi, Vol. No 2, July 1988, p-73-78.

This article deals with the concept of public sector and discusses its needs in various fields of socioeconomic activities. The article also highlights the magnitude and growth of central public enterprises since independence and discusses the achievements and the failures of public sector undertakings in India. Some of the limiting factors inhibiting the success of public enterprises include interference either from the ministries and respective departments or from the so-called backward driving concept of autonomy and accountability, administered price policy of government etc. Discussion as regards the prospects of public enterprises in India highlights the various steps taken by the government in the matter of improvement of performance of public sector enterprises. The paper dwells on the following areas; 1) meaning of public sector 2) need for the state to enter into the field of economic activities 3) concept of public sector 4) achievements of public sector in fields like export promotion, generation of employment and socioeconomic goals 5) problem of public sector undertaking, frequency of strikes and lock outs, shortage of inputs, interface from industries, administered pricing policy of government, indifference manpower policies, high output ratio.

Standing Conference of Public Enterprises

This has been established to serve as a counterpart of Federation of Indian Chambers of Commerce and Industry (FICCI). It takes care of the common interests of all the public sector undertakings. So far as their problems and interests are concerned for building up the image of these undertakings. Government of India has committed itself for establishing a pioneering role for the public sector in the Indian economy and has taken adequate steps to improve the working of these undertakings. Sufficient power has been delegated to public sector undertakings in the following fields. 1) PSU's need not submit their revenue budget for approval to the government and expects when the government has to make good the deficit. 2) Full powers have been allocated to these undertakings for capital expenditure from their gross block up to Rs. 10 crores. 3) Public sector undertakings are permitted to directly approach IFC, IDBI, UTI etc. for expansion programme provided they have sufficient declared dividends. 4) The undertaking without reference to the government can make all appointments below the board level. Approval is required to the appointment of the chief executive. 5) Government has given clearance to some public sector undertakings to declare dividends, to go in for accepting public deposits. 6) To provide more autonomy in day to day functioning, the government has negotiated MoUs with few PEs such as BHEL and SAIL. 7) Government is intending to have an experiment of privatization of some select public sector undertakings like Air India and Scooters India Limited.

Sastry, K.S., Concept of Political will in the Context of Evolving a Suitable Performance Evaluation System for Public Enterprises—Some Explanations, International Centre for Public Enterprise Quarterly, Ljubljana, 11(4), December 1991, p. 223-234.

The problem of performance evaluation in public enterprises still considered a tricky one to date is examined. Specially two issues namely social profitability and political will, their quantification and inclusion in the performance evaluation, continue to be most critical are described. Attempts to understand and quantify social profitability but political will continue to be an elusive area is described. The concept of political will and its impact on public enterprise performance crucial for evolving a suitable performance evaluation system for public enterprises is explored. It is felt that there is a need for mechanism through which cases of political intervention can be distinguished from political interference. In conclusion it is suggested that it should be possible to develop such mechanism through further research, given the fact that a similar mechanism to combine financial and non-financial performance does exist in the form of an organisation index.

Satyamurthi, Y., Image of Public Sector, Lok Udyog, 6(2), New Delhi, May 1972, p. 17-21.

In this article, the author describes performance of public enterprises as not commendable, and the quality and price of public sector manufactured goods as unsatisfactory. He feels the reason behind this is lack of managerial talent in the public enterprises. Thousands of crores of rupees are invested in public enterprises with marginal amount spent on training of human resource. The author describes the key factors leading the losses in public enterprises as lack of objectives, ill conceived organisation, multiplicity of levels and grades, personnel policies, delegation of authority, autonomy, motivational factors and systems and procedures adopted and suggested remedial measures to overcome the problems.

Saxena, A.N, Productivity in Public Enterprises, A Multi-Pronged Approach in Sankar, T.L, Mishra, R.K, Ravishankar, S, (ed.) in Productivity in Public Enterprises, Himalaya, Bombay, 1986, p- 11-17.

Public sector accounts for over 60 percent of investment in the industrial sector. This is likely to increase further and the efficiency of public sector is going to determine an industrial growth process. The role and responsibility of public sector is crucial. However, certain constraints which are not conducive to this sector continue to operate in the same manner as the private sector. While profit cannot be dominant motive, but at the same time a reasonable rate of return is expected from them. Improvement of productivity performance in the public sector requires a multi pronged approach on the part of government, management and involvement and cooperation and trade union. The paper incorporates discussion on 1) role of government 2) productivity of capital 3) productivity measurement 4) organizational factors 5) productivity factors etc.

Sengupta P. R., Social Commitment and Efficiency in Indian Public Enterprises, Public Enterprise, International Centre for Public Enterprise Quarterly, Ljubljana, Vol.8, No. 4, December 1988.

As in other countries, PEs in India also have their twin objectives economic and social. This dual set of responsibilities of public enterprises makes efficiency measurement difficult and sometimes impossible: there has been hardly any attempt from any corner to define the two areas of public enterprise performance with much clarity. The Administrative Reforms Commission (ARC) recommended that a comprehensive and clear statement on the objectives and obligations of public undertakings be made. The government from time to time has issued guidelines and clarification regarding various aspects of public enterprise management. This, however, cannot be regarded as a categorical statement of the objectives and obligations of Indian PEs. In India, as in UK, a broad understanding of the extent and quantity of social obligations does not exist. Due to this vagueness PEs are judged by vague indices. An enterprise overburdened by non-economic considerations cannot justify itself on an economic test. An enterprise might be socially inefficient and is able to hide its commercial inefficiency with a curtain of social obligations.

Sengupta, Palas R., Social Performance of Public Enterprises: An Indian Perspective, New Delhi, Kanishka, 1993, XV, p-167.

While deciding on issues questioning the rationale of public enterprises in India, the concentration is more on the economic performance. The study involves a random sample survey of 25 central government public enterprises for enterprise analysis and a questionnaire survey of 50 private enterprises out of the top giants, on the basis of capital employed. The study attempts to find out the extent of social obligation of the Indian public enterprise, how far these social goals are incorporated in their annual plans, the difference between public and private sector, where do the Indian public sector stand individually in meeting their social responsibilities the impact of the broader social burden on the commercial performance of the enterprise and finally whether public enterprises adopt any performance measurement technique.

Sikorsky, Douglas, Public Enterprise: How It is Different from the Private Sector, IPE Journal, Hyderabad, April-June 1987, p-41-48.

This paper discusses how public enterprises are different from the private sector. The author's main concern here is with government enterprise as a competitor with private enterprise, which broadens the issue in general, context. The author compares both public sector and private sector in different parameters like, 1) Economic efficiency in public sector with regard to monopoly situation. The author also feels that inefficiency in public sector stems from poorly defined objectives which tend to increase the cost level and reduce profits. The author also feels that wider objectives than economic efficiency and profitability tend not to be stated in clear, consistent and stable way. The second parameter which the author has taken into consideration is ownership right a) state ownership is advised on grounds like balanced social and commercial cost; exploit profit from scarce resources; promotes national security and national prestige; improves productivity. The author feels that divorce of ownership and control in the private sector leads the firm away from the pursuit of profit. This is noticed in public enterprises where citizens are real owners. Given this situation of competitive environment the author feels that public enterprise can operate more efficiently responding to the stimulus. According to the author, like to take more where social costs are involved unlike private enterprise.

Srinivasan, A.V & Viramini, B R, Action Learning Programme: An Effective Concept in Developing Executives, Lok Udyog, April 1997.

One of the objectives of an Executive Development Programme (EDP) is continuing up-gradation of new knowledge and skill. Such programme also includes attitudinal change, which may be considered desirable for a practising executive. In the context of Industrial organizations one must differentiate between training and development, wherein training is acquisition of knowledge, skills and attitudinal changes.

In most EDPs the training and development is normally limited to course work. This may increase managers' awareness and remove their inhibitions and prejudices. In a conventional EDP the trainer decides the level of knowledge and formulates the design of the programme. Apart from training skills, EDP is also a development process.

Srivastava, S S, Performance Appraisal of Public Enterprises in India, Indian Journal of Public Enterprise, Allahabad, Vol. 2-3, December 1987, p-15-21.

PEs in India and also elsewhere have developed out of necessity as there has been no choice before the government in furthering the economic growth of the nations. They involve huge financial commitments, as a result they are subject to close scrutiny to pin point their strengths and weaknesses to improve their performance. The financial objective of share prize maximization of private sector does not apply to public sector because of its multiplicity of goals. Public sector undertakings in India are not bothered about profitability and risk taking and they have no obligation to declare dividends.

Issue of public verses private sector gained significance only after independence. The Industrial Policy Resolution 1956, states that all industries of strategic and basic goods/ services should come under the purview of the PEs and PEs should play an important role in the development of the country while serving the public enterprises.

Indian PEs are multifaceted institutions having for further fulfillment a set of multiple goals. These enterprises have to function within the broader environment of sociopolitical system. The goals of these enterprises are determined by political system, which also exercises controlling influence over the operation of the organization. In their overall performance the PEs have fulfilled the objective of their establishment. The total number of PEs stood at 5 in 1951, which increased, to 214 as on March 31st 1985. These enterprises have exhibited excellent performance in matters of turnover, export earnings, volume of production, capacity utilization and return on investment. Out of 214 enterprises 113 enterprises earned profit and 91 incurred losses. The performance appraisal of PEs requires complete harmonization of norms of evaluation of managerial effectiveness and appraisal of social benefits. Profit and production alone cannot judge effective functions of public sector enterprises, which must fulfill public expectations also. The public enterprises must not be judged by economic profitability but should be evaluated by their performance, fulfillment of their social responsibility. These enterprises should be established at uneconomic sites for balance regional development. For efficient functioning of PEs it is desirable to bring about the maximum operational economy and more rational personnel management. There must be autonomous corporation at the center and also in the state. This will facilitate functional coordination among public enterprises. The departmental enterprise must be non-bureaucratic to make them more efficient and result oriented. PE objectives must be very clear because they provide the thrust required to eliminate problems and give directions for performance of PEs.

Subba Rao and Gangadhara Rao M, Performance of Public Enterprise as a Model Employer in India, Indian Journal of Industrial Relations, New Delhi, 23(2), October 1987, p-.217-228.

The paper attempts to examine whether the public sector has been acting as a model employer in respect of a) existence of sound personnel policies; b) implementation of labour laws; c) maintenance of industrial harmony. It observed that these were some public units which violated the labour legislation's. 2) The number of man-days lost per thousand workers employed is lower in public sector compared to that in private sector. Further it is pointed out that the functioning of negotiating and grievance machinery is improper and ineffective mostly due to the conflicting attitudes and approaches of management. It suggests that the public sector units have to evolve a correct policy after thorough thinking and deliberations about the concept of model employer and then strive hard to prove itself as a model employer, model producer and accelerator of the economy.

Suresh Kumar, Public Enterprise Policy and Reform Measures: The Indian Experience, Public Enterprise, 11(4), June 1991, p-327-333.

The paper describes the crucial role of the public sector in the Indian economy. Combining the public and enterprise dimensions, a more comprehensive system of assessing the performance of public enterprise is sought. Where disinvestment is considered unsuitable the strategy adopted is that of performance contracts or MoU's. This paper proceeds to discuss about MoU which takes into account both commercial and non-commercial criteria in their static and dynamic aspects; while ensuring performance by making the autonomy aspects more transparent. It is felt while privatisation involves privatisation of public assets, MoUs imply privatisation of the public style management. This methodology which has been refined, over the years by assigning weights and values to the indicators are examined. Issues relating to the objectives of public enterprises, which are more transforming, are discussed, the improvement of performance incentive system is assessed and possible comparison of the performance of essentially dissimilar enterprises is presented.

Trivedi Prajapathi & Mookerjee Rajen, Comparative Impact of Monetary Incentives on Productivity in Public and Private Enterprises: A Case Study of the Indian Economy, Indian Journal of Industrial Relations, 25(1), New Delhi, July 1989, p-1-22.

The paper tests whether such conclusion is in fact, valid in the public enterprise sector of a developing country like India.

Additionally, by way of contrast, this paper also examines the relationship between monetary incentives and productivity in the private sector. It is generally accepted that private sector productivity is greater because of its practice of offering the right price in order to obtain the best available personnel. This paper has two basic goals. It attempts to determine whether monetary incentives are a solution to the poor productivity problems in the public enterprise sector. The statistical analysis of this issue is conducted at the aggregate level for both sectors. The analysis in this paper, however enables us to derive broad generalisations which we hope will be helpful to planners and policy makers in India as well as other LDCs also.

Venkatachalam, G & Dakshinamurthy, D, Performance of Public Enterprises in India: Impact of Heavy External Finance, International Centre for Public Enterprise Quarterly, Ljubljana, Vol. 6, February, 1986, p-147-155.

In this an attempt is made to analyze the broad pattern of financing of public enterprises in India. The study specifically aims at analyzing the various structural components of external sources. It also aims at examining the impact of heavy external finance on the financial performance of the enterprises and suggest some measures to rectify the imbalances in the financial pattern in order to make these enterprises financially sound. Public enterprises in India have grown tremendously since their inception both in terms of size and their volume of investment. It was observed that public enterprises in India heavily depended on external sum of financing during the period of study. Among the structural component accounted a major share of total external source of finance during the period of study. Among the structural component accounted a major share of total external source of finance. The heavy dependence on external source of finance and particularly as borrowing resulted in high interest burden and a problem of liabilities, which led to the poor performance of enterprises. The following areas were touched in this article. 1) source of finance- external and internal 2) effects of heavy external finance 3) interest burden a) interest as percentage of total income b) interest as a percentage of growth c) liquidity d) current rates e) quick ratio.

The study concludes that public sector enterprises in India increasingly depended upon external sources. Greater preference had been accorded to short term funding. Imbalance in capital structure was caused by heavy debts. The study suggests private equity participation, issuing redeemable preference shares, conversion of loans into equity, and improvement in operative effectiveness.

Verma, Prabhat Kumar, Operational Efficiency of Public Enterprises in India, Lok Udyog, New Delhi, 19(5), August 1985, p. 35-39.

Discusses that public enterprises can succeed in achieving their basic objectives through efficiency alone. Efficiency is to be brought about from various sides such as productivity efficiency, barrier efficiency and human efficiency is considered. It is felt that each of these efficiencies depends on factors over which the organisations may or may not have controls. The study argues that the public may or may not always be guided by purely commercial aims due to their present socio-economic objectives become secondary issue. However, it is imprinted out that in the competitive markets, profit making cannot be totally abandoned, warranting for a proper pricing policy of the public sector to enable them as self financing units. All such type of business efficiency has got a direct bearing on the productive efficiency and human efficiency. Overall the paper deals with the inter-linkages of each of their factors and tries to bring about a coordinated approach, which may help in achieving operational efficiency.

Victor, Powel, Improving Public Enterprise Performance, Oxford Publication, Oxford, 1987.

There is considerable evidence that the economic and financial performance of many public enterprises in developing countries is not as good as it could be. Often these enterprises have vague or even conflicting objectives ever short of professional managerial staff and suffer from frequent bureaucratic interference. Some of them are excessively politicized. Government tolerates their poor performance although, their financial losses constitute a heavy drain on state exchequer.

Improved public enterprise performance has thus become a key development issue and major condition for recovery of stagnating economies. This publication has been written to help in these efforts. It reflects the experience of several countries and projects that have aimed at making public enterprises more effective, efficient and profitable. Drawing on their experience of performance improvement programmes in several public enterprise, the author suggests how to improve definition of enterprise objectives, the process of strategic planning, relation with supervisory bodies and evaluation of performance. He pays particular attention to performance improvement programmes started and implemented by public sector enterprises themselves.

Vinayshil, Gautam & Narayan, S, Perspective for Understanding Effectiveness The Case of a Public Sector Enterprise, International Centre for Public Enterprise Quarterly, Ljubljana, 6(1), October -December 1985, p-41-48.

The paper discusses that the applications of socio technical theory have been somewhat restricted to the analysis of lower levels of organisations. It is possible to view organisations as constituting a number of inter-related sub-systems, each performing complex tasks to achieve together the multiple goals of the organisation. Using the socio-technical framework of analysis, the paper suggests that the efficiency and effectiveness of task performance of sub-systems, which would help determine the effectiveness of the organisation could be examined. It is felt that this approach looks at internal efficiencies of the organisation which would meaningfully be adopted for the study of public sector enterprises operating under environmental constraints such as state controls externally set goals. As an illustration the paper proceeds to discuss, the usage of this methodology for analysing a sub-system relating to industrial relations in a public sector enterprise in India.

2. On Autonomy and Control

Mishra R. K, Geeta, P & Navin B, (ed.) The Role of Memorandum of Understanding in Public Enterprise Management, Vikas Publishing House, New Delhi, 2002.

The editors in their book argue that MoU has emerged as a potent mechanism to facilitate a smooth government-public enterprise interface. This book elucidates the objectives of MoU to increase performance, autonomy and accountability of public enterprises. The book explores the foundations, theories and methodologies of MoU, its implementation and institutionalization in the public enterprise system in India. Further, it outlines the government policy on MoU and the views of researchers and public enterprise executives on its various aspects and identifies the issues and problems experienced at the managerial level.

Om Prakash, Public Sector Performance Evaluation, in edited vol. of Sankar, T. L, Mishra , R. K, & Ravishankar, S, Leading Issues in Public Enterprise Management, Himalaya Publication, Bombay, 1985, p-55.

Om Prakash emphasizes the need for objectivity in evaluating the performance of public enterprises on the basis of given objectives. He observes that the vagueness in objectives would be a major constraint on the judicious evaluation of the public undertaking performance. He proposes a qualitative and quantitative evaluation to ensure a balance between the autonomy and accountability of the public enterprises.

Prasad Jagadish Autonomy And Accountability of Public Enterprise - Facts And Issues in (ed.) Vol. of Sankar, T. L, Mishra, R. K, & Ravishankar, S. Leading Issues In Public Enterprise Management, Himalaya Publication, Bombay, 1985, p-50.

Jagadish Prasad discusses the dilemma of maximum control, which is desired by the parliament and public, and the maximum autonomy desired by the public enterprise management. Accountability according to the author has been organized through two channels, the ministerial as well as from the parliament. The author is of the opinion that the public enterprise should not be under the control of the minister for day to day operations, though it should be broadly accountable on policy matters. The author suggests the need for a healthy practice in the area of legislative provisions and conventions.

Sankar, T. L, The Government Executive and the Public Enterprise: A Study of the Supervisory Control System, in (ed.) Vol. of Sankar, T. L, Mishra, R. K, & Ravishankar, S, Leading Issues in Public Enterprise Management, Himalaya Publication, Bombay, 1985, p-30.

T. L, Sankar, examines the extent, scope and necessity of executive controls, with special reference to the Indian case. He holds the view that the relative weights of social responsibility in the overall objectives of public enterprise influences the degree of autonomy and accountability. In the units that are purely commercial in nature there is more autonomy for they are provided with detailed guidelines spelling out the role of the government executives and that of the professional, managers. In such undertakings there is a greater possibility to determine objectives clearly and prioritize them. The author emphasizes a need for greater understanding between the public enterprise as well as the government so that the conflicts are resolved amicably.

3. Government-Enterprise Interface

Adih, Doctor, Striving for Autonomy: A Study of Public Sector Enterprises, State Enterprise, 1988, p- 91-99.

The paper discusses the need to build right culture in public enterprise functioning. Public enterprises will not be able to enjoy autonomy, even the little that is statutorily confirmed unless those in charge of these enterprises make an effort to change the prevailing administrative culture and learn to stand up on their rights to turn the enterprises.

Gadhak, D N, Accountability of Public Enterprises to Parliament: Working & Impact of Parliamentary Committee on PSUs, Sterling Publishers, New Delhi, 1980, vii, p-147.

In a democratic system an essential feature of public accountability is the supervision and control exercised by parliament. Parliament exercises control through various means like questions, discussion on "Presidents Address", budget debates, short duration discussions etc. But they have never been considered complete and perfect. Parliament being an amalgam of large number of interests and ideologies has never been able to devote time and attention to specific issues, which come before it. Moreover parliament has no time to spare for detailed examination. Like other democracies the judiciary system also provides for the constitution of Parliamentary Accounts Committee (PAC), Estimates Committee (EC), Committee on Public Undertakings (COPU) to perform function of financial control and scrutiny on behalf of parliament. COPU composed of members of both houses of Parliament was set up in May 1964 to take over the function vested in the PAC and EC in relation to the public undertaking. Effectiveness of functioning of Parliamentary Committee has become the subject of scholarly discussion and analysis.

Prakash, Jagdish, Leading Issues in Public Enterprise Management on Autonomy and Accountability of Public Enterprises, Himalaya Publications, Bombay, 1985, p-320-338.

The author in his paper discusses the dilemma of maximum control, which is desired by the public and parliament and maximum autonomy, which is desired by PE management. Accountability according to author has been organized through two channels the minister and parliament. While there is no conflict on the desirability of ministerial control the extent to which management should be more accountable continues to be a highly controversial issue. The author is of the opinion that for efficient operation the management should not be made accountable to the minister for day to day operations. It should be broadly accountable for policy matters. The author decries two present practices under which the ministerial control, formal or informal is often extensively exercised and minister interference not only in broad policy matter but also in matters concerning personnel management, labour relations, stores and purchase policy. The best convention to be followed is that the minister should not think that the enterprise concerned is the limb of his ministry and the chairman of the board should not be allowed to become an arbitrary emperor of industry resentful of public criticism. The need for parliamentary control of PEs is better established than ministerial control. PE should be set up in the form of public corporation.

Premchand, A, Public Enterprises and Autonomous Agencies in Govt. Budgeting and Expenditure Control, International Monetary Fund, Washington, 1983, p. 415-463

Public Enterprises and autonomous agencies have grown in size and scope during recent years. Their working reveals many problems common to both Industrial and developing countries. It appears that Public Enterprises have added to the budgetary pressure by shifting same burdens to the government budget, thus endangering its already fragile balance. The sick units taken over by the government have become in many cases, permanent liability on the government. Instead of contributing additional resource these enterprises have become more dependent on government budget. Instead of fulfilling development task they have contributed to delay in investment choices, capital intensive technology, cost escalation, credit expansions, presentation of credit to other needing sector and over all to our inefficiency.

Sengupta, A., Accountability of Enterprises: Performance Evaluation, Institute of Public Enterprise Journal, Hyderabad, July-September, 1986, p. 26-34.

This paper deals with accountability of PEs. The author feels that PEs should be made more accountable for their performance. The present system which operates through the evaluation of performance in the government, through audit and through parliamentary scrutiny needs to be modified and strengthened. On the basis of agreed plans for investments, production, capacity utilization, profit, dividends etc for a period of five years, the government in administrative ministry and holding company would enter into a memorandum of understanding. Accordingly this certain obligations would cast on the government in terms of procession of equity, price level. MoU is updated every year. The financial criteria for measuring the performance would be 1) Gross margin on assets (for all enterprises) 2) net profit on net worth (for core sector and profit making enterprises) 3) gross margin on sales (service enterprises). In respect of core sector enterprises, the role of net profit should be at stipulating percent and gross margin on capital should be improving overtime. In non-core sector, enterprises should be judged against the Industry average for both gross margin on capital employed and role of net profit. In service enterprises attention must be on gross margin on sales. In case of loss making enterprises gross margin should be positive. 1) ratio of loan liabilities to assets b) ratio of wages to value added per worker c) cash loss per worker.

Swamy, Dorai P K, Public Enterprise Autonomy from the Legislature's Point of View, International Centre for Public Enterprise Quarterly, Ljubljana, Vol. I, 1983, p- 36-55.

The article examines the basic motives of the intervention of the government in the working of SLPE and can be reviewed in the following context;

- To implement Government policies
- To increase the percentage of political party in power
- To enhance the prestige of Minister concerned.
- To satisfy the regional demands of reserved classes.

The author discusses about the agencies, which interfere with the working of PEs. External agencies a) Governor (b) Chief Minister (c) Other Ministers (d) Minister concerned and internal agencies: (a) Chairman (b) Board Member (c) Trade union leader (d) Employee.

He also discusses in length the area of intervention and control exercised by government vis-a vis SLPEs; *Official or Formal:* (1) Directives (2) Circular and office order (3) Reporting Rules and Meets (4) Power of Suspension. *Non-official & Informal*: (1) Personal visit (2) telephonic message (3) Relative and friend (4) Informal gathering

The author expresses the need for an effective nodal agency in the form of Bureau of Public Enterprise and that the government must delegate authority and encourage the enterprises to take decisions at the enterprise level.

The paper highlights a few principles for government-enterprise relationship;

- The government should be concerned with ensuring that public enterprise operate in public interest.
- The government should seek to ensure the efficiency of public enterprise exercising control.
- The public enterprise must be left as free as possible.

- There should be clear demarcation of responsibilities both between the government department and between the ministries concerned.
- The nature of control need not be wholly formal
- The government and public enterprise should be publicly accountable.
- The measure of management should not be purely commercial success or social achievement.
- The ultimate penalty for bad management may be dismissal or non-reappoint in post, but implementation of management should be prior.

Swamy Dorai, P.K, Public Enterprise Autonomy from the Legislative Legislature's Point of View, International Centre for Public Enterprise Quarterly, Ljubljana, Vol. 3, No.4, 1983.

A controversy that has become almost a reference in any discussion as public enterprise relates to their so-called autonomy. While the executive, the legislature, the public enterprises and the academicians each have their own point of view on public enterprise autonomy there is as yet no generally accepted synthesis of these views. The present paper is an attempt to apply a corrective to this impression and to do justice to the concept of legislative supremacy in a parliamentary democracy.

The Legislature: A watchdog role – In the classical model of parliamentary democracy based on the separation of power the legislature plays the role of watchdog vis-a-vis the executive which includes the cabinet and secretary. The latter's accountability to the former is supposed to be essence of democratic process.

Why autonomy? Matching each manager's responsibly with authority and autonomy appropriate to his operating microenvironment is essential in any organization, which seems to be effective. It might be imagined that unjustified interference in the day to day working of public enterprise would result in greater loss or harm to the society at large than a similar interference in a government department.

The paper also discusses the Role of Legislature;

- Legislative supremacy is the essence of parliamentary democracy.
- The Executive using the public enterprise system as a screen to evade legislative scrutiny is as real as and more so as the public enterprise system being demoralized by executive legislative scrutiny.
- What demoralizes the public enterprise manager is not really legislature scrutiny but the danger of a weak executive panicking and letting down by over reacting to such scrutiny.
- Civil servants and public enterprise manager should look upon the legislature as a guardian of their operational autonomy.

Venkat, Swamy G, State Government Enterprise: Factors Curbing Autonomy, Economic Times, September 18, 1987.

This paper discusses the problem of state enterprises with regard to autonomy. There are about 780 state government enterprises with an investment of 40.000 crores in 24 states. Like central PE they are also facing problems in their effective day to day operation and some of these relate to autonomy and accountability: structures, style and culture, personnel. This paper discusses in length the various issues regarding autonomy in these state enterprises.

Venkat, Swamy G, State Government Enterprise: The Politics of Inefficiency, Economic Times, September 19, 1987.

The practice of appointing civil servants to top position in state government enterprises hampers autonomy in two ways.

Firstly the enterprise relies heavily on the government to fill these posts and officials who man these posts often lack initiative and the capacity to take decisions independently. Secondly, they bring with them what is called civil service culture as against industrial culture, which percolates downwards and spreads to the entire organisation. It has been observed that "The association of secretariat official with the Board of Directors vitiate the very purpose for which autonomous enterprise are formed. In this paper it is mentioned in details regarding factors which inhibits the autonomy and which is responsible for ineffective performance of State Government enterprise.

Venkat, Swamy G, Interface between Government and State Enterprises, in Satish, K Batra & Tej, K Jain, State Enterprise: The Emerging Scenario, Printwell Publishers, Jaipur, 1988.

One of the most important aspect having a bearing on the performance of the public enterprise is the relationship between the public enterprise and the external environment, more particularly the government. In this paper it is proposed to study the nature of relationship between Government of Andhra Pradesh (GOAP) and Andhra Pradesh State Level Public Enterprise (APSLPEs), sources of government control on them, areas of government control, the instruments of control and the overall impact of these control and interference.

Even though the study deals with APSLPEs, the observations are relevant to other state enterprises also. The public enterprise-government relationship is perhaps one of the most sensitive issues in democratic societies, infact some state government enterprise have close and continued relationship with the government. The government has to convey to the public enterprise the need for better performance, coordination and control their operations in view of their importance in the development of economy. Notably, the government-public enterprise relationship is determined not only by the fact that government is sole or major shareholder but also to see that public enterprise are compatible with national and state priorities and objectives.

4. On Management Development & Training

Acharya M.R, Recruitment and Training in Public Sector, in Batra Satish. K & Jain K, (ed.) State Enterprises an Emerging Scenario, Printwell Publishers, Jaipur, 1988, p- 125-138.

The author discusses the need and importance of training for an industrial undertaking. He divides the training requirement into two different areas namely vocational training and training for management.

Chowdhary, A S, Professionalisation among Managers in Industrial Organisation in Public Sector, Lok Udyog, New Delhi, March 198, p-35-67

There is a continuing trend towards professionalization of management professionals, which has brought in serious changes in the status, functioning and responsibility of managers. Professionalism involves two basic elements viz. the acquisition of certain knowledge and skill and (2) the right mental attitude. Both the requirements will have to be interpreted in terms of management as a profession being different from other professions due to its distinct nature. Professionlism in management is not essentially identified with acquisition of theoretical knowledge and application of expertise. It must translate into practice the moral, ethical and social standards that are expected of a person in high position of business administration. The present study is confined to measure the degree of professionalism among managers operating at three levels viz., higher, middle and lower.

Khanna, K. K., Management of Public Sector Enterprise in India, Himalayan Publishers, Bombay, First Edition, 1988.

Experiences of the process of professionalization in some Public and Private sectors have revealed some critical issues, such as attitude change in favour of professionlization has to percolate from top to the bottom, Disharmony between preaching and practice, Unwillingness on the part of manager of accept and exercise the delegated authority, unwillingness to take risks, Leadership-style-not strong and courageous enough when it comes to implementation, Time Lag between conceptualization and implementation.

From this one can see that conceptualization and implementation of the process of professionalization of management in any enterprise is very challenging and demanding task, and more so in public sector enterprise with unique feature of gigantic size, public accountability and lack of autonomy.

Thus viewed from the point of view of social and national economic relevance any input material developed with coverage and emphasis in the area of "Management of State enterprise", will be a step forward and facilitate grasping and in producing a basic management perspective in Public Sector Enterprise.

Parekh, Udai, Human Resource Development in Public Enterprises, in (ed.) Vol. of Sankar, T. L, Mishra , R. K, & Ravishankar, S, Leading Issues in Public Enterprise Management, Himalaya Publication, Bombay, 1985, p-42.

Udai Parekh discusses the practices of human resource development in the public enterprises. After examining the distinctive features of public enterprise management, he feels that only a systematic management of human resources will help public enterprises achieve the objectives for which they have been set up. The most important features that need to be taken care of are the management of rewards.

Ramu Shiva, Improving Public Enterprise Performance Through Appraisal, Training and Management Development, in (ed.) Vol. of Sankar, T. L, Mishra , R. K, & Ravishankar, S, Leading Issues in Public Enterprise Management, Himalaya Publication, Bombay, 1985, p-48.

Shiva Ramu is of the opinion that manpower planning in public enterprises has been a neglected function. He deplores the prevalence of unhealthy practices in the appraisal of public enterprise personnel. He believes that the training systems need to be toned up to develop competent individuals to accomplish organizational goals.

5. On Performance Evaluation

Mishra, R.K, Performance Evaluation of Public Enterprises in India, Institute of Public enterprises Journal, Hyderabad, 1988, Volume XI No.4, p-1.

R.K Mishra reiterates the importance of public enterprises in the planned economic development in India. It is therefore, vital that the public sector enterprises accelerate the socio-economic growth. The paper deals with how educational and training programmes for the public enterprise board members, executives and removal of external barriers, may be used as tools to secure a better performance evaluation for the public enterprises in the future.

Murthy, K.R.S, More Memorandum Less Understanding, Economic and political Weekly, Bombay, 26th May 1990.

K.R.S. Murthy evaluates the effectiveness of the MOU system introduced in the Indian public sector enterprise after considering the recommendations of Sengupta Committee Report, 1985.

Powell Victor, Improving Public Enterprise Performance (Concepts and Techniques), Management Development Series No.22, International Labour Office, Geneva, 1982.

Victor Powell discusses about the public enterprise systems in developing countries. It has a concern about the operations of these systems and the constraints of the environment in which the public enterprises have to operate. It discusses about various dimensions of performance and operating effectiveness and how they can be measured. By 'effectiveness' is implied to the enterprise objectives and the extent to which these are achieved. Since public enterprises in developing countries seldom have clearly defined, unambiguous and consistent objectives, the attempts to assess their effectiveness are frequently met with frustration.

Emphasis is given on the need for the public enterprise to add wealth to the community, and to help raise the standard of living and undertake investment, which will generalize opportunities for, improved consumption. It also emphasizes the need for improving planning, control at the enterprise level and develop action plan for performance improvement of the enterprise.

Ramanadham, V V, The Basic Purpose of a Performance Contract, Paper presented at International conference on performance contracting, New Delhi, 13-15 January 1997.

Ramanadham focuses on the basic purpose of a performance contract in the case of a public enterprise. It has by design, not gone into the many important aspects of implementing it, which are usually considered, important. The author highlights the point that the performance contract must spring from a consideration of its basic purpose, or else it operates on loose foundations. The autonomy with which the managers operate in the circumstances of their markets makes the full success of a performance contract. This depends again on the nature of publicness of a given public enterprise. The performance contract helps the parliament and the public in visualizing the rationale of a public enterprise, its operating efficiency, and the government's own role in its management. Thus, it helps in drawing up detailed provisions of the contract, specially relating to the responsibilities of the government under the contract.

Ramanadham, V. V, (ed.), The Efficacy of Public Enterprise, Allied Publishers Pvt. Ltd., Bombay, 1963, pp-230.

This volume contains basic papers and discussion at the second all India seminar on public enterprise, organized by the Department of Commerce, Osmania University, Hyderabad in February 1962. An important objective of the seminar was to provide the necessary synthesis between academic ideas and practical views on a subject of growing importance in India, namely, the public sector. Three topics were mainly discussed public enterprise and regional development, social and economic returns of public enterprises and management of boards of public enterprises.

Sharma, Sreedhar J, The Enterprise Contract System in Public Enterprise Management, Institute of Public Enterprise Journal, December 1982. Hyderabad.

This paper is based on Shreedhar Sharma's thesis on state Financial Corporation submitted for University of Paris. Here, the author discusses the nature of the public enterprises, being enterprises they are expected to perform specific functions and at the same time unlike their counterparts in the private sector they are supposed to subserve the 'public interest'. The evolution of the contractual system is traced in the annals of the French public enterprises. The objectives with which the contracts originated are discussed which are essentially improving their financial situation, fixing investment of these enterprises over a given period of time and at the same time fixation of productivity norms. The author also discusses the advantages of contractual system for the betterment of public enterprises; i.e., by codifying relationships between government and enterprise by target setting, specifying nature of government aid. At the enterprise level the advantages of performance contracting is manifold, it helps in strategic planning, greater sense of satisfaction to personnel introduces a sense of commercial functioning in the enterprise introduces Management by Objectives (MBO) and enhances autonomy.

Trivedi, Prajapathi, Theory and Practice of Contractual Approach: Lessons From Lower Developed Countries With Performance Contracting, International Centre for Public Enterprise Quarterly, Ljubljana Vol.8 No.1, 1988, Yugoslavia.

Prajapathi Trivedi, surveys the theoretical basis and country experiences of the French system of contracts as a technique to rationalize government controls of public enterprise's in order to improve their performance. Starting with the theoretical foundations of the system, the paper describes its nature, history and practice in France and makes a critical analysis of the theoretical justifications for its design and listing a set of preconditions for its successful implementations. The experiences in less developed countries (LDC's) with the use of the French model or variations thereof are surveyed. These include Senegal, Gambia, Pakistan, Korea, Bangladesh and India. The paper concludes with a summary of lessons or conditions for successful implementation of the contractual approach. They include political commitment at the highest level as well as throughout various levels of government and emphasize the importance of training.

Venugopal, Reddy Y, Public Enterprise Reform and Privatisation, Himalaya Publishing House, Bombay. 1992.

Y.Venugopal Reddy discusses the highlighting features of Memorandum of Understanding in India. He discusses how the MOU formalizes the relationship between ministry and the public enterprises. By signing the MOU greater transparency is expected. The author refers to the performance contracting in France. The experiences with performance contracting in France were dissatisfactory, though contractual system cannot be totally refuted it has certainly initiated thought process in the enterprises regarding their own objectives of policy and the instruments of execution.

6. On Country-Specific Experiences

Iyer, Ramaswamy R., Past Experiences With Public Performance Evaluation System In India: Lessons for MOU's, paper presented at International Workshop on MOU's organized by Bureau of Public Enterprise and Indian Institute of Management, Calcutta, March 6-9th 1989.

Ramaswamy Iyer discusses the experiences of India with Performance Evaluation Systems in relation to public enterprises. The past experiences and efforts are highlighted in the Central Public Sector Enterprises.

Jones, Leroy P, Towards a Performance Evaluation Methodology for Public Enterprises: Special Reference to Pakistan, Paper presented at the International Symposium on Economic Performance of Public Enterprises, Islamabad, Pakistan, 1981.

Leroy Jones argues about the need for improving the efficiency of the public enterprise sector. A basic indicator of efficiency is first derived and then modified to account for some of the exogenous factors beyond the control of management. Given a criterion, which is broadly applicable across enterprises, it is necessary to establish criteria values deviating 'good' from 'bad' performance. The next step would be to allow for non-commercial objectives and growth for dynamic effects. The need in fact is to implement the performance evaluation method in a phased manner for enterprises. Finally, the feasibility of proposed methodology is examined by its application to one Pakistani public enterprise.

Jones, Leroy P, Improving Korea's Public Enterprise Evaluation Efforts, Korean Development Institute, Korea, 1985.

Leroy Jones gives due importance to the Korean effort for improving their public sector enterprise performance. Though Korea has developed the world's most sophisticated system for evaluating performance of its public enterprise the implementation of the system has been done in such a way that the enterprise behaviour has actually changed as a result. The author attacks the indicator categorization, i.e., qualitative Vs quantitative, results Vs processes, non-duplicative Vs duplicative indicators. The problems existing with criteria value determination, criteria selection is also highlighted. The problem of duplication is dealt with in details. The need is also highlighted for improving qualitative, indicators by focussing on marginal changes, staffing etc.

Mahnot, S.R. Basic Issues in Performance Contracting Systems with Special Reference to Indian Case, Paper presented at the International Conference on Performance Contracting, New Delhi, 13-15th January 1997.

Mahnot talks about the concept of performance contracting, as to why was the need felt for a contract and how it originated as an effective instrument for improving the performance of public enterprises. The contents of a contract are discussed that it should thrust to accountability, generate more autonomy, and contain targets to be measured in a fixed span.

The Indian model of performance contracting (MOU), is

discussed at length. The government claim as per the authors reference to a DPE Survey that MOU System has now stabilized. The public sector enterprises signing MOU's have achieved the targets fixed by the Finance Ministry and the Planning Commission, the MOU Policy seems to have been successful as per a report given by The Government of India, DPE, Public enterprises surveys.

Mehdi, Istaqbal, Setting Targets For Improving Cost Efficiencies in Public Enterprises, Paper presented at a seminar on 'Elimination of Waste through Cost Effective Management for Public Enterprises in Developing countries', Karachi, 1-4th July, 1985.

Istaqbal Mehdi deals with the most important aspect of contracting system i.e., target setting. Setting targets for operating units is an exercise of reviewing the annual operational plan of enterprises, identification of cost inefficiency areas and a negotiated agreement to improve performance by way of agreeing to a set of targets for the enterprise management. Negotiation and establishment of acceptable and achievable targets reflecting good performance is a challenge both to the management of an enterprise as well as to evaluating agency (EAC), Experts Advisory Cell. The exercise of target negotiation provides an occasion to identify weak areas in the enterprise operations. This paper attempts to illustrate Pakistan's efforts to improve cost efficiency in public enterprises by way of target setting for evaluating performance. The first section deals with the concept of target setting, the second with performance evaluation exercise in Pakistan's context, the third section highlights the process of target setting in the context of Pakistan.

Park, Young C, System for Evaluating the Performance of Government Invested Enterprises in the Republic of Korea, World Bank Discussion Paper, November 1986.

Park Young reviews role of the GIE's in Korea, which is

represented by far the most important category of public corporations. It traces the unsatisfactory performance of the Government-Invested Enterprises, leading to the promulgation of the Government Investment Enterprise Management Act, which introduced extensive institutional and legal reforms. The paper then goes on to describe the various characteristic features of the system and reviews the results of the evaluation conducted for its first two operational years, 1983 and 1984. Finally, the paper assesses the system's performance and attempts to draw some conclusions that will be useful for other countries, which may consider adopting a simi'ar system.

Rammurthi, Ravi, Observations on the South Korean System for Performance Evaluation of Public Enterprises, Report submitted to the Ministry of France, Government of Bangladesh and United Nations, April 1986.

Ramamurthi discusses the main features of the Korean system of performance evaluation for public enterprises. The various aspects are discussed like the technical aspects of the Korean System, which comprises of target setting, giving weightages and values ending up with an evaluation and reward. The organizational aspects like the structures of the contractual system and staffing is also mentioned. The second part deals with some observations on the system citing the examples of Korean Telecom Authority discussing how the performance criteria and weightages are decided upon and how the evaluation begins and ends with a reward or punishment.

Ramamurthi, Ravi, Performance Contracting System in Bangladesh, Report submitted to Ministry of France, Government of Bangladesh and the United Nations, April 1986.

Ramamurthy briefly reviews the fundamental problems governments' face in controlling the public enterprises. The report recommends an innovative approach to the strategic planning and control of non-financial public enterprises (PE's) in Bangladesh. The report offers the performance contracting system as a possible solution. Further, it describes the units of applying the performance contracting system or an experimental basis to two public enterprises (NBPM AND GENCO)

Ramamurthi, Ravi, Methods for Controlling Public Enterprises: International Comparators, Report submitted to the Ministry of Finance, Government of Bangladesh and the United Nations, April 1986.

Ravi Ramamurthy in this paper, compares the programme contract used in the France and Senegal and the signaling system, which is used in Pakistan and South Korea is discussed at length.

Sankar, T L, Memorandum of Understanding: The Wrong End of the Stick, Journal of Public Enterprise, Volume 13, No.2, 1990, p- 72- 78.

T.L.Sankar systematically analyses the MOU system in India. He has brought out the hard facts about the MOU system and has highlighted the total set up of the system right from the institutional arrangements, contents and implementation.

Shahrokh, Roya Jone, The Contract Plan Experience in Africa, Paper submitted for partial fulfillment of MBA, Graduate School of Business Administration, University of California, Berkeley, December, 1987.

Shahrokh, Roya prepared a census of the contract plan experience in Africa. Issues on the contract plans expansion across Africa, and the industries using them are explored. Fact finding objectives in individual country reports highlighting the known facts and the lesson learned in the process does an assessment of the contract plans. The positive and negative points of the contract plan and a list of recommendations for the future users is given. Alternative mechanisms for controlling public enterprises are also brought out.

Ninety-six instances of contract plans in the public utility sector were explored. The various lessons learned by them are highlighted and a need is expressed to find an alternative to the signaling system as a better mechanism for controlling the public enterprises.

Shaikh, Hafeez, Performance Evaluation of Public Enterprises: Lessons from the Pakistan Experience, paper presented at the Association of Indian Economic Studies (AIES), New Orleans, December 1986.

Shaikh Hafeez provides an overview of the public enterprise sector in Pakistan. It traces how the contracting system originally developed in Pakistan's enterprises and also highlights how the system was actually implemented by the government of Pakistan. It explains the deviations from the system, actually proposed and the system implemented. The paper includes with an assessment of the success of the contracting system in Pakistan's public enterprise performance improvement.

Shirely, Mary M, Public Enterprise Performance Evaluation System in Pakistan, World Bank Discussion Paper, World Bank, 1988.

Mary Shirley provides an assessment of Pakistan's performance evaluation system for its Industrial Public Enterprise (IPE's). The paper gives a brief history and description of the system. It calculates the impact of the system on performance and management of enterprises. The paper concludes with recommendations to adopt the system in other countries. The assessment is carried out to: (i) provide suggestions on ways to strengthen the system (ii) inform officials of other countries interested in replicating the system (iii) suggests ways to adopt it in other countries.

Song, Dae-lee, New Public Enterprise Policy and Efficiency Improvement, Korean Development Institute Working Paper No.8811, September 1988, KDI, Seoul, South Korea.

Song, Dae-Lee essentially highlights the economic development of Korea during the last 30 years, and the role of public sector played in the economy. The paper reassesses the importance of the Korean public enterprise sector and the impact of the new Korean public enterprise policy. The policy for the Government Invested Enterprise in 1984, brought in the contractual system for the 25 industries (GIE's). An assessment is made at the end as to how the policy has worked and its impact on the Korean economy is also highlighted. The utility of the Korean system of performance evaluation to other developing countries is discussed at the end.

Trivedi, Prajapathi, Institutional Arrangements For Designing And Implementing Memorandum Of Understanding, Management in Government Journal, New Delhi., 1990.

Trivedi brings an overview of the complete institutional structure for the MOU Policy. The various organs for designing MOU's as well as for implementing them are discussed at length. The author justifies the present set up for the MOU.

Trivedi, Prajapathi, Methodological Issues Relating to Recent Changes in the MOU Policy, Quarterly Journal of AIMA, Vol.29, No.7, July 19, 1990.

Trivedi highlights through this article, highlights the changes which MOU policy underwent relating to i) format ii) institutional arrangements for drafting and monitoring MOU iii) differences relating to process and procedures involved.

Trivedi, Prajapathi, Public Enterprises In India: If Not for Profit then for What, Economic and Political Weekly, Volume XXI, No.48, November 29, 1986.

Prajapathi Trivedi discusses about the evaluation system

for the public enterprises. He is of the view that though the public enterprises must be evaluated like the private enterprises, they should not be evaluated on the basis of same criteria as the private enterprises.

Trivedi, Prajapathi & Suresh, Kumar, Memorandum of Understanding and the Korean Performance Evaluation System, Institute of Public Enterprise Journal, Volume 13, No.2, 1990, p-567.

Prajapathi Trivedi in this paper essentially deals with the experience of the Korean enterprises with the signaling system and makes a comparison of the signaling system with MOU system adopted in India. The paper descriptively gives the public sector scenario in Korea and how the GIE's were initiated into the performance contracting with the Act of 1984. It also highlights the post contract scene in Korea. The differences and similarities between the Indian MOU system as well as the Korean system are discussed at length.

7. Corporate Governance, Boards

Mukund, R. Dixit, Into the Future: Some Issues for Management, Vikalpa, Vol. 25, No.1, January-March 2000, p- 21-28

Developments in the business environment in the last decade of the 20th century and the responses of corporations to these have set the stage for entering the first decade of the 21st century. This perspective attempts to anticipate the developments in the new decade and identify a set of issues for management. The expectation is that the change process will accelerate further. The overall import of the issues is that the Indian corporations should take a proactive approach to strategy formulation and implementation. Their response should be based on the strengths they have and would like to build and not on the weakness that they developed in the past. They should create a distinctive attribute of their own, and not jump into the bandwagon to try out whatever is internationally popular or fashionable.

Venugopalan, S, Director's Papers- Its Scope, Contents and Legal Recruitment's, Chartered Secretary, Vol. XXXII, April 2002, p-493-501.

This paper examines the association between board size and corporate financial performance using data on 504 corporations belonging to 18 industries. The results suggest that the size of the board plays an important role in influencing the financial performance of corporations. The analysis shows that the performance improves if the board size increases, but the contribution of an additional board member decreases as the size of the corporation increases. The results however fail to indicate any significant role of director's equity ownership in influencing the performance.

8. On Performance Contracting for State Owned Enterprises

Beesely, M E, Likierneas, A & Bloomfield, S, Commentaries on State Enterprise Control Problems, Discussion Paper No.302, Economic Council of Canada, Ontario.

This paper is a commentary by Beesely, M.E, Likierneas, A, Bloomfield, dealing with United Kingdom, France and Italy. It reflects the levels of dissatisfaction with the performance of government enterprise. The issues addressed are relating to accountability, efficiency, policy direction etc. These are common to all the countries in Europe.

Mallon, Richard D, Performance Contracts With Sate Owned Public Enterprises, Development Discussion Paper No.143, Harvard Institute for International Development, February 1983.

Mallon Richard deals with the performance contracts

between government and SOE's to regulate the hierarchical exchange of reciprocal commitments. The simplest form of contracts is mentioned as the single period contracts, the multiple period contracts prove expensive. Performance contracting is not a panacea for improving the performance of SOE's, instead they should be viewed as a step towards creating self correcting organizations.

Menon, Krishna, & Umapathy, Srinivasa, Control Systems for SOE'S: Conceptual Framework, Working paper No. 5/85, School of Management Working Paper Series, Boston University.

Menon and Srinivasa discuss that there is no unique control system that is suitable for all SOE's that is appropriate to all types of organizations. The type of control system needed is a function of certain organizational objectives and the measurability of organizational outputs. This paper classifies SOE's into four groups on the basis of their features and suggests improvements for the design of organizational control system.

Sankar, T L, Mishra, R. K, & Nandagopal, R, MOU's for the State Level Public Enterprises in India, Economic and Political Weekly, August 31st, 1991.

Sankar, Nanadgopal, Mishra, discuss at length the background for working of State Level Public Enterprises (SOEs) and a need to take initiatives to improve their performance. The need for the introduction of MOU system in the (SOEs) is felt as a necessary prerequisite for their proper functioning.

Shirley, Mary M, Contracts Between the State and It's Enterprises, The Experience of France & Senegal, World Bank Staff Working Papers on Managing State Owned Enterprises, No.577, Washington, 1983.

Shirley, Mary discusses Senegalese government negotiated

controls with 5 SOE's since 1980. This paper studies the experience of the contracts and points out the fact that SOE's were forced to do strategic planning for preparing the contracts and simultaneously made the government systematically compare their cost of social objectives and investment proposals with their benefits.

Vernon, Raymond, Linking Managers With Ministries: Dilemma's of the SOE'S, Journal of Policy Analysis and Management, Volume 4, No.1, 1984.

Vernon Raymond says that in relation with their SOEs governments try to capture the advantages that are thought to exist in operating through autonomous organizations. At the same time, they attempt to push the enterprises towards a set of governmental goals. The interface between ministries and managers of SOE's has to be considerably different from those of the private enterprises. Thus governments are attempting to improve the relationship with their SOE's through contracts. This step cannot be ruled out as a significant one.

9. On United Nation Publications

A Handbook For Managers: Commonwealth Secretariat, United Nations. New York, 1995

Another book on Performance contract deals with the concept and rationale of performance contracting in public enterprises, the institutional arrangements needed for designing and implementing the contracts, as well as the monitoring and evaluation procedures involved in it, country experiences of specific enterprises are also included in the publication.

Bureaucrats in Business, Oxford University Press, 1995.

A World Bank Policy Research Report, discusses the various aspects of reform in the state owned enterprises. The contracting system for the SOE's have been studied in detail and an evaluation is made of their success functionally. It deals with specifically the dynamic factors like the political will and economic factors in a country, which help in shaping the policies for reform.

Department of Development and Support Management Services, United Nations, New York, 1995.

The book entitled Performance Contracting for public Enterprises deals with each country experiences with contracting system giving a complete picture of the economy's policy of the country and the need felt for the system.

Department of Development and Support Management Services, United Nations, New York, 1995.

Another publication Guidelines for Performance Contracting deals with how performance contracting is dealt with in different countries. It gives a guideline for preparing performance contracts with country specific needs

Gaps in Literature

The performance contracting system in the global context has received great attention in the academic circles. There are a few gaps in the literature that has been identified during the course of the study. Firstly most of the writings are of the time when the system was hardly introduced in the public enterprises. After a system is introduced it takes at least 5 to 6 years for the system to become operational and highlight results. Secondly, all the literature that has been available only focuses about the 'quantitative' target setting and their evaluation. There are very few articles, which highlight the 'qualitative' aspects of an enterprise, which are equally important. This study is conducted keeping these gaps in view and an attempt is made to reduce, if not fill these gaps through this study.

Appendix I

Committee on Public Undertakings (COPU)

Backdrop

Constitution

The Committee on Public Undertakings is a Parliamentary Committee consisting of 22 members—fifteen elected by the Lok Sabha and seven by the Rajya Sabha, from amongst their members, according to the principle of proportional representation by means of single transferable vote. The Chairman is appointed by the Speaker from amongst the members of the Committee.

Functions

The functions of the Committee on Public Undertakings are:

(a) To examine the reports and accounts of Public Undertakings specified in the Fourth Schedule to the Rules of Procedure and Conduct of Business in Lok Sabha.

(b) To examine the reports, if any, of the Comptroller and Auditor General of India on Public Undertakings

(c) To examine, in the context of the autonomy and efficiency of the Public Undertakings whether the affairs of the Public Undertakings are being managed in accordance with sound business principles and prudent commercial practices; and

(d) To exercise such other functions vested in the Public Accounts Committee and the Estimates Committee in relation to the Public Undertakings as are not covered by clauses (a), (b) and (c) above and as may be allotted to the committee by the Speaker from time to time.

Working of the Committee

The Committee selects from time to time for examination of such public Undertakings or such subjects as they may deem fit and as fall within their terms of reference.

The Ministry/Undertaking concerned is asked to furnish necessary material relating to those subjects for the information of the members of the Committee.

The Committee may from time to time appoint one or more Study Groups for carrying out detailed examination of various subjects.

List of Reports - Committee on Public Undertakings (COPU)

Third Lok Sabha

Sl. No.	*Report*	*Year*	*Particulars*
1	1st Report	1965	National Building Construction Corporation
2.	2nd Report	1965	Hindustan Insecticides Ltd.
3.	3rd Report	1965	Shipping Corporation of India Ltd.
4.	4th Report	1965	Life Insurance Corporation of India
5.	5th Report	1965	Oil & Natural Gas Commission
6.	6th Report	1965	Fertilizers Corporation of India Ltd.
7.	7th Report	1965	Action taken on 32nd Report of the Estimates Committee (3rd L.S) on

(Contd...)

			National Coal Development Corporation
8.	8th Report	1965	Townships and Factory Buildings of Public Undertakings
9.	9th Report	1965	Action taken on 157th Report of the Estimates Committee (2nd Lok Sabha) on National Newsprint & Paper Mills
10.	10th Report	1965	Action taken on 36th Report of the Estimates Committee(3rd L.S) on Industrial Finance Corporation of India
11.	11th Report	1965	Rurkela Steel Plant of Hindustan Steel
12.	12th Report	1965	Action taken on 28th Report of the Estimates Committee(3rd L.S) on Indian Oil Company
13.	13th Report	1965	Management and Administration of Public Undertakings
14.	14th Report	1965	Action taken by Government on the recommendations contained in the 34th Report of the Estimates Committee, 3rd Lok Sabha
15.	15th Report	1966	Action taken by Govt. on the recommendations contained in the 120th Report of the Estimates Committee, 2nd Lok Sabha
16.	16th Report	1966	Travancore Titanium Products Ltd. Trivandrum
17.	17th Report	1966	Travancore Cochin Chemicals Ltd. Trivandrum
18.	18th Report	1966	The Platinum Corporation of Kerala Ltd. , Kottayam
19.	19h Report	1966	Trivandrum Rubber Works Ltd., Trivandrum
20.	20th Report	1966	The Kerala Ceramics Ltd. Kundra
21.	21st Report	1966	Air India, Ministry of Transport and Aviation
22.	22nd Report	1966	Indian Drugs & Pharmaceuticals Limited
23.	23rd Report	1966	Indian Airlines

(Contd...)

24.	24th Report	1966	Neyveli Lignite Corporation Ltd.
25.	25th Report	1966	The Kerala Premo Pipe Factory Ltd., Trivandrum
26.	26th Report	1966	Traco Cable Co. Ltd. Ernakulum
27.	27th Report	1966	Planning, Management & Administration of Kerala State Govt. Companies
28.	28th Report	1966	Head Office of Hindustan Steel Ltd.
29.	29th Report	1966	Durgapur Steel Plant of Hindustan Ltd.
30.	30th Report	1966	Bhilai Steel Plant of Hindustan Ltd.
31.	31st Report	1966	Alloy Steel Projects and Coal Washeries Project of Hindustan Steel Ltd.
32.	32nd Report	1966	State Trading Corporation of India
33.	33rd Report	1966	Action taken by Govt. on the recommendations contained in the 11th Report of the COPU on the Rourkela Steel Plant of the Hindustan Steel Ltd.
34.	34th Report	1966	Action taken by Govt. on the recommendations contained in the 124th Report of the Estimates Committee, 2nd L.S, Hindustan Aircraft Ltd. Bangalore
35.	35th Report	1967	Indian Oil Corporation Ltd. (Marketing Division)
36.	36th Report	1967	Indian Oil Corporation Ltd. (Refineries Ltd.)
37.	37th Report	1967	Hindustan Shipyard Ltd.
38.	38th Report	1967	Pyrite & Chemicals Development Co. Ltd.
39.	39th Report	1967	Bharat Heavy Electricals Limited.
40.	40th Report	1967	Materials Management in Public Undertakings

Fourth Lok Sabha

Sl. No.	*Report*	*Year*	*Particulars*
1.	1st Report	1967	Action taken by Govt. on the recommendations contained in the

(Contd...)

			47th Report of the EC, 3rd LS (Export Risks Insurance Corp. Ltd. Bombay)
2.	2nd Report	1967	Action taken by the Govt. on the recommendations contained in the 35th Report of the EC, 3rd LS (Heavy Electricals (I) Ltd. Bhopal)
3.	3rd Report	1967	Action taken by Govt. on the recommendations contained in the 4th Report of the CPU, 3rd LS, Life Insurance Corporation of India
4.	4th Report	1967	Action taken by the Govt. on the recommendations in the 2nd Report of the CPU, 3rd LS, Hindustan Insecticides Ltd.
5.	5th Report	1967	State Trading Corporation of India Ltd.
6.	6th Report	1967	Rourkela Steel Plant of Hindustan Steel Ltd with M/S B. Patnaik Mines (P) Ltd and others for the supply of Iron Ore and Manganese Ore.
7.	7th Report	1967	Action taken by Govt. on the recommendations contained in the 51st Report of the EC, 3rd LS. Heavy Engineering Corp. Ltd.
8.	8th Report	1967	Hindustan Aeronautics Ltd.
9.	9th Report	1967	Central Warehousing Corp.
10.	10th Report	1967	National Coal Development Corporation Ltd.
11.	11th Report	1967	National Mineral Development Corporation Ltd.
12.	12th Report	1967	Heavy Electricals (India) Ltd.
13.	13th Report	1967	Ashok Hotels Ltd.
14.	14th Report	1967	Heavy Engineering Corp. Ltd.
15.	15th Report	1967	Financial Management in Public Undertakings
16.	16th Report	1967	Action taken by Govt. on the recommendations contained in the 39th Report of the CPU, 3rd LS (BHEL)

(Contd...)

17.	17th Report	1967	Action taken by Govt. on the recommendations contained in the 15th Report of the PAC, 3rd LS, Ref: Audit Report on the Accounts of Damodar Valley Corp. for the year 1961-62.
18.	18th Report	1967	Action taken by the Govt. on the recommendations contained in the 3rd Report of the CPU, 3rd LS, Shipping Corp. of India Ltd.
19.	19th Report	1967	Action taken by the Govt. on the recommendations contained in the 8th Report of the CPU, 3rd LS (Township and Factory Building of Public Undertakings)
20.	20th Report	1967	Action taken by the Govt. on the recommendations contained in the 1st Report of the CPU, 3rd LS (National Buildings Construction Corp. Ltd.)
21.	21st Report	1967	Action taken by the Govt. on the recommendations contained in the 15th Report of the EC, 3rd LS on Public Undertakings-accommodation rented in principle cities, and guesthouses, staff cars etc maintained by them.
22.	22nd Report	1967	Action taken by the Govt. on the recommendations contained in the 21st Report of the CPU, 3rd LS (Air India)
23.	23rd Report	1967	Action taken by the Govt. on the recommendations contained in the 24th Report of the CPU, 3rd LS (Neyveli Lignite Corp. Ltd. Ministry of Steel and Mines)
24.	24th Report	1967	Action taken by the Govt. on the recommendations contained in the 36th Report of the CPU, 3rd LS (Indian Oil Corp. of India Ltd., Refineries Division)

(Contd...)

25.	25th Report	1967	Pragya Tools Ltd.
26.	26th Report	1967	Trombay Unit of Fertilizer Corporation of India Ltd.
27.	27th Report	1967	Hindustan Cables Ltd.
28.	28th Report	1968	Action taken by the Govt. on the recommendations contained in the 38th Report of the COPU, 3rd LS (Pyrites and Chemicals Development Co. Ltd.)
29.	29th Report	1968	Action taken by the Govt. on the recommendations contained in the 37th Report of the COPU, 3rd LS (Hindustan Shipyard Ltd.)
30.	30th Report	1968	Action taken by the Govt. on the recommendations contained in the 22nd Report of the COPU, 3rd LS (IDPL)
31.	31st Report	1969	Action taken by the Govt. on the recommendations contained in the 28th Report of the COPU, 3rd LS (Head Office of Hindustan Steel Ltd.)
32.	32nd Report	1969	Action taken by the Govt. on the recommendations contained in the 9th Report of the COPU, 4th LS (Central Warehousing Corporation)
33.	33rd Report	1969	Action taken by the Govt. on the recommendations contained in the 29th Report of the COPU, 3rd LS (Durgapur Steel Plant of Hindustan Steel)
34.	34th Report	1969	Action taken by the Govt. on the recommendations contained in the 30th Report of the COPU, 3rd LS (Bhilai Steel Plant of Hindustan Steel Ltd.)
35.	35th Report	1969	Action taken by the Govt. on the recommendations contained in the 7th Report of the PAC, 3rd LS (Food Corporation of India & Hindustan Steel Ltd.)

(Contd...)

36.	36th Report	1969	Action taken by the Govt. on the recommendations contained in the 23rd Report of the COPU, 3rd LS (Indian Airlines)
37.	37th Report	1969	Action taken by the Govt. on the recommendations contained in the 5th Report of the COPU, 3rd LS (ONGC)
38.	38th Report	1969	Action taken by the Govt. on the recommendations contained in the 40th Report of the COPU, 3rd LS (Materials Management in Public Undertakings)
39.	39th Report	1969	Action taken by the Govt. on the recommendations contained in the 35th Report of the COPU, 3rd LS (IOC Ltd. Ministry of Petroleum & Chemicals & Mines & Metals)
40.	40th Report	1969	Action taken by the Govt. on the recommendations contained in the 23rd Report of the COPU, 3rd LS
41.	41st Report	1969	Action taken by the Govt. on the recommendations contained in the 6th Report of the COPU, 3rd LS (Fertilizer Corporation of India Ltd.)
42.	42nd Report	1969	Mazagon Dock Ltd.
43.	43rd Report	1969	Sindri Unit of Fertilizers Corporation Ltd of India
44.	44th Report	1969	Fertilizers and Chemicals, Travancore Ltd.
45.	45th Report	1969	Action taken by the Govt. on the recommendations contained in the 31st Report of the CPU, 3rd LS (Alloy Steel Projects & Coal Washeries Project of Hindustan Steel Ltd.)
46.	46th Report	1969	Indian Drugs & Pharmaceuticals Ltd.
47.	47th Report	1969	Public Relations Publicity in Public Undertakings
48.	48th Report	1969	Action taken by the Govt. on the

(Contd...)

			recommendations contained in the 13th Report of the CPU, 3rd LS on (Management and Administration of Public Undertakings)
49.	49th Report	1969	Industrial Finance Corporation of India
50.	50th Report	1969	Action taken by the Govt. on the recommendations contained in the 52nd Report of the EC, 3rd LS on (Personal policies of Public Undertakings)
51.	51st Report	1969	State Trading Corporation of India Ltd.
52.	52nd Report	1969	Action taken by the Govt. on the recommendations contained in the 6th Report of the CPU, 4th LS (Ministry of Steel & Heavy Engineering)
53.	53rd Report	1969	Action taken by the Govt. on the recommendations contained in the 5th Report of the CPU, 4th LS (Ministry of Foreign Trade)
54.	54th Report	1969	Action taken by the Govt. on the recommendations contained in the 51st Report of the CPU, 4th LS on STC.
55.	55th Report	1969	Action taken by the Govt. on the recommendations contained in the 11th Report of the CPU, 4th LS on NMDC.
56.	56th Report	1969	Action taken by the Govt. on the recommendations contained in the 15th Report of the CPU, 4th LS on Finance Ministry
57.	57th Report	1969	Action taken by the Govt. on the recommendations contained in the 43rd Report of the CPU, 4th LS, Sindhri Unit of Fertilizers Corporation of India Ltd.
58.	58th Report	1969	Action taken by the Govt. on the recommendations contained in the

(Contd...)

			25th Report of the CPU, 4th LS (Praga Tools)
59.	59th Report	1969	Action taken by the Govt. on the recommendations contained in the 44th Report of the CPU, 4th LS (Fertilizers & Chemicals, Travancore)
60.	60th Report	1969	Action taken by the Govt. on the recommendations contained in the 8th Report of the CPU, 4th LS (Hindustan Aeronautics Ltd.)
61.	61st Report	1970	Action taken by the Govt. on the recommendations contained in the 10th Report of the CPU, 4th LS (NCDC)
62.	62nd Report	1970	The Central Road Transport Corporation
63.	63rd Report	1970	The National Industrial Development Corporation
64.	64th Report	1970	Action taken by the Govt. on the recommendations contained in the 47th Report of the CPU, 4th LS (Public Relations and Publicity in Public Undertakings)
65.	65th Report	1970	Mining and Allied Machinery Corporation
66.	66th Report	1970	Indian Oil Corporation Ltd.
67.	67th Report	1970	Production Management of Public Undertakings.
68.	68th Report	1970	Bokaro Steel Plant
69.	69th Report	1970	Air India
70.	70th Report	1970	Indian Tourism Development Corporation

Fifth Lok Sabha

Sl. No.	*Report*	*Year*	*Particulars*
1.	1st Report	1971	Hindustan Steel Limited
2.	2nd Report	1971	Bharat Earth Movers Ltd.
3.	3rd Report	1971	Bharat Electronics Limited
4.	4th Report	1971	Action taken by the Govt. on the

(Contd...)

			recommendations contained in the 46th Report of the CPU, 4th LS.
5.	5th Report	1971	Action taken by the Govt. on the recommendations contained in the 12th Report of the CPU, 4th LS.
6.	6th Report	1971	Action taken by the Govt. on the recommendations contained in the 70th Report of the CPU, 4th LS.
7.	7th Report	1971	Action taken by the Govt. on the recommendations contained in the 42nd Report of the CPU, VLS 4th LS.
8.	8th Report	1971	Action taken by the Govt. on the recommendations contained in the 27th Report of the CPU, VLS 4th LS.
9.	9th Report	1971	Action taken by the Govt. on the recommendations contained in the 67th Report of the CPU, 4th LS.
10.	10th Report	1971	Action taken by the Govt. on the recommendations contained in the 69th Report of the CPU, 4th LS.
11.	11th Report	1971	Action taken by the Govt. on the recommendations contained in the 49th Report of the CPU, 4th LS (IFCI)
12.	12th Report	1971	Food Corporation of India
13.	13th Report	1971	Action taken by the Govt. on the recommendations contained in the 14th Report of the CPU, 4th LS (Heavy Engineering Corporation)
14.	14th Report	1971	Action taken by the Govt. on the recommendations contained in the 68th Report of the CPU, 4th LS (Bokaro Steel)
15.	15th Report	1971	Action taken by the Govt. on the recommendations contained in the 13th Report of the CPU, 4th LS (Ashoka Hotels (ITDC)
16.	16th Report	1971	Oil and Natural Gas Commission, ONGC
17.	17th Report	1971	Personnel Policies and Labour Management Relations in PU's
18.	18th Report	1971	Heavy Engineering Corporation

(Contd...)

19.	19th Report	1971	Heavy Electricals India Ltd.
20.	20th Report	1971	Shipping Corporation of India Ltd.
21.	21st Report	1972	BHEL
22.	22nd Report	1972	On paragraph 1.17, 63rd Report of the CPU, 4th LS, NIDC
23.	23rd Report	1972	Action taken by the Govt. on the recommendations contained in the 63rd Report of the CPU, 4th LS (NIDC)
24.	24th Report	1972	Action taken by the Govt. on the recommendations contained in the 63rd Report of the CPU, 4th LS (MAMC)
25.	25th Report	1973	Action taken by the Govt. on the recommendations contained in the 3rd Report of the CPU, 5th LS (BEL)
26.	26th Report	1973	Action taken by the Govt. on the recommendations contained in the 2nd Report of the CPU, 5th LS (BEML)
27.	27th Report	1973	National Newsprint & Paper Mills Ltd.
28.	28th Report	1973	Indian Airlines
29.	29th Report	1973	Action taken by the Govt. on the recommendations contained in the 20th Report of the CPU, 5th LS, Shipping Corp.
30.	30th Report	1973	Action taken by the Govt. on the recommendations contained in the 17th Report of the CPU, 5th LS, Personnel Policies and Labour Management Relations in PU's
31.	31st Report	1973	Action taken by the Govt. on the recommendations contained in the 62nd Report of the CPU, 4th LS (CRTC Ltd.)
32.	32nd Report	1973	Action taken by the Govt. on the recommendations contained in the 19th Report of the CPU, 4th LS (HEL)
33.	33rd Report	1973	Action taken by the Govt. on the recommendations contained in the

(Contd...)

			66th Report of the CPU, 4th LS (IOC)
34.	34th Report	1973	Indian Telephone Industries
35.	35th Report	1973	Action taken by the Govt. on the recommendations contained in the 26th Report of the CPU, 4th LS, Trombay unit
36.	36th Report	1973	Action taken by the Govt. on the recommendations contained in the 16th Report of the CPU, 5th LS (ONGC)
37.	37th Report	1973	NMDC
38.	38th Report	1973	HMT Ltd.
39.	39th Report	1973	Pyrites Phosphate & Chemicals Ltd.
40.	40th Report	1973	Role and Achievements of PU's
41.	41st Report	1973	Action taken by the Govt. on the recommendations contained in the 1st Report of the CPU, 5th LS (HSL)
42.	42nd Report	1973	Action taken by the Govt. on the recommendations contained in the 12th Report of the CPU, 5th LS (FCI)
43.	43rd Report	1973	Action taken by the Govt. on the recommendations contained in the 21st Report of the CPU, 5th LS (BHEL)
44.	44th Report	1973	Action taken by the Govt. on the recommendations contained in the 18th Report of the CPU, 5th LS (HEC)
45.	45th Report	1973	Action taken by the Govt. on the recommendations contained in the 27th Report of the CPU, 5th LS (National Newsprint & Paper Mills Ltd.)
46.	46th Report	1973	Action taken by the Govt. on the recommendations contained in the 40th Report of the CPU, 5th LS (BPE)
47.	47th Report	1973	Modern Bakeries (I) Ltd.
48.	48th Report	1973	Action taken by the Govt. on the recommendations contained in the 39th Report of the CPU, 5th LS Pyrites, Phosphates & Chemicals Ltd.

(Contd...)

49.	49th Report	1973	Indian Oil Corporation Ltd.
50.	50th Report	1973	Fertilizer Corporation of India Ltd.
51.	51st Report	1974	India Tourism Development Corporation Ltd.
52.	52nd Report	1974	Indian Oil Corporation Ltd.
53.	53rd Report	1974	Action taken by the Govt. on the recommendations contained in the 28th Report of the CPU, 5th LS (IA)
54.	54th Report	1974	State Farms Corporation of India Ltd.
55.	55th Report	1974	Hindustan Photo Films Manufacturing Co. Ltd.
56.	56th Report	1974	Indian Drugs & Pharmaceuticals Limited
57.	57th Report	1975	Action taken by the Govt. on the recommendations contained in the 34th Report of the CPU, 5th LS ITI Ltd.
58.	58th Report	1975	Action taken by the Govt. on the recommendations contained in the 38th Report of the CPU, 5th LS HMT Ltd.
59.	59th Report	1975	Action taken by the Govt. on the recommendations contained in the 47th Report of the CPU, 5th LS Modern Bakeries (I) Ltd.
60.	60th Report	1975	Action taken by the Govt. on the recommendations contained in the 37th Report of the CPU, 5th LS NMDC
61.	61st Report	1975	Action taken by the Govt. on the recommendations contained in the 51st Report of the CPU, 5th LS ITDC
62.	62nd Report	1975	Rural Electrification Corporation Ltd.
63.	63rd Report	1975	National Textiles Corporation
64.	64th Report	1975	Indian Petrochemicals Corporation Ltd.
65.	65th Report	1975	Action taken by the Govt. on the recommendations contained in the

(Contd...)

			52nd Report of the CPU, 5th LS, State Farms Corporation
66.	66th Report	1975	National Seeds Corporation Ltd.
67.	67th Report	1975	Fertilizers & Chemicals Travancore Ltd.
68.	68th Report	1975	Cotton Corporation of India Ltd.
69.	69th Report	1975	Cement Corporation of India Ltd.
70.	70th Report	1975	Action taken by the Govt. on the recommendations contained in the 55th Report of the CPU, 5th LS, HPFM Co. Ltd.
71.	71st Report	1975	Action taken by the Govt. on the recommendations contained in the 50th Report of the CPU, 5th LS, FCI Ltd.
72.	72nd Report	1975	Action taken by the Govt. on the recommendations contained in the 40th Report of the CPU, 5th LS, Role & Achievements
73.	73rd Report	1975	Action taken by the Govt. on the recommendations contained in the 49th Report of the CPU, 5th LS, IOC
74.	74th Report	1975	Action taken by the Govt. on the recommendations contained in the 54th Report of the CPU, 5th LS, State Farms Corporation of India (SFCI)
75.	75th Report	1975	National Coal Development Corporation Ltd.
76.	76th Report	1975	Action taken by the Govt. on the recommendations contained in the 56th Report of the CPU, 5th LS, IDPL
77.	77th Report	1975	Steel Authority of India Limited
78.	78th Report	1976	Action taken by the Govt. on the recommendations contained in the 62nd Report of the CPU, 5th LS, REC Ltd.
79.	79th Report	1976	Film Finance Corporation Ltd.
80.	80th Report	1976	Hindustan Antibiotic Ltd.
81.	81st Report	1976	Action taken by the Govt. on the recommendations contained in the 67th Report of the CPU, 5th LS,

(Contd...)

			Fertilisers & Chemicals, Travancore.
82.	82nd Report	1976	Action taken by the Govt. on the recommendations contained in the 68th Report of the CPU, 5th LS, Cotton Corporation of India Ltd.
83.	83rd Report	1976	Indian Dairy Corporation
84.	84th Report	1976	Action taken by the Govt. on the recommendations contained in the 64th Report of the CPU, 5th LS, IPC Ltd.
85.	85th Report	1976	Hindustan Paper Corporation Ltd.
86.	86th Report	1976	Action taken by the Govt. on the recommendations contained in the 66th Report of the CPU, 5th LS, NSC Ltd. (Seeds)
87.	87th Report	1976	Action taken by the Govt. on the recommendations contained in the 63rd Report of the CPU, 5th LS, NTC Ltd.
88.	88th Report	1976	Hindustan Zinc Ltd.
89.	89th Report	1976	Foreign Collaboration in Public Undertakings
90.	90th Report	1976	Action taken by the Govt. on the recommendations contained in the 69th Report of the CPU, 5th LS, Cement Corporation of India Ltd.

Sixth Lok Sabha

Sl. No.	*Report*	*Year*	*Particulars*
1.	1st Report	1978	Extravagant and Infrastructure Expenditure on Entertainment by PUs'.
2.	2nd Report	1978	Central Inland Water Transport Corporation
3.	3rd Report	1978	Jute Corporation of India Ltd.
4.	4th Report	1978	Extraordinary High Expenditure on Publicity by PU's
5.	5th Report	1978	Procurement of vacuators under mysterious circumstances.

(Contd...)

6.	6th Report	1978	Galloping rise in foreign tours and costs thereof undertaken by the officials of the PU's
7.	7th Report	1978	CIWTC, Inland Water Transport Objectives and River Services
8.	8th Report	1978	Jute Corporation of India Ltd.
9.	9th Report	1978	CIWTC, Mismanagement in Organisation Administration and Financial Matters
10.	10th Report	1978	Unusually high expenditure by PSU's for their head officers
11.	11th Report	1978	Extravagant expenditure on guest houses incurred by PU's
12.	12th Report	1978	Jute Corporation of India
13.	13th Report	1978	- do -
14.	14th Report	1978	- do -
15.	15th Report	1978	Central Inland Water Transport Corp.
16.	16th Report	1978	Jute Corporation of India
17.	17th Report	1978	Action taken by the Govt. on the recommendations contained in the 4th Report of the CPU, 6th LS, extraordinary high expenditure of PU's
18.	18th Report	1978	Action taken by the Govt. on the recommendations contained in the 7th Report of the CPU, 6th LS, CIWTD Corp.
19.	19th Report	1978	- do-
20.	20th Report	1978	Structure of Boards of Management of Public Undertakings & Others
21.	21st Report	1979	Action taken by the Govt. on the recommendations contained in the 1st Report of the CPU, 6th LS, Extravagant Infrastructure Expenditure
22.	22nd Report	1979	Action taken by the Govt. on the recommendations contained in the 10th Report of the CPU, 6th LS, Unusually high expenditure by PU's

(Contd...)

23.	23rd Report	1979	Action taken by the Govt. on the recommendations contained in the 6th Report of the CPU, 6th LS, Galloping rise in foreign tours
24.	24th Report	1979	Expenditure on hiring and storage space by Public Undertakings
25.	25th Report	1979	Jute Corporation of India
26.	26th Report	1979	Action taken by the Govt. on the recommendations contained in the 2nd Report of the CPU, 6th LS, CIWT Corp.
27.	27th Report	1979	Action taken by the Govt. on the recommendations contained in the 88th Report of the CPU, 5th LS, Hindustan Zinc Ltd.
28.	28th Report	1979	PU's-delays in commencement of production, business, under utilisation of capacity & related matters
29.	29th Report	1979	Action taken by the Govt. on the recommendations contained in the 85th Report of the CPU, 5th LS, Hindustan Paper Corp Ltd.
30.	30th Report	1979	Action taken by the Govt. on the recommendations contained in the 79th Report of the CPU, 5th LS, Film Finance Corporation Ltd.
31.	31st Report	1979	Action taken by the Govt. on the recommendations contained in the 89th Report of the CPU, 5th LS, foreign collaboration in PUs
32.	32nd Report	1979	Action taken by the Govt. on the recommendations contained in the 8th Report of the CPU, 6th LS, JCI
33.	33rd Report	1979	- do -
34.	34th Report	1979	Purchase of Tobacco by the STC of India
35.	35th Report	1979	Export of leather and leather goods by STC Ltd. of India
36.	36th Report	1979	Action taken by the Govt. on the recommendations contained in the

(Contd...)

			5th Report of the CPU, 6th LS, Procurement of Vacuators under mysterious circumstances.
37.	37th Report	1979	Action taken by the Govt. on the recommendations contained in the 18th Report of the CPU, 5th LS, Hindustan Antibiotics Ltd.
38.	38th Report	1979	Action taken by the Govt. on the recommendations contained in the 77th Report of the CPU, 5th LS, SAIL
39.	39th Report	1979	Action taken by the Govt. on the recommendations contained in the 15th Report of the CPU, 6th LS, CIWT Corp.
40.	40th Report	1979	Action taken by the Govt. on the recommendations contained in the 75th Report of the CPU, 5th LS, NCDC
41.	41st Report	1979	Action taken by the Govt. on the recommendations contained in the 12th Report of the CPU, 6th LS, JCI
42.	42nd Report	1979	Perquisites enjoyed by public sector executives & AI executives
43.	43rd Report	1979	Action taken by the Govt. on the recommendations contained in the 11th Report of the CPU, 6th LS, extravagant expenditure on guesthouse incurred by PU's.
44.	44th Report	1979	Tea Trading Corp. of India
45.	45th Report	1979	- do -
46.	46th Report	1979	Action taken by the Govt. on the recommendations contained in the 13th Report of the CPU, 6th LS, JCI
47.	47th Report	1979	Action taken by the Govt. on the recommendations contained in the 14th Report of the CPU, 5th LS, SAIL
48.	48th Report	1979	International Airports Authority of India
49.	49th Report	1979	Central Fisheries Corp. Ltd.
50.	50th Report	1979	Bharat Heavy Electricals Limited
51.	51st Report	1979	Action taken by the Govt. on the

(Contd...)

			recommendations contained in the 16th Report of the CPU, 6th LS, JCI
52.	52nd Report	1979	Air India- working results
53.	53rd Report	1979	Air India- Commercial & Staff Matters
54.	54th Report	1979	Andaman and Nicobar Islands Forest
55.	55th Report	1979	Appointment of Auditors in Govt. Co.

Seventh Lok Sabha

Sl. No.	*Report*	*Year*	*Particulars*
1.	1st Report	1980	Action taken by the Govt. on the recommendations contained in the 25th Report of the CPU, 6th LS, JCI
2.	2nd Report	1980	Action taken by the Govt. on the recommendations contained in the 55th Report of the CPU, 6th LS, Appointment of Auditors in Govt. Co.
3.	3rd Report	1980	Action taken by the Govt. on the recommendations contained in the 24th Report of the CPU, 6th LS, Expenditure on Hiring of storage space by PUs
4.	4th Report	1980	Action taken by the Govt. on the recommendations contained in the 54th Report of the CPU, 6th LS, Andaman & Nicobar Islands
5.	5th Report	1980	Action taken by the Govt. on the recommendations contained in the 45th Report of the CPU, 6th LS, TTCI
6.	6th Report	1980	Action taken by the Govt. on the recommendations contained in the 34th Report of the CPU, 6th LS, STC (Tobacco)
7.	7th Report	1980	Action taken by the Govt. on the recommendations contained in the 44th Report of the CPU, 6th LS, TTCI
8.	8th Report	1981	Action taken by the Govt. on the

(Contd...)

			recommendations contained in the 20th Report of the CPU, 6th LS, Structure of Boards of Management
9.	9th Report	1981	Action taken by the Govt. on the recommendations contained in the 42nd Report of the CPU, 6th LS, Perquisites enjoyed by public sector expenditure & AI executives
10.	10th Report	1981	Action taken by the Govt. on the recommendations contained in the 28th Report of the CPU, 6th LS, PUs delays in commencement
11.	11th Report	1981	Action taken by the Govt. on the recommendations contained in the 52nd Report of the CPU, 6th LS, Air India
12.	12th Report	1981	Action taken by the Govt. on the recommendations contained in the 48th Report of the CPU, 6th LS, IAAI
13.	13th Report	1981	Action taken by the Govt. on the recommendations contained in the 35th Report of the CPU, 6th LS, STC Exports of Leather
14.	14th Report	1981	Action taken by the Govt. on the recommendations contained in the 83rd Report of the CPU, 5th LS, IDC
15.	15th Report	1981	Action taken by the Govt. on the recommendations contained in the 53rd Report of the CPU, 6th LS, Air India
16.	16th Report	1981	Damodar Valley Corporation
17.	17th Report	1981	Coal India Ltd.
18.	18th Report	1981	Hindustan Copper Ltd. – Khetri Copper Complex
19.	19th Report	1981	Electronic Corporation of India Ltd.
20.	20th Report	1981	Tannery & Footwear Corporation of India Ltd.
21.	21st Report	1981	Rashtriya Chemicals & Fertilizers Ltd.
22.	22nd Report	1981	Food Corporation of India
23.	23rd Report	1981	Steel Authority of India Limited, Import of Steel

(Contd...)

24.	24th Report	1981	Industrial Development Bank of India
25.	25th Report	1981	Delhi Transport Corp- Accidents & Operation of Pvt. Buses
26.	26th Report	1981	Housing & Urban Development Corp.
27.	27th Report	1981	Hindustan Teleprinters Ltd.- New Projects
28.	28th Report	1981	HMT Ltd.- Tractors Division
29.	29th Report	1981	Jessop & Company Ltd. – employment and overheads
30.	30th Report	1981	Action taken by the Govt. on the recommendations contained in the 17th Report of the CPU, 7th LS, Coal India Ltd.
31.	31st Report	1981	Action taken by the Govt. on the recommendations contained in the 21st Report of the CPU, 7th LS, RCF Ltd.
32.	32nd Report	1981	Action taken by the Govt. on the recommendations contained in the 19th Report of the CPU, 7th LS, ECIL
33.	33rd Report	1981	Action taken by the Govt. on the recommendations contained in the 20th Report of the CPU, 7th LS, IFCI Ltd.
34.	34th Report	1981	Action taken by the Govt. on the recommendations contained in the 49th Report of the CPU, 6th LS, CFC Ltd.
35.	35th Report	1981	Action taken by the Govt. on the recommendations contained in the 23rd Report of the CPU, 7th LS, SAIL (import of steel)
36.	36th Report	1981	Action taken by the Govt. on the recommendations contained in the 22nd Report of the CPU, 7th LS, FCI
37.	37th Report	1981	Action taken by the Govt. on the recommendations contained in the 6th Report of the CPU, 7th LS, DVC

(Contd...)

38.	38th Report	1981	Indian Telephone Industries Ltd.- R&D New Projects
39.	39th Report	1981	Action taken by the Govt. on the recommendations contained in the 50th Report of the CPU, 6th LS, BHEL
40.	40th Report	1981	National Textile Corporation Ltd.
41.	41st Report	1981	Hindustan Photo Films Manufacturing Corp.
42.	42nd Report	1981	Indian Airlines
43.	43rd Report	1981	Shipping Corporation of India Ltd.
44.	44th Report	1981	Bharat Heavy Electricals Limited
45.	46th Report	1981	Electronics Trade & Technology Development Corp. Ltd.
46.	47th Report	1981	Oil Companies- Imports
47.	48th Report	1981	India Tourism Development Corp.
48.	49th Report	1981	Public Undertakings- Management & Controls
49.	50th Report	1981	Engineering Project India Limited
50.	51st Report	1981	Action taken by the Govt. on the recommendations contained in the 25th Report of the CPU, 7th LS, DTC
51.	52nd Report	1981	Action taken by the Govt. on the recommendations contained in the 26th Report of the CPU, 7th LS, HUDCO
52.	53rd Report	1981	Action taken by the Govt. on the recommendations contained in the 29th Report of the CPU, 7th LS, Jessop & Company
53.	54th Report	1981	Action taken by the Govt. on the recommendations contained in the 28th Report of the CPU, 7th LS, DTC
54.	56th Report	1981	Action taken by the Govt. on the recommendations contained in the 38th Report of the CPU, 7th LS, ITI
55.	57th Report	1981	Action taken by the Govt. on the recommendations contained in the 42nd Report of the CPU, 7th LS, IA
56.	58th Report	1981	Action taken by the Govt. on the recommendations contained in the 40th Report of the CPU, 7th LS, NTC

(Contd...)

57.	59th Report	1981	Action taken by the Govt. on the recommendations contained in the 48th Report of the CPU, 7th LS, ITDC
58.	60th Report	1981	Action taken by the Govt. on the recommendations contained in the 60th Report of the CPU, 7th LS, Hindustan Copper Limited
59.	61st Report	1981	Central Cottage Industries Corp. Limited
60.	62nd Report	1981	Cotton Corporation of India Ltd.
61.	63rd Report	1981	Action taken by the Govt. on the recommendations contained in the 41st Report of the CPU, 7th LS, HPF
62.	64th Report	1981	Action taken by the Govt. on the recommendations contained in the 43rd Report of the CPU, 7th LS, SCI
63.	65th Report	1981	National Fertilizers Limited
64.	66th Report	1981	Action taken by the Govt. on the recommendations contained in the 50th Report of the CPU, 7th LS, Engineering Project India Limited
65.	67th Report	1981	Hindustan Antibiotics Ltd.
66.	68th Report	1981	Scooters India Limited
67.	69th Report	1981	Action taken by the Govt. on the recommendations contained in the 44th Report of the CPU, 7th LS, BHEL
68.	70th Report	1981	Action taken by the Govt. on the recommendations contained in the 49th Report of the CPU, 7th LS, Public Undertakings- Mgt. & Controls
69.	71st Report	1981	Bharat Aluminum Co. Ltd.
70.	72nd Report	1981	Hindustan Petroleum Corp.
71.	73rd Report	1981	Action taken by the Govt. on the recommendations contained in the 47th Report of the CPU, 7th LS, Oil companies
72.	74th Report	1981	Mazagon Dock Ltd.
73.	75th Report	1981	National Film Development Corp.
74.	76th Report	1981	Minerals and Metals Trading Corp.
75.	77th Report	1981	Action taken by the Govt. on the recommendations contained in the

(Contd...)

			46th Report of the CPU, 7th LS, Electronics Trade & Technology
76.	78th Report	1981	Forms of consolidated statements to be annexed to civil appropriation accounts.
77.	79th Report	1981	Action taken by the Govt. on the recommendations contained in the 71st Report of the CPU, 7th LS, Bharat Aluminum Co.
78.	80th Report	1981	Action taken by the Govt. on the recommendations contained in the 72nd Report of the CPU, 7th LS, HPCL
79.	81st Report	1981	Action taken by the Govt. on the recommendations contained in the 75th Report of the CPU, 7th LS, NFDC
80.	82nd Report	1981	Action taken by the Govt. on the recommendations contained in the 76th Report of the CPU, 7th LS, MMTC
81.	83rd Report	1981	Action taken by the Govt. on the recommendations contained in the 65th Report of the CPU, 7th LS, NFL
82.	84th Report	1981	Action taken by the Govt. on the recommendations contained in the 61st Report of the CPU, 7th LS, CCI
83.	85th Report	1981	Action taken by the Govt. on the recommendations contained in the 67th Report of the CPU, 7th LS, Hindustan Antibiotics Limited
84.	86th Report	1981	Action taken by the Govt. on the recommendations contained in the 74th Report of the CPU, 7th LS, Mazagon Dock Ltd.
85.	87th Report	1981	Central Coal Washeries Organisation
86.	88th Report	1981	National Small Industries Corp.
87.	89th Report	1981	Durgapur Steel Plant
88.	90th Report	1981	Action taken by the Govt. on the recommendations contained in the

(Contd...)

			68th Report of the CPU, 7th LS, Scooters India
89.	91st Report	1981	Bharat Petroleum Corporation Ltd.
90.	92nd Report	1981	National Thermal Power Corporation
91.	93rd Report	1981	Action taken by the Govt. on the recommendations contained in the 62nd Report of the CPU, 7th LS, CCI
92.	94th Report	1981	HMT Ltd.
93.	95th Report	1981	Central Warehousing Corp.
94.	96th Report	1981	Rehabilitation Industries Corp. Ltd.
95.	97th Report	1981	Productivity in Public Enterprises
96.	99th Report	1981	Action taken by the Govt. on the recommendations contained in the 88th Report of the CPU, 7th LS, NSIC
97.	100th Report	1981	Action taken by the Govt. on the recommendations contained in the 94th Report of the CPU, 7th LS, HMT Ltd.
98.	101st Report	1981	Action taken by the Govt. on the recommendations contained in the 95th Report of the CPU, 7th LS, CWC

Eighth Lok Sabha

Sl. No.	*Report*	*Year*	*Particulars*
1.	1st Report		Action taken by the Govt. on the recommendations contained in the 92nd Report of the CPU, 7th LS, NTPC
2.	2nd Report		Action taken by the Govt. on the recommendations contained in the 91st Report of the CPU, 7th LS, BPCL
3.	4th Report	1987	Mineral Exploration Corporation Ltd.
4.	5th Report	1987	Action taken by the Govt. on the recommendations contained in the 44th Report of the CPU, 8th LS, Shipping Corp.
5.	6th Report	1987	General Insurance Corporation
6.	7th Report	1987	Action taken by the Govt. on the recommendations contained in the

(Contd...)

			89th Report of the CPU, 7th LS, Durgapur Steel Plant
7.	8th Report	1987	Oil & Natural Gas
8.	9th Report	1987	Bharat Electronics Limited
9.	10th Report	1987	Hotel Corporation of India
10.	11th Report	1987	Indian Dairy Corporation
11.	12th Report	1987	Oil & Natural Gas Corporation
12.	13th Report	1987	Bharat Electronics Limited
13.	14th Report	1987	Air India- working results and traffic growth
14.	15th Report	1987	Indian Petrochemicals Corp.
15.	16th Report	1987	Action taken by the Govt. on the recommendations contained in the 11th Report of the CPU, 8th LS, IDC
16.	18th Report	1987	Mineral exploration corporation Ltd. (Action taken on 4th Report, 8th Lok Sabha)
17.	19th Report	1987	Hotel Corporation of India Ltd. (Action taken on the 10th report of 8th Lok Sabha)
18.	20th Report	1987	Trade Fair Authority
19.	21st Report	1987	Indian Petrochemicals Corporation Limited working results
20.	22nd Report	1987	Bharat Heavy Plate and Vessels Ltd.
21.	23rd Report	1987	General Insurance Corporation of India, Action taken by '
22.	24th Report	1987	Air India, Agency System and Passenger Service
23.	25th Report	1987	Eastern Coal-fields Ltd.
24.	26th Report	1987	Cochin Shipyard Ltd.
25.	27th Report	1987	Nomination of Directors by financial institutions
26.	28th Report	1987	ONGC head office survey and exploration, action taken on 12th COPU Report of 8th LS
27.	29th Report	1987	Indian Drugs & Pharmaceuticals Ltd.
28.	30th Report	1987	Steel Authority of India Ltd., Salem Steel Plant
29.	31st Report	1988	Bharat Electronics Ltd., objectives and implementation of projects, action taken on 9th report of COPU, 8th LS

(Contd...)

30.	32nd Report	1988	Accountability and autonomy of public undertakings
31.	33rd Report	1988	BEL capacity utilisation, production and pricing, research and development, action taken on 13th report, 8th LS
32.	34th Report	1988	Indian Airlines - Passenger Service
33.	35th Report	1988	Air India – working results and traffic growth, action taken on 28th report, 8th LS
34.	36th Report	1988	Nomination of Director by financial institutions , action taken on 27th report of COPU, 8th LS
35.	37th Report	1988	Trade Fair Authority of India, action taken on 20th report, 8th LS
36.	38th Report	1988	Indian Drugs and Pharmaceuticals Limited. Action taken on 29th report, LS
37.	39th Report	1988	SAIL, Salem Steel Plant, action taken on 30th report, LS
38.	40th Report	1988	Air India – Agency system and passenger services, action taken on 24th report, 8th LS
39.	41st Report	1988	Cochin Shipyard Ltd., action taken on 26th report, 8th LS
40.	42nd Report	1988	Bicco Lawrie Ltd.
41.	43rd Report	1988	Eastern Coalfields Ltd., action taken on 25th report , COPU, 8th LS
42.	44th Report	1988	Shipping Corp. of India Ltd.
43.	45th Report	1988	Bharat Earth Movers Ltd.
44.	46th Report	1988	Bharat Gold Mines Ltd.
45.	47th Report	1988	Indian Airlines – Fair and Cost aspects, Ministry of Civil Aviation
46.	48th Report	1988	Indian Petrochemicals Corp. Ltd., action taken on the 15th report, 8th LS
47.	49th Report	1989	Bharat Heavy Plates Vessels Ltd. Action taken on 22nd report, 8th LS
48.	50th Report	1989	Accountability and autonomy of public undertakings, action taken on 32nd report, 8th LS

(Contd...)

49.	51st Report	1989	Air India- fare aspect
50.	52nd Report	1989	Indian Petrochemicals Corp. Ltd. Action taken on 21st report CPU, 8th LS
51.	53rd Report	1989	Action taken by the Govt. on the recommendations contained in the 47th Report of the CPU, 8th LS, IA
52.	54th Report	1989	Indian Airlines- passenger services, action taken on 34th report, 8th LS
53.	55th Report	1989	Indian Oil Corp., installation of two LPG bottling plants at Bangalore
54.	56th Report	1989	Oil & Natural Gas Commission, undue benefit of Rs. 5.10 crores to a contractor
55.	57th Report	1990	Food Corporation of India, dispatch of sub standard wheat
56.	58th Report	1990	Air India undue benefit to private operators
57.	59th Report	1990	ONGC- extra expenditure of Rs. 70 .31 lakhs on purchase of depressant
58.	60th Report	1990	State Trading Corp. India Ltd.
59.	61st Report	1990	Indian Tourism Development Corp.
60.	62nd Report	1990	Biecco Lawrie Ltd.
61.	63rd Report	1990	Cochin Refineries Ltd. , Ministry of Petrochemicals and Natural Gas
62.	64th Report	1990	Bharat Gold Refineries Ltd. , Ministry of Steel and Mines, AT on 40th Report, 8th LS

Ninth Lok Sabha

Sl. No.	*Report*	*Year*	*Particulars*
1.	1st Report	1990	Bharat Earth Movers Ltd.
2.	2nd Report	1990	Action taken by the Govt. on the recommendations contained in the 51st Report of the CPU, 8th LS, AI
3.	3rd Report	1990	Action taken by the Govt. on the recommendations contained in the 61st Report of the CPU, 8th LS,ITDC
4.	4th Report	1990	Action taken by the Govt. on the

(Contd...)

			recommendations contained in the 60th Report of the CPU, 8th LS, STC
5.	5th Report	1990	Shipping Corp. of India Ltd.
6.	6th Report	1987	Oil & Natural Gas Commission
7.	7th Report	1990	Indian Oil Corp., installation of 2 LPG bottling plants at Bangalore
8.	8th Report	1990	Food Corp. of India, dispatch of sub standard wheat
9.	9th Report	1990	ONGC- avoidable payment of Rs. 89.06 lakhs made to a foreign contractor beyond the terms of the contract.
10.	10th Report	1990	Air India undue benefits to private operators
11.	11th Report	1990	Cochin Refineries Ltd., AT on 63rd report, 8th LS

Tenth Lok Sabha

Sl. No.	*Report*	*Year*	*Particulars*
1.	1st Report	1993	Steel Authority of India Ltd., import of defective bullets, Ministry of Steel and Mines, Dept. of Steel
2.	2nd Report	1993	
3.	3rd Report	1993	Tea Trading Corp. of India, setting up of joint venture co., export contracts and regular payment of advance
4.	4th Report	1993	NTC Ltd. Avoidable payment of commission of Rs. 148.80 lakhs due to appointment of agents for supplies to defence and other government departments
5.	5th Report	1993	Hindustan Fertilizer Corp. Ltd., Ministry of Chemicals & Fertilizers, Dept. of Fertilizers
6.	6th Report	1993	National Mineral Development Corporation, Ministry of Steel.
7.	7th Report	1993	Coal India Ltd.

(Contd...)

8.	10th Report	1993	ONGC construction of NR- 1 and NH well platforms
9.	11th Report	1993	ONGC avoidable payment of Rs. 89.06 lakhs made to a foreign contractor beyond the terms of the contract.
10.	8th Report	1993	Bringing RBI, Nationalized Banks including SBI & its subsidiaries and other financial institutions within the purview of CPU
11.	9th Report	1993	Litigations pending for settlement in public undertakings, Ministry of Industry, Dept. of Public Enterprises
12.	7th Report	1991-1992	Coal India Ltd.
13.	10th Report	1991-1992	ONGC Construction of Platforms
14.	11th Report	1991-1992	ONGC- avoidable payment of Rs. 89.06 lakhs made to a foreign contract beyond terms of contract
15.	28th Report	1993-1994	Tea Trading Corporation of India Ltd.- Setting up of a Joint Venture Co. Export Contracts
16.	29th Report	1993-1994	Litigation's pending for settlement in PUs
17.	30th Report	1993-1994	STC of India Ltd.- Import of Newsprint
18.	31st Report	1993-1994	Industrial Development Bank of India
19.	32nd Report	1993-1994	Delhi Transport Corp.- Including comparative analysis of transport in metro's
20.	33rd Report	1993-1994	Indian Airlines
21.	34th Report	1993-1994	Cement Corporation of India Ltd.
22.	35th Report	1993-1994	Educational Consultants India Ltd.
23.	36th Report	1993-1994	Gas Authority of India Ltd.
24.	37th Report	1993-1994	SAIL, Bokaro Steel Plant
25.	38th Report	1994-1995	Social Responsibility & Public Accountability of Public Undertakings, Ministry of Industry, DPE
26.	39th Report	1994-1995	Bharat Cooking Coal Ltd. Ministry of Coal

(Contd...)

27.	40th Report	1994-1995	Educational Consultants India Ltd., Ministry of HRD (Dept. of Education)
28.	41st Report	1994-1995	Cement Corporation of (I) Ltd., Ministry of Heavy Industry
29.	42nd Report	1994-1995	Indian Oil Corporation Ltd., Ministry of Petroleum & Natural Gas
30.	44th Report	1995-1996	Indian Airlines, Ministry of Civil Aviation & Tourism (Dept. of Civil Aviation)
31.	45th Report	1995-1996	Gas Authority of India Ltd., Ministry of Petroleum & Natural Gas
32.	46th Report	1995-1996	Hindustan Organic Chemicals Ltd. Ministry of Chemicals & Fertilizers & Dept. of Chemicals & Petrochemicals
33.	47th Report	1995-1996	Burn Standard Co. Ltd. , Ministry of Industry, Dept. of Heavy Industry
34.	48th Report	1995-1996	Indian Oil Corp. Ltd. (Ministry of Petroleum & Natural Gas)
35.	49th Report	1995-1996	-
36.	50th Report	1995-1996	-
37.	51st Report	1995-1996	-
38.	52nd Report	1995-1996	-
39.	53rd Report	1995-1996	Steel Authority of India Ltd., Bhilai Steel Plant(Ministry of Steel)
40.	54th Report	1995-1996	Rural Electrification Corp. Ltd. (Ministry of Power)

Eleventh Lok Sabha

Sl. No.	*Report*	*Year*	*Particulars*
1.	1st Report	1996-1997	Mazagon Dock Ltd. (Ministry of Defence Production & Supplies)
2.	2nd Report	1996-1997	Rural Electrification Corp. Ltd. (Ministry of Power)
3.	3rd Report	1996-1997	Power Finance Corp. Ltd. (Ministry of Power)
4.	4th Report	1996-1997	Hindustan Organic Chemicals Ltd.

(Contd...)

			(Ministry of Chemicals & Fertilizers, Dept. of Chemicals & Petrochemicals
5.	5th Report	1996-1997	Steel Authority of India Ltd.- Bhilai Steel Plant (Ministry of Steel)
6.	6th Report	1996-1997	National Hydroelectric Power Corporation Ltd. (Ministry of Power)
7.	7th Report	1996-1997	National Small Industries Corporation Ltd., Ministry of Industry, Dept. of Small Scale Industries and Agro and Rural Industries
8.	8th Report	1996-1997	Bharat Cooking Coal Ltd. Ministry of Coal
9.	9th Report	1996-1997	Buran Standard Company Ltd. (Ministry of Industry, Dept. of Heavy Industry)
10.	10th Report	1996-1997	ITI Ltd., Ministry of Communications, Dept. of Telecommunications
11.	11th Report	1997-1998	Sickness in Public Undertakings, Ministry of Industry, Dept. of Public Enterprises
12.	12th Report	1997-1998	Oil & Natural Gas Corp. Ltd., Setting up of Single Buoy Mooring Project

Twelfth Lok Sabha

Sl. No.	*Report*	*Year*	*Particulars*
1	1st Report	1998-1999	Sickness in Public Undertakings, Ministry of Industry, Dept. of Public Enterprises
2	2nd Report	1998-1999	Follow up action on the reports of CAG of India (Commercial) Ministry of Industry, Dept. of Public Enterprises
3	3rd Report	1998-1999	ONGC Ltd. – Setting up of single Buoy Mooring Project, Ministry of Petroleum & Natural Gas

(Contd...)

4	4th Report	1998-1999	Senior Level Posts in Public Undertakings- Appointment & Related Matters, Ministry of Industry, Department of Public Enterprises
5	5th Report	1998-1999	-
6	6th Report	1998-1999	ITI Ltd., Ministry of Communications, Dept. of Telecommunications

Thirteenth Lok Sabha

Sl. No.	*Report*	*Year*	*Particulars*
1.	1st Report	1999-2000	Follow up action on the report of AG India(Commercial), Ministry of Heavy Industries & PEs (DPEs)
2.	2nd Report	1999-2000	Senior Level Posts in PUs- Appointment & related matters, Ministry of Heavy Industries & Public Enterprises & PEs, Department of Public Enterprises
3.	3rd Report	1999-2000	-
4.	4th Report	2000-2001	Air India Ltd., Ministry of Civil Aviation

Thirteenth Lok Sabha XIII LS

13th Lok Sabha	1st Report	1999-2000	Follow up action on the report of AG India (Commercial), Ministry of Heavy Industries & PEs (DPEs)
13th Lok Sabha	2nd Report	1999-2000	Senior Level Posts in PUs- Appointment & related matters, Ministry of Heavy Industries & Public Enterprises & PEs, Department of Public Enterprises
13th Lok Sabha	3rd Report	1999-2000	-
13th Lok Sabha	4th Report	2000-2001	Air India Ltd., Ministry of Civil Aviation

Appendix II

Report of the Committee to Review Policy for Public Enterprises [Arjun Sengupta Committee Report]: A Summary

In September 1984, the Government of India set up a Committee to analyse the performance of the public sector enterprises to identify the problems they face and suggest measures for their improved functioning. In over three months the Committee presided over by Dr. Arjun Sengupta, then Special Secretary to the Prime Minister, submitted its report in December 31, 1984. The report deals with the Organisational Structure of Public Enterprises, Autonomy and Accountability of Public Enterprises, Technology Upgradation, Financial Viability of Loss Making Units, Capital Restructuring and Closure, Pricing in Public Enterprises.

Summary of Recommendations

1. Careful dovetailing of all plans of public enterprises with the National Plan is required only in a few core sectors as below;

   Coal and Lignite

   Crude Oil, petroleum and natural gas

Power

Primary steel production

Primary productions of aluminum, copper, lead, zinc and nickel

Fertilizers

Primary production of petrochemical intermediates

- The plans of enterprises in the non-core sector are to be integrated with the National Plan to finance their investment requirements by raising funds from the public through deposits or debentures or by borrowing from the financial institutions, they need not be subjected to any process of governmental clearance and the public sector plan should include only the flows through the budget. (para 4.5 & 4.6)
- For the core sector, investment approvals by government should be built around two stage clearance. In the first stage, besides conveying approval in principle and sanctioning preliminary expenditure, a 'Task Force' should be set up by PIB to go into all aspects relating to indigenous availability of equipment, capability of manufacture by public enterprises, need for import and quantum of imports. In the second stage, detailed scrutiny regarding technology, costs, etc. should take place. Based on the report of the 'task force' on indigenous availability of equipment the need for import, foreign exchange requirements, price preference, etc. should be finalsied by PIB. (Paras 4.7 & 4.8)
- Single window clearance by PIB is recommended in the second stage, including approvals for financing packages, external credits, collaboration agreements, capital goods imports, location and environmental aspects etc. (Para 4.9)
- It is recommended that the present limits for investment approval by the EFC and PIB be enhanced as below,
  (i) **EFC**- Investment proposals costing over Rs. 5 crores but not above Rs. 25 crores.

(ii) **PIB**- Investment proposals costing over Rs. 25 crores.

Corresponding changes must be made in the delegated powers of the public enterprises. (Para 4.10)

- Project Appraisal Division of the Planning Commission should be nodal agency for submitting a comprehensive appraisal report for consideration of EFC and PIB. PAD should be suitably strengthened for effective discharge of this additional responsibility. Investment proposals may be sent to PAD and Administrative Ministry simultaneously, by public enterprises after approval by their Boards, (Paras 4.11 & 4.12)
- For financially viable enterprises in the non-core sector government would contribute only towards equity. Investment approvals for equity participation in such cases would be dependent on the enterprise meeting the performance criteria and payments of dividend at the prescribed rates. The remaining requirements for project investment should be raised outside the budget through borrowing or non-convertible debentures but without government guarantee. (Para 4.13 & 4.17)
- Where non-core enterprises are used as agencies for other than commercial objectives, either government should undertake additional equity contribution or the additional net cost of such activities should be reimbursed. (Para 4.14)
- Since selling of shares may create problems of ownership without giving the public sector enterprises any greater advantages the Committee does not recommend selling of shares to the public enterprises. (Para 4.16)

B. Wage Policy in Public Enterprises

- It is recommended that basic wage structure of employees of public enterprises should be determined on industry basis or industry-cum-region basis by a wage commission or through the mechanism of industry wise Wage Boards for a period of 5 years. (Para 4.26)

- In addition to the basic wage there should be a component of earning linked with productivity. The total amount involved may be determined by the enterprise in consultation with the government on the basis of profits earned or substantial reduction achieved in losses. Within the guidelines indicated by the government the Board of Directors of an enterprise would have full authority to devise a scheme in consultation with the workers. Thus, the main portion of increase in wage would be linked with productivity. Existing bonus scheme would continue and no change in procedure is recommended. (Paras 4.27 & 4.28)

C. Executive Appointments and Remuneration

- It is recommended that Chief Executives and Functional Directors of public enterprises should be given a tenure of 5 years subject to a probationary period of one year and removal at three months notice for unsatisfactory performance. (Para 4.31)
- It is recommended that proposal for removal of Chief Executive or Functional Director should be put up to the Appointments Committee of the Cabinet with the view of the Public Enterprise Selection Board. (Para 4.31)
- Part time Directors of public enterprises should be appointed after consulting the respective Chief Executives. Non- official Directors should have tenure of three years. Vacancies on the Board should not be left unfulfilled for a long time. (Para 4.32)
- It is recommended that filling up of all posts other than those of Chief Executives & Functional Directors should be left to the Boards of Directors. (Para 4.34)
- It is recommended that there should be flexibility for giving a higher scale of pay to the Chief Executive or the Functional Director of a sick unit on a personal basis. (Para 4.35)
- There is a strong case for narrowing the gap in the remuneration of Chief Executives and Functional Directors

as between the public and private sector enterprise. It is recommended that a Working Group be set up, at an appropriate time after the receipt of the Fourth Pay Commission's recommendations to specify scales and prerequisites of Chief Executives and Functional Directors. The present rental ceiling for Chief Executives, Functional Directors and Executive Directors also needs revision. The same Working Group may look into this also. (Para 4.36 & 4.37)

- Disciplinary proceedings against Board Level appointees would be the responsibility of the government. In respect of all others, the Board of Directors would have the final authority. (Para 4.38)
- It is recommended that performance of a Chief Executive of the enterprise, evaluated according to agreed parameters, should form his performance record for the year. In the case of Functional Directors, no review of the Confidential Report by the Ministry is necessary. (Para 4.39)
- Every enterprise must submit to its Board of Directors, each year, a manpower budget and training plan for the executives and others. (Para 4.40)
- It is recommended that mobility of management personnel between public enterprises should not be discouraged. (Para 4.41)

ACCOUNTABILITY OF PUBLIC ENTERPRISES

A. Performance Evaluation

- On the basis of agreed plans for investments, production, capacity utilisation, profits, dividends, etc., for a period of five years, the Government in the Administrative Machinery and the Holding Company or Apex Company, as the case may be, would also be cast on the Government in terms of provision of equity, price level, etc. This Memorandum would be reviewed each year and updated. The performance of the Holding Company or Apex

Company, as the case may be, would be reviewed each year and evaluated on this basis making due allowance for the failure, or otherwise, of the Ministry or Department to fulfill its part of the Understanding. (Paras 3.23 & 5.3)

FINANCIAL PERFORMANCE

- It is recommended that for evaluating financial performance of public enterprises, the following criteria should be used:

  (i) Gross Margin on assets(for all enterprises)

  (ii) Net Profit on net worth (for core sector and profit making enterprises)

  (iii) Gross Margin on Sales (Service enterprises)

  (Para 5.5)

- In respect of core sector enterprises, the rate of net profit should be atleast a stipulated percent and gross margin on capital should be improved over time. (Para 5.7)

- In the non-core sector, enterprises should be judged against the industry average for both gross margin on capital employed and the net profit. (Para 5.8)

- In evaluating the performance of Service Enterprises, attention should be focussed on direction of change in the gross margin on sales. (Para 5.9)

- In loss-making enterprises, gross margin should be positive. In addition, the following to be monitored:

  (a) Ratio of loan liabilities to assets

  (b) Ratio of wages to value added per worker

  (c) Cash loss per worker (Para 5.10)

Productivity and Cost Reduction

- In the core sector enterprises, monitoring unit cost and productivity should be undertaken by examining the direction of change in indicators like capacity utilisation and raw materials costs (at constant prices). Wherever possible, an overall index of cost of production should be evolved for monitoring changes in costs and productivity. In Service Enterprises, productivity can be monitored by the direction of change in the utilisation of fixed assets, number of days of inventory and manpower per unit of turnover. (Para 5.11)

Technical Change

- It is recommended that attempts should be made to evolve technology development indices even on a rough basis. (Para 5.12)

Project Implementation

- It is recommended that the following indices should be monitored for project implementation in the core sector:

  (a) Percentage utilisation of plan funds.

  (b) Average slippage in the ongoing projects, the weights for the averages being defined by the cost of each project.

  (c) Percentage cost revision for the approved investment programme relative to the previous year. (Para 5.1)

- A group constituted by Administrative Ministry with representatives from the Ministry, Bureau of Public Enterprises and the Planning Commission should prepare an annual Performance Evaluation Report based on these performance indicators for each enterprise and submit it to the Planning Commission for arriving at the investment decisions and PESB for appointment, promotion, confirmation and extension of top management. (Para 5.15)

- Detailed monitoring of subsidies and divisions should be carried out by the Holding or Apex Company. (Para 5.17)

- A Working Group may be set up to evolve appropriate information system based on the above performance evaluation criteria. (Para 5.17)

Audit: Role of the Comptroller and Auditor General

- It is recommended that accounting policies and accounting standards should be evolved for public enterprises with the help of C&AG, professionals in the filed and BPE. Thereafter supplementary audit of C&AG may not be considered necessary for profitable, non-core enterprises. Amendment to Companies Act would be necessary for this. However, the periodical performance audit of public enterprises conducted by C&AG would be continued. (Para 5.19 & 5.22)
- For large companies, especially in the core sector, supplementary audit of C&AG may continue, if necessary provision can be made only for audit by C&AG. (Para 5.23)

C. *Relations with the Parliament*

- It is submitted that
  - (i) parliament questions on day-to-day operation and management of public enterprise may be avoided
  - (ii) COPU can examine and probe the working of public enterprises in depth and in direct contact with the management of public enterprises
  - (iii) Debates on the Demands for Grants of the Administrative Ministries or Departments, tabling of Annual Reports, and Annual accounts of public enterprises and tabling of Public Enterprise Survey in both houses of Parliament for discussing the performance of individual public enterprises as well as the performance of public enterprises as a whole.

(Para 5.26)

TECHNOLOGY UPGRADATION

- The transfer of know how of imported processes and designs should take into account availability of product design, product engineering and production engineering groups of high caliber. This is essential for effective transfer of 'Know-How' from a collaborator. Where monopoly producers are catering to the needs of monopoly users, the selection of technology, product size and product design by import should be decided upon jointly by them. (Para 6.1)

- It is recommended that appropriate mechanism should be adopted to ensure prompt absorption and improvement of imported technology, through association of R&D personnel from the very beginning. Adequate investment in R&D should be made in the enterprise to facilitate technology absorption and upgradation. (Para 6.2)
- All major projects include technology adaptation programmes and for this purpose the government should consider providing part of this expenditure as grant. (Para 6.3)

FINANCIAL VIABILITY OF LOSS MAKING UNITS

A. Capital Restructuring

- It is recommended that where a company has suffered cash losses for a number of years, after excluding the interest burden, Bureau of Public Enterprises should examine such cases, suo moto, for capital restructuring. (Para 7.3)

B. Closure

- BPE should undertake special studies of the operations of public enterprises incurring cash losses which fulfill the following criteria;
  - (a) Units should have incurred cash losses over a continuous period of not less than 5 years.
  - (b) Value added per employee per month should be less than the average monthly emoluments per employee.
  - (c) Equity capital should have been wiped out by mounting deficits.

BPE would, thereafter, submit a comprehensive report to PIB

which would then make suitable recommendations to the Cabinet for reviving or closure of the unit. (Para 7.5 to 7.7)

- Proposals for investment by loss making units should not be considered without BPE having undertaken the exercise indicated in para 10.53
- Where healthy public enterprises are willing to voluntarily, take over sick enterprises, suitable package of measures in favour of volunteering public enterprises would be considered and government procedures for such takeovers or mergers should be simplified. (Para 7.8)
- Where closure is recommended, a liberal compensation scheme for the workers should be evolved. It is recommended that a suitable fund or an insurance scheme should be evolved for financing expenditure on compensation to retrenched workers. An Expert Group of representatives of the Labour Ministry, General Insurance Corporation, BPE etc. should be set up for this purpose. (Paras 7.9 & 7.12)
- Where taking over, a sick private sector unit is mooted, a study similar to the one in respect of closure of sick units should be undertaken by BPE and a comprehensive report brought before PIB which may make suitable recommendations to the government. (Para 7.11)

PRICING IN PUBLIC SECTOR

- Where public enterprises are functioning under price controls, it is recommended that the periodicity of revision should be reasonable. Government's decision on the recommendations of bodies like BICP on price fixation should be taken within a reasonable time or an additional element in price should be added to allow for the delays.
- It is recommended that:
  - (i) Price control must be retained only in areas where the nature of product justifies;
  - (ii) Where public enterprises operate in competition with

the private sector, the former should be left free to fix prices on commercial considerations; and

(iii) In areas, where prices are uncontrolled, government should not get involved, formally or informally, in approving or fixing prices (Para 8.3)

- It is recommended that BICP should be explicitly asked to take into account the need to provide incentives for improvement in efficiency and for replacement of equipment, while fixing prices. (Para 8.4)
- It is recommended that in fixing prices of products of public enterprises operating under monopoly conditions, particularly intermediates, attention should be paid to ensure international competitiveness and reducing costs. (Para 8.5)

PRICE PREFERENCE

It is recommended that price preference to public enterprises should be phased out over a period of 4-5 years. If necessary, government may give subsidies to such units. (Para 8.6)

OTHER ISSUES

Award of Contracts

It is recommended that Ministries or Departments of the government shall not interfere in areas of decision making which are well within the delegated powers of the public enterprises. It is recommended that public enterprises should process their cases directly through Capital Goods Committee, Foreign Investment Board, RBI, CCI & E etc, as done by private enterprises. (Para 9.2)

Expenditure on Township and Residential Quarters

- Within the framework of BPE's guidelines public sector enterprises should be free to invest on township and residential accommodation without prior approval of the government within the limits of delegated powers subject to the constraints of the approved capital budget. (Para 9.3)

BPE Guideline

- It is recommended that BPE guidelines on norms and standards in various areas of operations may be reviewed. BPEs instructions based on recommendations of COPU accepted by the government decisions of the Cabinet and its committees etc are mandatory for all public enterprises. It is also recommended that in the case of public enterprises generally, economy instructions for filling up of posts, stoppage of advertisements etc may not be applied ipso facto. (Para 9.4)
- It is recommended that a Group consisting of the representatives of C&AG, professionals in the filed including public enterprises and BPE should evolve accounting policies and standards for the public enterprises.

Appendix III

Report of the Committee on Disinvestment of Shares in Public Sector Enterprises

1. Introduction

1.1 It has been decided by the Government of India that the scheme of disinvestment of equity in Public Sector Enterprises which commenced in 1991 – 92 would continue through 1992-93. In view of the above, the Ministry of Finance, Department of Economic Affairs vide their Office Memorandum No. 14/1/SE//92 dated 26.2.92 had appointed a Committee with Shri V. Krishnamurthy, Member, Planning Commission as its Chairman, with Sarvashri K.P. Geetha Krishna, Montek Singh Ahluwalia, Suresh Kumar, Ashok Desai, S.S. Nadkarni as Members and Shri Kamal Pande of Department of Economic Affairs as its Member Secretary. The terms of reference of the Committee are as follows:

(i) To devise criteria for public sector Enterprises for disinvestment during 1992-93

(ii) To advise on limits on the percentage of equity to be disinvested in respect of such public Sector Enterprises;

(iii) To suggest the target clientele including Mutual Funds,

Financial Institutions. Banks, Employees, Resident Investors, Non-Resident Indians, Foreign Institutional investors etc.

(iv) To make suggestions on the modus operandi of disinvestments, whether through public offer or private placements.

(v) To lay down the criteria for valuation of equity shares of Public Sector Enterprises.

(vi) To make recommendations on any other subject matter germane to the disinvestment plan.

1.2. The committee held three meetings on March 31st 1992, April 24th 1992 and May 13th 1992. On the advice of the then governor of RBI, the committee temporarily co-opted Mr. D. Basu, Deputy Managing Director, State Bank of India as a member because of his expert knowledge on the subject. The committee also had the benefit of detailed analysis done by the officers of the Department of Economics Affairs and Department of Public Enterprises.

1.3. The Government reconstituted the committee in November 1992 with Dr. C. Rangarajan, Member, Planning Commission as Chairman and Dr. Y Venugopal Reddy as member secretary. The chairman and member secretary held informal meetings with some members of the committee discussed issues with selected managers of PSUs pursued recent publications, reports of seminars, letters/ suggestions received from individuals, institutions, trade union leaders at Ministry of Finance obtained the advice of chairman, SEBI in the light of subsequent development sought advice of Dr. L C Gupta of the secretary for the capital market research and development and drew upon the research work already conducted by the Institute of Public Enterprise, Hyderabad. The Committee then met on December 31st 1992 and January 1st 1993 for detailed discussions

1.4. In its general approach, the committee was guided by several important factors such as

(a) The contributions made by the public sector in general to economic development, and entrepreneurial skills.

(b) The institutional, technological and fiscal compulsions that have led to a review of Public sector investment.

(c) The exercise gained in disinvestment in the recent past, taking into account the unusual circumstances in capital markets.

(d) The need to enhance the competitive strength and ensure expansion of these enterprises while protecting the interest of workers and

(e) Above all, the requirement of constituency with the on going economic reforms in the areas of industrial licensing, foreign trade and investment and financial sector

Criteria for Selection of Public Sector Enterprises Disinvested during 1992-93.

2.1. The committee noted that the government disinvested its shareholding in 30 public sector enterprises during 1991-92. The extent of disinvestment worked out to 8 percent of the government shareholding in these enterprises and the total amount realised was Rs. 3038 crores.

2.2. The present status of disinvestment during 1992 –93 may be summarised as follows

(a) Advertisement was given inviting tender for purchase of shares of 8 central PSUs, namely, Steel Authority of India Ltd., Bharat Petroleum Corp. Ltd. Hindustan Petroleum Corp. of India Ltd., HMT Ltd, National Aluminum Company Ltd. and Neyvely Lignite Corp. of India Ltd. The last date for receipt of tenders was extended to 14.10.1992 to enable a wider response.

(b) A minimum reserve prices fixed on the basis of recommendations of three merchant bankers-Industrial Credit and Investment Corporation of India,

Industrial Development Bank of India and SBI Capital Market Ltd.

(c) Having this criterion, the bids eligible for acceptance amounted to a total share value of Rs. 681.95 crores for 12. 87 crore shares in eight companies.

(d) Advertisement was again issued on November 28, 1992 for disinvestment of shares of 14 PSEs. The extended terminal date for reviving the bids was December 22, 1992. The bids for 12 of this companies for a value of Rs. 1183.3 crores were accepted. The average price realisation per share disinvested in the second round was subsequently lower than the price realised in October 1992.

(e) The government invited a third round of bids for sale of equity in 15 PSEs for a total of 533 million shares in March 1993. While bids were received, it was decided to accept bids for a total of 10.1 million shares only aggregating to Rs. 46.73 crore. The referral price was fixed as earlier on the recommendations of the three agencies.

(f) The government has also decided in principle to disinvest shares in selected companies in favour of employees during 1992-93.

2.3. The committee further noted the following features relevant to the policy of disinvestment for the rest of the financial year.

(a) The financial year 1992-93 is about to end.

(b) The listing of shares of many PSEs has been completed, there is a little or no trading in most of them. In fact, many of the mutual funds and financial institutions, which have acquired PSEs shares, have not been able to sell them in the market. This could adversely affect forthcoming trances of disinvestment.

(c) The weaknesses in stock markets such as low trading volumes and non-transparent trading practices have come to the fore. The stock market themselves have shown unusual volatility.

(d) As of now, it has to be recognised that there is no trading history for most public enterprise shares.

(e) The restricted tendering and handling of shares had to be resorted to in the past due to unusual circumstances but more recently, enterprise – specific bids have been invited and financial limits for bidding have also been lowered.

(f) It is generally agreed that a public issue by way of an offer to the members of public would be the most desirable option. However, if time and market circumstances do not permit it, bid mechanisms close to a public offering should be devised.

(g) By the time this Report was finalised and submitted, the new financial year had commenced.

3. Limits on the Percentage of Equity to be Disinvested

3.1. The Committee recognises the need to broadly indicate the objectives that are sought to be achieved through disinvestment in public sector equity:

(a) As an immediate objective to mop up resources of non-inflationary character to meet the budgetary needs which include requirements of developmental activities and social obligations.

(b) To subserve, in the medium term, the overall fiscal objective of gradually reducing the fiscal deficit and bringing about a positive overall impact on future liabilities and income flows to Government.

(c) To improve the overall economic efficiency by bringing about a more competitive atmosphere with emphasis on the cost and quality of product and service to the customers of public enterprise sector.

(d) To enhance the efficiency of individual enterprises by imparting a new dynamism in the management of these enterprises through diversification of ownership and control as also larger and freer access to the expanding capital markets in India.

(e) To realign the extent of ownership, control and regulation in different activities consistent with the technological needs and developments in Industrial Policy.

3.2 The Committee, therefore, recommends that limits to the level of disinvestment should be derived from the target level of government ownership in each enterprise in the medium term. Thus:

(a) The target levels of ownership could be zero; 26% to ensure limited control over special resolutions brought in general body meetings of the enterprise; 515 to have effective control and 1005 for full ownership.

(b) While determining the final level of government ownership, it must be recognised that there may be group specific or enterprise-specific intermediate levels of disinvestment depending on the state of preparedness of each enterprise, stock market conditions and the requirements of government.

(c) The desirable levels of public ownership may be reached with greater advantage to PE concerned and government by expanding the equity base through public offering than disinvestment.

(d) The economic efficiency and financial gains to government through disinvestment in respect of leach tranche in leach enterprise need to be continuously assessed so that there is no compulsive disinvestment merely to reach the target levels of ownership by government.

3.3 The Committee recommends the following considerations in determining the target level of disinvestment:

(a) Target level of disinvestment for the medium term (say 5 years) should be derived from desirable level of public ownership in an activity or unit consistent with Industrial Policy

(b) Target level of ownership should be attained through disinvestment after fully recognising the preparatory actions; mentioned in para 3.6 below.

(c) The target level of ownership in respect of all units reserved for public sector should be 51% to enable control over management. A target level of 26% of public ownership may be considered in exceptional cases. Such cases may include enterprises which currently have a dominant market share or where separate identity has to be maintained for strategic reasons. In others, it could be zero.

(d) There should be a set of specific reasons for continued government ownership of enterprises except in sectors which are reserved for public ownership. In all other sectors, government should justify its continued holding of equality on considerations as fan investor and not as owner. The government may hold more than 26% of the total equity in enterprises with outstanding prospects, but the investment would need to be justified on the basis of growth potential and the scope for larger realisation and not on the basis of desirability of government control. The effort should, therefore, be to disinvest the holding at the best available price at the opportune time.

3.4 Arising from the above, the Committee considers that the percentage of equity to be disinvested should be generally under 49% in industries reserved for the public sector and over 74% in other industries.

3.5 In realising such target levels, no year-wise target for disinvestment need be rigidly prescribed but action plans have to be evolved as indicated in Chapter & of the Committee's Report.

3.6 The Committee strongly recommends the following preparatory steps:

(a) Where the PSE is not in a company form, (i) determine whether it should be converted into a single or multiple companies; (ii) decide upon the capital structure differentiating between debt and equity; and (iii) evaluate whether an independent Regulatory Commission should be established for the concerned sector and, if necessary, put such a Commission in place.

(b) Estimate firmly the ongoing investment plans for expansion or modernisation or technical collaboration.

(c) Project the pattern of financing of such expansion through additional debt or expanded equity.

(d) Review existing debt-equity structure including scope for bonus issue to government to capitalise accumulated reserves where the reserves are disproportionately large in relation to the paid-up capital; where loans are disproportionately high, review scope for conversion of such loans into equity or consider other ways of distributing/lowering the burden of debt so as to keep the equity base at a level attractive to the capital market.

(e) Examine the feasibility of issuing convertible bonds as a measure of raising adequate resources for the PSEs.

(f) Decide in the light of the above, the desirable level of equity base and the targeted level of government ownership.

(g) Settle the modalities and accounting procedures for settlement of large arrears, if any, of dues payable receivable between PSEs and the government, among the PSEs or between PSEs, government and financial institutions.

(h) Appoint a merchant banker for each of the PSEs to assist in initiating some of the preparatory measures mentioned above.

(i) Arrange to create a market-friendly image for PSEs by projecting and publicising the strong points of each PSEs among the investing public in advance of the next disinvestment exercise.

3.7 In making the above recommendations, the Committee explicitly recognised the following:

(a) The introduction of Golden Share' as in UK, where government holds a share with special voting rights amounting to veto in some matters of importance was considered. The Committee felt that there may be constitutional problems of discrimination and did not pursue it further. Instead, 26% ownership is suggested wherever such control is necessary.

(b) The current organisational structure of the enterprise viz., whether it is departmental or statutory corporation or company, by itself is not material for determining the target level of ownership. In fact, organisational change where needed, is part of preparatory work for disinvestment. Similarly, the strategic importance of a unit should not be determined by the nature of the Ministry to which it is affiliated.

(c) It is possible to visualise asset stripping(i.e. sale of either non-income generating assets or one of the production units in a multi-unit company) by a PSE. This may be one of the preparatory exercises before disinvestment in the case of some enterprises.

(d) In some cases, it may be necessary to put a regulatory framework in place. In some other cases, the regime of administered prices may have to be altered. Further, the procedures for evaluation of bids for large value contracts by PSEs may need to be changed in some cases so as to let PSEs reap the entire benefits of any credit package for the contracts instead of government sharing such benefits. It is necessary to complete such vital actions before and not after disinvestment.

(e) The existing status of profitability(or loss) is not material as long as it is ensured that the price realised for shares offered represents a net gain in terms of future cash flows to the Government.

4. Modus Operandi of Disinvestment

4.1 The procedure of bundling share, combining different public enterprises in lots and restricting the disinvestment in favour of public sector mutual funds, was adopted in 1991- 92 as this was the first exercise in disinvestment. For the year 1992 – 93, the sale of shares was made enterprise-wise and to a wider clientele in order to get optimum benefits.

4.2 There are two acceptable and transparent processes for divestiture of government's shareholding:-

(a) Offering shares of public sector enterprises at a fixed price through the medium of recognised market intermediaries.

(b) Sale of equity through auction of shares amongst predetermined clientele whose number could be as large as necessary or practicable. The reserve price for the public sector enterprises' equity is determined with the assistance of merchant bankers.

4.3 In addition, a third method practised worldwide for disinvestment is to transfer the controlling interest in an enterprise to a specific firm or group of persons based on a negotiated price, the entire process being finalised based on certain pre-determined objective criteria.

4.4 Two important considerations for the government in deciding the precise mode of disinvestment are the best means to realise the highest price and the best course which would save the highest number of jobs in the enterprise disinvested.

4.5 All the above methods have their own merits and demerits. In the first alternative of 'offer for sale', difficulties may be encountered in estimating and determining the 'fixed' price if it is offered for the first time and the shares have not actually been trading in the stock exchange. On the other hand, this method has the advantage of spreading the ownership widely amongst the general public and in a transparent manner. A pre-requisite for the method is to list the shares of enterprises in the stock exchange and establish a track record of trading. In the case of those PEs for which the first sale of equity is yet to be made, or those where the track record of trading in shares is yet to be established, the tender system would be advantageous. The last method of negotiated sale has the advantage of direct interface with potential new owners so as so specify the manner of future operation of the enterprise to achieve the best social objectives. But it has the demerit of the potential for long drawn out negotiations and allegations of favouritism.

4.6 The committee, in the light of experience gathered to date recommends the following modus operandi:

(a) Once a reasonable market price is established in a normal trading atmosphere over a reasonable period of time and a public enterprise completes the preparatory work, the fixed price method would be appropriate. In any case, for expanding the equity base through capital markets, the fixed price method has to be adopted.

(b) In all other cases, the auction method with wide participation may be adopted.

(c) Close and continuous involvement of public enterprises concerned and the merchant banker appointed for the purpose of devising the modus operandi is essential. In fact, disinvestment should be planned and implemented for each enterprise separately and not in groups.

(d) PEs should have the freedom to engage merchant bankers and other intermediaries to ensure effective and efficient exploitation of market opportunities.

(e) Where employee-takeover is involved, appropriate modus operandi would have to be devised, essentially through negotiations.

(f) Where it is proposed to offer equity stake to existing technical collaborators in the PSEs, it needs to be ensured that such equity link-up is based on strategic considerations. The choice of partner, extent of equity stake, terms of offering, timing etc. would need to be based on objective criteria such as access to newer technology, scope for increasing export turnover and possibilities of setting up third country operations. The modus operandi would thus have to be uniquely devised.

(g) In respect of PEs which are operating as holding company structures(for example, SAIL) or companies with multiple production units (like the Cement Corporation of India), the modus operandi could be similar but the processes have to be devised in detail and actively implemented by the PE concerned.

(h) An enterprise-specific approach in the modus operandi, including timing of issue and choosing intermediaries, is essential to meet the needs of the government, the enterprise concerned and stock markets.

(i) Costs of floatation have to be explicitly assessed, and reasonableness of costs ensured.

4.7 The committee recommends that 10% of the proceeds appears a reasonable amount to be set apart by the government for lending to the PEs concerned on concessional terms to meet their expansion / rationalisation needs. The Committee recognises the need to use a part of the proceeds of disinvestment for effecting improvements in the PEs concerned in a manner similar to earmarking a part of the gross proceeds for the National Renewal Fund. Such an approach provides incentives to the PE management to augment receipts from disinvestment.

4.8 The Committee also recognised that disinvestment of government equity could be tailored to an informed process of management of external debt of the country. By allowing

PEs to swap the entire or a portion of their outstanding external debt with lenders for an equity stake at negotiated prices, the twin benefits of reduction in debt service obligations to the country as well as to the enterprise concerned and a better debt equity gearing for the entity may be achieved.

4.9 The Committee, however, recognised that there are practical limitations to such an approach. Debt equity swaps have been practised as part of privatisation in certain countries with acute problems of debt overhang and servicing. Especially countries which have defaulted on external payment obligation and whose debt is traded in secondary markets at substantial discounts have resorted to this option.

4.10 The Committee concluded that the above factors are not relevant in the Indian context. There is no comparable external debt problem for India. Therefore, there is no practical utility in encouraging recourse to debt equity swaps in the context of privatisation. However, it is recommended that where an individual enterprise finds unique advantages in adopting this approach, such enterprise could be enabled to do so.

5. Criteria for Valuation of Equity Shares of Public Sector Enterprises

5.1 Valuation of shares in the past was generally based on the guidelines formulated by the Controller of Capital Issues. Currently, however, these are no longer in vogue. In general, three methods for valuation of shares are adopted, viz., Net Asset Value method, Profit Earning Capacity Value method and Discounted Cash Flow method. While the NAV would indicate the value of assets, it would not be in a position to indicate the profitability or income to the investors. The profit earning capacity is generally based on the profit actually earned or anticipated. The discounted cash flow is a far more comprehensive method of reflecting the expected income flows to the investors. However, in the context of valuation of shares of public enterprises, none of the traditional methods would by themselves be adequate. The special circumstances that require to be assessed in the context of valuation of shares of public enterprises are:

(a) In the management of the public enterprises, the focus has been on discharging economic and social responsibilities indicated by the government rather than on projecting profitability to the investor.

(b) In regard to valuation of some of the assets, the book value might reflect land and other facilities provided to such enterprises at lower than market cost.

(c) The structure of the debt and equity of public enterprises had not necessarily followed commercial norms.

(d) Many enterprises have had gains or losses in the past due to the effect of administered prices. Further, recent policy measures are also affecting immediate business prospects of some PEs (e.g. STC due to decentralisation).

(e) A number of public enterprises have been already invested heavily in projects under construction and some of them have ambitious expansion programmes.

(f) No effort has been made to project in the public eye and in the market, the strengths of these enterprises in the past for a variety of reasons.

(g) While in some activities such as cement, there are private enterprises whose shares are listed and traded in the market, there are certain other activities where there are no private enterprises involved in the same activity to provide appropriate basis for valuation.

5.2 The Committee wishes to record the following relevant factors in the context of valuation of shares:

(a) Valuation is a difficult exercise, whether in the private or public sector, in India or in other countries; and more so when there are wide divergences in valuation by different merchant bankers in respect of the same public enterprise.

(b) The price at which a share can be sold is determined more by investor perception of the worth rather than any mechanical measure of intrinsic worth. Hence the importance of information gathering and full disclosure to generate credibility and investor interest.

(c) Rise or fall in share values of an enterprise soon after disinvestment does not by itself indicate that shares were underpriced or overpriced at the time of disinvestment.

(d) Difficulties of valuation in a multi-unit and multi-product scenario have to be reckoned.

5.3 In assessing the intrinsic worth of a share, the Committee recommends the following:

(a) Among the three criteria viz. Net asset value, profit earning capacity value and discounted cash flow value, discounted cash flow has the greatest relevance, though it is the most difficult.

(b) An explicit assessment of the scope and limits for selling non-income generating assets(land or buildings) and rationalising labour force (Voluntary Retirement Scheme etc.) should be made.

(c) Government policies affecting future profitability (such as disappearance of guaranteed off-take or guaranteed rate of return) may have to be spelt out. Such assurances wherever required may be extended only after careful assessment of the implications of such assurances on the economic efficiency rather than immediate attractiveness of the shares to investors.

(d) The influence of social constraints in the past working of the PEs and the extent of benefit accruing due to provision of certain under-priced facilities like land should be captured and presented. Likewise, costs of projects under construction should be evaluated on a realistic basis and presented while reckoning the intrinsic worth of the PEs.

5.4 As regards investor perception, the Committee recommends the following:

(a) Each company has to be studied carefully with the help of a merchant banking firm taking into account factors such as value of assets, its market share, potential profit earning capacity and the prevailing price in the market for shares of similar enterprises in the private sector.

(b) It is essential that the PE and merchant banker concerned present all positive aspects of the enterprise in the prospectus.

(c) While fielding PEs in the capital market, the main line of activity of the PE concerned and the extent of investors' fancy for the particular industry at the material time may have to be taken into account.

(d) In the offering memorandum and during investor presentations, the likely improvements in the efficiency of the PE concerned as a result of changed management attitudes and other relevant factors may need to be emphasised.

(e) Wherever disinvestment is made through public issues, the offering price would need to be fixed with a close assessment of the need to project the issues as a success to pave way for subsequent offering and at the same time avoiding any criticism of under-pricing.

6. Target Clientele for Disinvestment

6.1 The Committee adopted the following approach in determining the relative roles of target clientele:

(a) The target clientele should include Mutual Funds, Financial Institutions, Merchant Bankers, Brokers, Employees of the respective public enterprises,

Resident Investors, Non-resident Indian investors, as also Foreign Investors. In fact, there is no necessity to restrict the disinvestment among any particular groups or categories. Ideally, the purpose is best served by the shares being held by the widest cross section of the Indian public.

(b) Ceilings may be imposed in respect of preferential allotments of shares to the employees in all production / manufacturing oriented companies. However, such preferential allotments should not exceed 200 shares for each employee subject to an overall ceiling of 5%. In the case of "consultancy" companies, preferential allotment to the employees can extend upto 20 per cent again with a ceiling per employee. In case where employee-take-over is sought by employees, the ceilings and payment arrangements could be flexible.

(c) There can also be a ceiling for allotment if any to Non-resident Indian investors or the extent of foreign holding that can be permitted. The same rules as are applicable to NRIs and foreign investors to buy the equity in private industry in India may be extended to the foreign investors to buy shares in PEs.

(d) The question of reserving a portion of the government shareholding proposed to be disivested in favour of Foreign Institutional Investors may be considered when the role of FIIs expands in the Indian capital markets.

(e) It may be desirable to allow shareholding by technical collaborators in PEs on a preferential basis as part of modernisation and expansion. The new Industrial Policy allows foreign equity participation upto 51% in Indian enterprises. Rather than encouraging them to set up new units for the same purpose, it should be open to the existing foreign collaborators to buy into the equity of PEs operating in such areas. The public sector will derive two advantages through this method, viz. (I) continued technological and possibly fresh managerial involvement from foreign collaborators and (ii) scope for optimising the use of existing plant and other facilities to stage a global presence with the help of the foreign collaborators.

(f) There may be restrictions on the extent of equity sold to particular group of clients. For example, foreign investors may not be allowed to buy more than 24% of equity except on those PEs concluding strategic alliances with overseas firms on terms approved by the government.

6.2 The Committee, therefore, recommends the following target clientele:

A. Where auction method or public offer is adopted, the target clientele should include:

(i) The general public;

(ii) Mutual funds;

(iii) NRIs and foreign investors on par with general principles governing their participation in the Indian equity market with no reservation for either of the categories;

(iv) Reservation restricted to employees who would get upto 200 shares per employee at a discount of 15% on the market price, enabling funding arrangements and a lock in period that is normally prescribed for reserved allocation of shares. While a ceiling is prescribed for each employee, where a trust or cooperative of employees is formed for the specific purpose, individual ceilings could be aggregated for the purpose;

(v) Under special circumstances, reservation for other stakeholders such as dealers in select activities like fertilisers depending on the extent of interest of such stake-holders, upto 500 shares per applicant at market price and subject to lock-in restriction as normally prescribed for reserved allocations.

B. In regard t technical collaborations;

- Technical collaborators may be existing or new;
- Emphasis on identification of enterprises that would benefit from conversion into joint venture;
- Transparency through competitive offers (i.e. not restricting negotiations only to existing collaborator);
- Expanded equity base or disinvestment by negotiated price as well as stock options subject to any SEBI regulations;
- Where domestic industrial houses have synergy and offer collaboration arrangements to ensure efficiency, they should be treated at least on par with foreign technical collaborators.

C. Merchant bankers and stock brokers are essentially intermediaries and should not be treated as target-clientele. However, assistance of internationally renowned merchant bankers may be employed if the enterprise concerned expressly requests that this be done. Assistance of such foreign merchant bankers may be useful when foreign collaborations or investments have to be examined (including BIFR cases).

7. Other Issues

7.1 The Committee noted some important lessons of international experience in PSU disinvestment viz.

(i) In many countries, separate apex agencies have been created to design and implement disinvestment. In some cases, such an agency was established by law, so that the concerned law overcomes existing legal impediments to PE disinvestment.

(ii) The process of disinvestment was spread over two to three years, and where it was done in a hurry, it resulted in undesirable concentration, sometimes described as crony capitalism.

(iii) In the case of some countries, where a rigid time-table for disinvestment was caused by prescription of donors, there was an erosion of the negotiating strength of government agencies and possible loss of revenue.

(iv) Interested parties, including managers, bureaucracy and unions resisted such disinvestement but this was overcome with the chief executives and boards being packed with pro-changers.

(v) Introduction of competition as part of the process of disinvestment was preferred. Consequently, to ensure competition and protection of consumers' interest, necessary policy/legal changes had to be brought about.

(vi) Concern with equity considerations has been an important issue in striking a balance between fiscal needs, consumers' interests and workers' welfare, but often special arrangements to protect income flows, if not jobs, were put in place for workers.

(vii) In some cases, quality of services and access of the poor to services suffered as a consequence of disinvestment but on the whole, results were positive.

(viii) There has been virtually universal criticism of underpricing of shares wherever disinvestment has taken place. In some cases, floatation costs or gains by financial intermediaries such as underwriters and merchant bankers were considered excessive.

(ix) Pursuance of multiple objectives blurred proper evaluation of the impact of disinvestment.

7.2 Keeping in view the international experience and our own requirements, a Standing Committee on Public Enterprise Disinvestment is recommended. The Committee may consist of both full and part time members and draw expertise from Government, Public Enterprises, Financial Sector, Professionals and academicians. The Commission's terms of reference may include;

(a) review of public enterprises with a view to recommending enterprise-specific actions for reforms, restructuring and disinvestment:

(b) suggesting, where appropriate, parameters for selection of Chief Executives Board of Directors to meet the requirements of reforms.

(c) Identifying the appropriate legal, institutional and procedural arrangements for protecting the interests of consumers, rural or backward areas while transforming organisational form into companies wherever needed and such arrangements may include breaking up of existing monopolies or encouraging new firms to promote competition;

(d) Proposing necessary incentives to enterprises to mobilise support for disinvestment;

(e) Applying the criteria suggested for establishing the percentage of disinvestment in regard to each enterprise;

(d) Providing guidance on modalities of disinvestment appropriate to each enterprise including share valuation;

(e) Monitoring the progress of disinvestment programme; and

(f) Arranging for independent evaluation of the progress of the disinvestment programme.

7.3 The proposed Committee would also be in a position to guide the public enterprises and the government in preparatory measures for disinvestment which include;

(a) financial restructuring especially debt / equity, accounting for and the settlement of dues between the government and public enterprises

(b) preparatory measures legally required for

diversification of ownership including assistance in obtaining lenders' consent (external commercial or aid)

(c) assessing the medium term corporate plan with special reference to the proposed equity structure

(d) ensuring that data is gathered by each public enterprise and prospectus is prepared with due care

(e) the employment of merchant bankers, timing and management of issue, listing, share transfer etc.

7.4 The Committee recommends for consideration of the government, establishing the Committee mentioned in para 7.2on a statutory basis in view of the financial magnitudes involved, multiple ministries concerned impact on economic reform and the need to monitor use of proceeds of such disinvestment.

7.5 The Committee further recommends for consideration, use of part of proceeds of disinvestment not only for National Renewal Fund (which may include financing of retraining of workers to enable redeployment), 10% incentive for PEs, and reduction in Government debt but also for channeling resources to social sectors like literacy, health and employment generation in rural area.

7.6 The Committee recommends that the following further measures in respect of PEs be initiated to ensure that the objectives of disinvestment are realised

(a) Government expectations from the PEs as majority / dominant shareholders should be documented in the form of MOUs but the focus of these MOUs will be different viz. Customers and capital markets.

(b) With diversified ownership coming into place after disinvestment, reconstituting PEs Boards with appropriate representation for non-government directors as may be necessary.

(c) Each enterprise should be encouraged to commence

work on corporate strategies and plans in alignment with ongoing reforms.

(d) Seminars and workshops could be held for the finance personnel and other senior executives of PEs on the subject of their new role in the liberalised economic environment, their relationship with the government, capital markets and their customers etc. SCOPE could take the initiative in organising such workshops/ seminars with guidance perhaps from SEBI.

(e) A deliberate policy of 'image building' through media and projecting performance is also necessary to ensure continuous entry in to capital markets for raising resources.

Appendix IV

Report of the Comptroller and Auditor General of India

Overview

The Government of India sold the shares of selected Public Sector Enterprises (PSEs) during 1991-92. The sale was carried out in two phases in December 1991 and February 1992. The disinvestment exercise was not preceded by adequate preparatory study. No efforts were made to generate widespread investor enthusiasm among the financial institutions / mutual funds about PSE shares to encourage good response from them.

(Paragraph 5.1)

Some of the PSEs were included in the programme of disinvestment of shares though exclusion of these was advised by PSEs / Administrative Ministries on specific grounds. The result was that in the case of shares of some PSEs such as Steel Authority of India Ltd (SAIL) and Indian Petro Chemicals Ltd (IPCL), there was gross under-realization of sale receipts.

(Paragraphs 5.1, 5.15 and 5.16)

The method adopted by Government for sale of shares of PSEs in bundles depressed value realization of "Very Good" / "Good" PSEs as a result of their being clubbed together with

"Average" PSEs. In four cases the average realization was even below the face value (Rs 10/-) of the share.

(Paragraph 5.3)

Offers received in the first phase of disinvestment were far below the reserve value of bundles based on reserve price fixed for share of each PSE. Reserve prices originally fixed on the basis of accepted criteria were reduced drastically without which the low offers received could not have been accepted. Such reduction ranged between 21.95 percent to 86.67 percent. In 24 out of 31 PSEs, reduction in valuation was above 50 percent. The reduction in original reserve price both at the time of first and second phase of disinvestment resulted in underrealization of value to the extent of Rs 3442 crores.

(Paragraphs 5.9, 5.10)

The Government had initially decided that in respect of PSE's, whose shares were already listed on the stock exchanges, their shares would be off-loaded directly to mutual funds / financial institutions at the market price of their shares. The shares of Cochin Refineries and Andrew Yule listed on the Stock Exchange, were, however, clubbed in bundles along with the other shares and sold to financial institutions / mutual funds in the first phase of disinvestment in December 1991.

(Paragraph 5.3)

Composition of bundles of shares of PSEs for disinvestment were determined even before fixation of the reserve price of the shares of each PSE. As a result the value of each bundle instead of being around Rs 5 crores, as approved by the Government, ranged between Rs 8.61 crores and Rs 12.91 crores. The financial institutions / mutual funds being presumably under the impression that the bundle value was Rs 5.00 crores, quoted lower rates.

(Paragraph 5.5)

In the first phase of disinvestment, the Government offered shares valued at Rs 8000 crores on the basis of the original reserve prices fixed. This was far in excess of the perceived investible resources of around Rs 2000-2500 crores available with the financial institutions / mutual funds.

(Paragraph 5.6)

Tenders received in the first phase of disinvestment were non-competitive. 72.61 percent of the bids received had only one bidder. Out of the 406 bundles sold, in respect of 289 bundles representing 71 percent of the total bundles sold, only single bids had been received.

(Paragraph 5.7)

In the second phase of disinvestment of shares undertaken in February 1992, tenders received were again non-competitive. Four out of 19 bidders contributed 68 percent of total bids received.

(Paragraph 5.11)

A claw back provision was not incorporated in the terms and conditions of the sale to ensure realization by Government of a part of the profits likely to be made by the buyers in a subsequent sale of the shares.

(Paragraph 5.12)

The disinvestment served only to contain the fiscal deficit.

(Paragraph 5.14)

Disinvestment of Government shareholding in selected Public Sector Enterprises (PSEs) during 1991-92.

1. Introduction

The public sector has been central to India's economic development. In the pursuit of development objectives in a mixed economy, public sector enterprises in critical sectors of the economy have played an important role in preventing the concentration of economic power, reducing regional disparities and ensuring that planned development serves the common good.

The total investment including equity, loans and deferred credits in 246 PSEs amounted to Rs 1,13,233.68 crores as on 31st March, 1991. As against this the profit earned by these PSEs during 1990-91 was Rs 2367.74 crores and the dividend paid was a mere Rs 364.86 crores. Such minimal generation of surplus has been perceived by the Government as responsible for the inability of the PSEs to regenerate themselves in terms of new investments as well as in technology development. Proposal of raising resources for the PSEs through investment by the public sector financial institutions / banks in a basket of shares of both profit and loss making enterprises had been under consideration of the Government since July 1990 and it was decided in March 1991 to undertake partial disinvestment of shares of PSEs.

In the aforesaid background the Union Government announced in their statement on Industrial Policy on 24th July 1991 and in the Union Budget for 1991-92 presented on the same day that apart from revitalising the public sector, a part of the Government's share-holding in the public sector would be offered to mutual funds, financial institutions, general public and workers so as to raise resources and encourage wider public participation.

The Union Budget for 1991-92 provided for receipts of Rs 2500 crores on this account. In the two phases of disinvestment carried out in December 1991 and February 1992 the Government realized a sum of Rs 3038 crores from the sale proceeds of its shares held in 30 selected PSEs.

2. Organizational set up

The PSEs are under the administrative control of the various Ministries and Departments of the Government of India. The Department of Public Enterprises (DPE) under the Ministry of Industry acts as the nodal agency for all PSEs and assists in policy formulation pertaining to the role of PSEs in the economy as also in laying down policy guidelines on performance improvement and evaluation, financial accounting, personnel management and in related areas. It also collects, evaluates and maintains information on several areas in respect of PSEs. The DPE also provides an inter-face between the administrative Ministries / Departments and the PSEs. In fulfilling its role it inter-acts with other Ministries and organizations as also premier management institutes in the country. The disinvestment of Government shares in selected PSEs during 1991-92 was carried out by the DPE in association with the concerned PSEs and their Administrative Ministries / Departments, Ministry of Finance and the Cabinet Secretariat.

3. Arrangement for valuation and sale of shares of PSEs

After the announcement of the proposal for partial disinvestment in the Union Budget 1991-92 and the Industrial Policy Statement 1991, the process of selection of PSEs whose shares were to be disinvested was undertaken by the Department of Public Enterprises (DPE). Out of the total 244 PSEs as on 1.4.1990, the DPE recommended disinvestment of shares of only 41 PSEs. PSEs which were (i) under construction stage, (ii) whose net asset value (NAV) per share was either negative or less than the face value, (iii) which were of insignificant size, (iv) where current level of profitability was low, (v) those falling under Section 25 of the companies act 1956, (vi) in which share-holding of the government was below 60 percent, (vii) those functioning in power generation / transmission sectors and (viii) those in the oil sector having special relationship with the Government and (ix) also those meeting defence needs of the country were excluded from the purview of disinvestment.

Out of these 41 PSEs, ten PSEs were later excluded at different stages for reasons such as some of them being consultancy firms, some having gone into losses during 1990-91 and the remaining engaged in production of strategic nature. Finally a list of 31 PSEs was drawn up in the first week of December 1991. Of the 31 PSEs, 8 were categorised as 'Very Good', 12 as 'Good' and 11 as 'Average'. The categorisation of these PSEs was apparently made on the basis of the Net Asset Value (NAV) / Share vis-à-vis face value Rs 10/- of the share of the PSEs as on 31st March 1991. The PSEs whose NAV was Rs 50/- per share and above were categorised as 'Very Good', between Rs 20/- per share to Rs 49/- per share as 'Good' and between Rs 10/- to Rs 19/- as 'Average'.

3.1 Formulation of guidelines for valuation of shares of PSEs

In August 1991, the Ministry of Finance constituted a Committee under the Chairmanship of the Secretary (DPE) for formulating guidelines for valuation of shares of PSEs which were to be disinvested.

Based on the recommendations of the Committee submitted on 5th September 1991, the DPE issued detailed guidelines to the Chief Executives of the PSEs identified for disinvestment for valuing the shares by three different methods namely:

(a) Net Asset Value (NAV) Method.

(b) Profit Earning Capacity Value (PECV) method at capitalisation rate of 4 to 8 percent.

(c) Discounted Cash Flow (DCF) method – based on the future expected free cash flow streams for a period of about 5 years discounted at appropriate rates.

The PSEs were asked to submit the necessary data by 25th October, 1991 to enable the DPE to fix the 'reserve price' for sale of shares in respect of each PSE.

3.2 Appointment of Consultant for valuation of shares

The Government also appointed a private Consultancy firm in September 1991 to advise on the pricing of the shares of selected PSEs. The Government's intention was that if the value of shares computed by the consultants was higher than the values arrived at by the other methods it would be taken to increase the valuation of the shares. The Consultants submitted their report in three volumes on 10th, 12th and 18th December 1991. The Consultants based their recommended values taking into account prevalent stock market sentiment specific to the industry in which each PSE could be classified.

3.3 Modus operandi for sale of shares

The following decisions were taken by the Government at the outset:

(a) Disinvestment would be done in phases, the first phase to be implemented in December 1991.

(b) Level of disinvestment would vary from 5 percent to 20 percent, keeping in view that Government shareholding would not fall below 51 percent.

(c) Shares of all selected PSEs would be offered in the form of bundles consisting of nine PSEs (3 PSEs from each category viz., very good, good and average) through a process of bidding.

(d) Shares would be sold to only mutual funds and investment institutions in the Public Sector who would gradually off load these shares into the market so as to finally ensure a wider holding of the ownership of these shares.

(e) DPE would finalise the list of PSEs for disinvestment in consultation with the Administrative Ministries and Ministry of Finance, value them and prepare bundles.

While taking the above decisions in November 1991 the Government also decided that the Controller of Capital Issues (CCI) norms for share valuation would not be applicable for the envisaged disinvestment since they tended to generally under value shares. The CCI norms provide for share valuation by computing the average of NAV and PECV at 15 percent capitalisation rate for manufacturing companies subject to suitable adjustment with reference to the stock market prices in respect of listed companies. The Government decided that the valuation of shares of selected PSEs would be according to the three methods indicated in para 3.4 above. The average of the two highest values so obtained would be taken as the 'fair' value or the 'reserve price' for that PSEs share. It was also decided that the total value of the equity in each bundle would be about Rs 5 crores based on the fair value of the shares of each PSE. In the case of PSEs already listed on the stock exchanges, it was further decided that disinvestment of Government equity shares would be made directly to mutual funds and investment institutions at the market price.

3.4 Invitation of bids, fixation of reserve prices

The DPE issued notices, inviting bids for the sale of shares of 31 selected PSEs from 10 financial institutions / mutual funds on 10th December 1991. All the PSEs shares were grouped into 825 bundles each consisting of the shares of 9 PSEs in certain proportions determined by the DPE. On the basis of data furnished by the PSEs for the valuation of shares and the report submitted by the consultancy firm, the 'reserve price' of shares of each selected PSE was fixed by the DPE in consultation with the representatives of the PSEs concerned, Administrative Ministry of PSE and Ministry of Finance between the 14th and the 18th of December 1991.

3.5 Revision of reserve prices

After the bids were opened on 18th December 1991, it was found that the bid prices were far below the value of bundle computed with reference to reserve price and the number of shares in the bundles and, therefore, could not be accepted. Approval of the Government was, therefore, obtained on 24th December 1991 for empowering the DPE to sell the shares of selected PSEs by accepting the highest of the bids including single tender received, so long as these were above the average of the NAV and PECV computed using an average capitalisation rate of 10 percent. The price of the bundle so arrived at could further be reduced upto 10 percent, if necessary. The need for reducing the reserve price of each PSE share fixed earlier was justified on the ground that the reserve prices fixed earlier had been inflated due to optimistic projections of future cash flows by the PSEs.

Out of the 825 bundles offered for sale, bids were received from 9 mutual funds / institutions for 533 bundles. The bids were evaluated against the reserve price of each bundle worked out on the basis of the revised reserve price fixed for each PSE share as included in the bundle. 406 bundles for a total value of Rs 1427 crores were sold. Acceptances were sent by the DPE to the mutual funds / investment institutions on 1st January 1992. The bid amounts had been credited earlier to the Government account on 23rd and 24th December 1991.

3.6 Second tranche of disinvestment

For the second tranche of disinvestment, (February 1992), the Government decided on the following:

(a) The bundles of shares of PSEs remaining unsold in the first tranche of disinvestment may be unbundled and fresh bundles of shares of 31 selected PSEs made with different proportion of shares of these PSEs.

(b) The fresh bundles of shares would be sold through the process of bidding to the mutual funds, financial institutions, investment institutions and banks in the public sector. The DPE would sell the bundles of shares for which the bids were equal to or above the price calculated according to the CCI guidelines.

(c) The DPE may sell shares in some selected PSEs beyond the 20 percent limit but in no case would this involve loss of Government control.

On 16th January 1992, the DPE orally requested the Delhi Regional Office of the Industrial Credit and Investment Corporation of India Ltd (ICICI) to evaluate and advise reasonable issue price for equity of selected PSEs. The ICICI submitted its recommendations on 29th January 1992 which inter-alia suggested non-inclusion of certain PSEs whose shares had been disinvested in the first phase. The prices suggested by the ICICI were higher than the earlier revised reserve prices in some cases. As a result of these recommendations a revised list of 16 PSEs for disinvestment was prepared by the DPE with the approval of Government. The valuation of the shares of these 16 enterprises was done with reference to the valuation done by the ICICI which was higher or equal to the revised reserve prices of the first phase of disinvestment.

The shares of the 16 PSEs were grouped in 120 bundles according to same categorisation as adopted earlier. Their reserve price was uniformly fixed at Rs 10.08 crores per bundle, which was also indicated in the notice inviting tenders and the bids were invited from 36 institutions, banks, on 11th February 1992. The terms and conditions stipulated in the notice inviting the bids for second phase were generally the same as those prescribed in the first phase of disinvestment. 273 bids were received from 19 institutions for all the 120 bundles. Bids for all the 120 bundles were accepted for a total value of Rs 1611 crores.

The shares of PSEs disinvested in the two phases taken together ranged from a minimum of 0.27 percent to maximum of 20 percent (Annexure I) and the total amount realised was Rs 3038 crores. The shares of one selected PSE namely Metal Scrap Trading Corporation remained unsold.

4. Scope of Audit

The arrangements made by the Government for the sale of shares of selected PSEs were examined in Audit to ascertain whether the preparation for sale had been adequate and satisfactory and whether the procedure for disinvestment was conducive to realizing the maximum receipts to the Exchequer. The records relating to disinvestment of Government shares in selected PSEs as supplied to Audit by the DPE and some of the concerned PSEs were examined in Audit and its findings based on these records are given in the succeeding paragraphs.

5. Audit findings and conclusions

5.1 Approach to disinvestment lacked necessary preparatory work.

Investors' enthusiasm for equity shares of a company is

dependent to a large extent on the knowledge about its inherent financial strength, including inter alia profits earned and dividends paid in the past, growth in sales and assets, future plans of expansion, risks involved, the future of the industry including demand / supply imbalances, locational advantages and the competence of its management. Public issues of equity by private enterprises are invariably preceded by wide publicity about such aspects. The requirement of familiarising the investors both institutional and individual was more essential for PSEs due to their earlier lack of exposure to the stock markets.

While the Government had decided as early as in March, 1991 to disinvest a part of its shares in PSEs, it was noticed in Audit that no efforts were made to generate investor enthusiasm through wide publicity about the PSEs. In fact the identification of the 31 PSEs was completed in November 1991. The Government had asked the financial institutions like the Unit Trust of India (UTI) who were the prospective buyers to do their own valuation of shares of PSEs for which purpose they were advised to obtain information from the PSE concerned. No efforts were made to generate wide spread investor enthusiasm among the FIs / MFs about the PSEs shares to encourage a good response from these institutions.

The Department of Public Enterprises (DPE) stated in March 1993 that since the shares were sold to MFs / FIs only it was not considered advisable to incur expenditure on publicity and that MFs / FIs were given access to annual accounts, balance sheet, etc. of the PSEs.

The fact remains that though the decision to disinvest had been taken quite some time back, the MFs / FIs were left with very little time to make a realistic valuation of shares after the issue of DPE circular of October 1991 advising the PSEs to give necessary information as and when asked for by the MFs / FIs. This together with the lack of information on the seller's perception of the reserve price for the shares / bundles led to the low offers as well as number of bids received as explained subsequently in para 5.5.

Suggestion had been received from some of the Ministries and Departments of the Government of India as well as PSEs for exclusion of some PSEs from the proposed disinvestment. The justification given by the Departments / PSEs for their exclusion is indicated below :

Name of PSE	*Justification for Exclusion*
i) Indian Petrochemicals Ltd (IPCL)	These PSEs were intending to raise funds directly from the market by issue of fresh equity shares which taken together with the proposed disinvestment would result in Government's share-holding falling below 51 per cent.
ii) Cochin Refineries Ltd (CRL)	-do-
iii) Andrew Yule & Co (AY)	-do-
iv) National Aluminium Co (NALCO)	The volatility of international price of aluminium and fluctuations in profitability were quite low at that time.
v) Hindustan Zinc Ltd (HZL)	Full scale commercial production was expected in a year or two with the commissioning of a new project costing Rs 617 crores in October 1991 which would increase the share price

(contd...)

	of the enterprise in future.
vi) National Fertilizers Ltd (NFL)	Profit of these enterprises in 1990-91 was low which was going to increase substantialy in 1991-92 and as such disinvestment should be considered after the finalization of accounts for 1991-92.
vii) Fertilizers & Chemicals (Travancore) Ltd (FACT)	-do-
viii) Steel Authority of India Ltd (SAIL)	The valuation of shares under the three methods would not reflect the real values of the SAIL and Government would not get fair price till 1994-95. On control of steel distribution and pricing as well as modernisation of the plants was likely to improve profitability.

There was nothing on record to show that their suggestions were given due consideration. These PSEs were, however, included in the first round of disinvestment. Only in the second round were some of the companies excluded on the advice of ICICI. The effect of this was that in the case of shares of IPCL and SAIL for example the realization turned out to be much lower than the original reserve price fixed as explained in paras 5.15 and 5.16.

The DPE stated that the Administrative Ministries / Departments and PSEs concerned were neither sellers nor buyers and the Government had to take a view for PSEs as a whole and as a seller based on macro considerations. The reply of the DPE is not convincing. It does not explain why the advice of the concerned Ministries / PSEs tendered, adducing specific grounds, was not accepted. As stated earlier, the Government subsequently, in the second phase, accepted the advice of ICICI for the exclusion of many PSEs from disinvestment.

5.2 Formulation of guidelines for valuation – Inadequacies

A scrutiny of the DPE's files relating to the setting up of the committee for formulating guidelines for valuation of shares of PSEs, revealed the following :

(a) The committee was to be assisted by Financial Advisers (FAs) of the Ministries as representative of the Department of Expenditure. The Chairman, however, decided not to associate the FAs on the ground that the committee had very little time and the selection of PSEs had not been finally completed.

The DPE stated that to complete the work in time, it was necessary to do away with the unwieldy size of the committee and to make maximum use of the available talents. It added that the absence of FAs of the Ministries in the committee was not of much consequence as representatives from available fields including PSEs were included in the committee. It was also stated that the disinvestment was not a normal activity for which rules were laid. The reply is not tenable as the committee constituted by the Ministry of Finance had, as its member, a representative of the Department of Expenditure. However, because of a subsequent decision by the Chairman, the expertise of the Department of Expenditure could not be availed of.

(b) The final report was signed by only four out of 14 members of the committee, including 5 co-opted members. It may be inferred that the deliberations and recommendations of the committee did not reflect fully the expertise available even within the Government. Some of their suggestions which could have had important bearing on the outcome of disinvestment are reproduced below :

(i) Shares should be offered not only to mutual funds and merchant banks but also to approved share brokers, public limited companies, approved pension funds, etc. for bringing more competition and better price and for preventing cartelisation. A limit should be fixed for purchase of shares by each financial institution for a wider dispersal of shares.

(ii) The book value of shares of PSEs being very low, the assets of PSEs should be revalued at current price or replacement value for calculating the NAV. If this was not possible due to time constraints, the weightage of NAV in computing fair value may be reduced from 50 per cent as per CCI norms to 25 per cent.

(iii) The rates of capitalisation for say the first ten among the best public sector units cannot be less than the average capitalisation rates obtaining in the first ten best private sector gilt edged shares.

(iv) The disinvestment should be considered in stages with pre-determined time schedule.

(v) In view of the absence of market value it may be advisable to transfer the shares to selected mutual funds / public financial institutions at a reasonable value with a stipulation that as and when these shares are offered to the general public 90 per cent of the price gained would be transferred back to the Exchequer.

(vi) If the Government have to raise the intended amount before 31.3.1992, the short term solution would be to raise a loan from the financial institutions against the collateral of shares which would in due course be offered to all parties including the financial institutions and the loan(s) be repaid.

Consideration of the above suggestions made by the various members representing different wings of the Government would have enabled an appraisal of the several options before embarking on disinvestment.

5.3 Effect of bundling of shares on prices of Very Good / Good PSEs

The Government had decided to offer for sale the shares of the selected PSEs in bundles consisting of shares of 9 PSEs each, 3 'Very Good', 3 'Good' and 3 'Average'. It was stated that bundling was to facilitate disinvestment of shares of the average PSEs as the potential buyers would be compelled to buy them along with the Very Good and Good shares.

The method of offering shares in bundles made it difficult for the Government to assess how each share had been evaluated by the bidders. This was evident from the wide variation in the prices of shares of PSEs furnished later by the financial institutions / mutual funds, after acceptance of bids. But for bundling, it would have been possible to reject the offers for individual shares of PSEs which were below the reserve prices fixed by the Government. Thus, while it is not clear whether the bundling exercise would facilitate sale of the average PSEs shares, it would result in depressing the value realization of the shares of Very Good / Good PSEs. Details of eight cases noticed in Audit where the average realizations were less than even the revised reserve prices is given below. In four cases the average realization was even below the face value of the share of Rs 20/- :

S No	*Name of the PSE*	*Revised reserve price December 1991*	*Average price per share realized*	*Loss per share Rs.*	*No. of shares sold (in lakhs)*	*Total loss Rs. Lakh*
1	IRCON	303	225	78	0.13	10.14
2	?	21	18.11	2.09	42.68	123.34
3	NCL	29	25.17	3.83	16.69	63.92
4	RCFL	13	9.87	3.13	311.36	974.56
5	NFL	10	8.46	1.54	111.63	171.91
6	NPF	10	8.00	2.00	191.90	383.80
7	CMC	10	8.00	2.00	25.28	50.56
8	DCI	36	10.00	26.00	4.02	104.52
					Total	1882.75

The invitation of bids for each PSE shares separately would have also resulted in higher value realisation for the Very Good and Good companies.

As mentioned in para 3.7 of the report, it was decided by the Government that in the case of PSEs already listed on the Stock Exchanges, their shares would be off loaded directly to mutual funds / financial institutions at the market price. Shares of Cochin Refineries and Andrew Yule which were already listed in the stock market were, therefore, not to be included for sale in the bundles. The inclusion of shares of these two PSEs in bundles was, therefore, contrary to the approval of the Government.

The DPE stated that sale of PSEs shares in bundles was considered as best method of realizing best prices in respect of all PSEs and it was not possible to say whether individual shares had been underpriced in this method of sale. The reply of the DPE is not convincing. The sale of shares in bundles definitely had the effect of depressing the value realization of shares of Very Good / Good PSEs. In fact, during the disinvestment made in 1992-93, the Government took a decision of off-loading the shares of individual PSEs and not in bundles.

The DPE also contended that inclusion of shares of Cochin Refineries and Andrew Yule in different bundles was not contrary to any Government approval and was tactically sound. This cannot be accepted as the Government had taken a decision to off-load shares of these two PSEs which were listed in the stock exchange and whose market prices were known.

5.4 Classification of PSEs – Basis inadequate

From a scrutiny of the files of DPE it emerged that the classification of PSEs as 'Very Good', 'Good' and 'Average' for the purpose of bundling of shares had apparently been done on the basis of NAV. This could not be considered as sufficient as the other financial criteria and macro economic parameters would substantially determine the market sentiment for each share. Reserve prices determined by the DPE and the valuation done by the consultants appointed by the Government were higher than the NAV of the PSEs used for the purpose of classification by the Government.

Taking into account the valuation done by the DPE and the consultants, classification made by the Government would have undergone a change. The table below indicates the classification as done by the Government, the consultant's valuation and the reserve price fixed by the DPE :

S No	*Name of PSE*	*Classification by the Government as per NAV*	*Valuation as per consultants report (Average of High & Low) (Rs)*	*Reserve price fixed by DPE (Rs)*
1	Madras Refineries Ltd	Good	65.25	65.00
2	MTN Ltd	Average	73.88	57.00
3	HMT Ltd	Good	56.62	46.00
4	Bongaigaon Refineries & Petrochemicals Ltd	Average	59.64	55.00
5	Hindustan Zinc Ltd	Average	88.76	85.00

From the above table it is clear that classifications of PSEs for the purpose of bundling of shares had not been done taking all factors into account. PSEs listed at Sr Nos 2,4 and 5 could have been classified as 'Good' as the valuation done by the DPE and the consultants in these cases was higher than the valuation done in respect of HMT Ltd at Sr No 3.

Further, a substantial number of PSEs whose shares were disinvested operated in fields such as telecom, oil, communications, etc enjoying virtual monopoly and cash cow status. There was, therefore, adequate justification for believing that these PSEs would continue to maintain their position and become more profitable in the future. Infact the lowest reserve price fixed by the Government was Rs 35 for SAIL and there were only two other PSEs whose reserve prices were determined less than Rs 50/-. As against this 23 of the 30 PSEs had NAV less than Rs 50 and they were, therefore, not categorised as 'very good'. Classification of PSEs on the basis of reserve prices rather than NAV would have enabled bundling of shares in a more rational manner.

The DPE stated that shares floated in the primary markets were judged / gauged by NAV which was also followed by the Government for classification of PSEs. The Audit view was also stated to be not supported by an expert study or commercial practice. The fact remains that NAV alone is not the indicator of the classification of a PSE. There are other factors also which could have been kept in view for deciding the classification on rational basis.

5.5 Constitution of bundles and inviting of bids without valuing the shares.

Government approved in November 1991 the offering of bundles of shares of 9 PSEs consisting of 3 very good, 3 good and 3 average, value of each bundle being kept around Rs 5 crores. The approval of Government also envisaged fixation of reserve price by taking the two highest values under the NAV, PECV and DCF methods.

The bids for all the 825 bundles were invited on 10th December 1991. Reserve prices of the shares of the selected PSEs were determined between 14th to 18th December 1991. Apparently, therefore, the bundles had not been valued before inviting bids and consequently the reserve price of bundle could not be indicated in the notice inviting the bids. As the approval of Government was for keeping the value of each bundle around Rs 5 crores, it was essential to fix the reserve price of shares to determine the value of each bundle before inviting bids.

Valuation done by Audit as a test check of bundle Nos 74, 90, 262, 277, 364, 385, 404, 460, 550, 580, 610, 674, 756, 788, 807 and 821 on the basis of reserve prices of shares of selected PSEs revealed that the value of these bundles ranged between Rs 8.61 crores to Rs 12.91 crores. Invitation of bids before fixation of reserve prices of shares, resulted in not keeping the value of each bundle around Rs 5 crores. There was also appreciable variation in the value of bundles, which was not in accordance with the approval of the Government.

The DPE had reported on 12th December 1991 that the financial institutions / mutual funds had been under the impression that each bundle of shares offered for sale would be around Rs 5 crores. It is not clear to Audit as to how the financial institutions / mutual funds gathered the impression that the value of each bundle was around RS 5 crores when the valuation of shares had not been made by the time the tenders were invited. The financial institutions / mutual funds quoted lower rates and the average realization per bundle worked out to Rs 3.51 crores.

The DPE stated that in the very first operation of its kind which had clear objective of raising resources, both underpricing and overpricing were obvious risks and it was for this reason that consultants' valuation and assessment of share prices by PSEs were not accepted. It was added that the value of internalized valuation of bundles without a buyer's perception, matching would not be material. The argument adduced are not convincing. The risks involved could have been minimised by a critical assessment of the best value of shares of individual PSEs by adequate preparatory company-wise / industry-wise study. The relevant factors indicated in consultants' report and the views of the PSEs could have been properly used to create favourable buyer's perception for realizing the best value.

5.6 Offer of shares for sale in excess of the perceived investible resources with the institutions.

On the basis of reserve price of shares determined by the Government between 14th – 18th December 1991, the average value of each bundle as worked out in Audit was about Rs 9.75 crores. The total value of 825 bundles was, therefore, around Rs 8,000 crores. From a note dated 18th December 1991 submitted by DPE before opening of the bids on that day, it was seen that the DPE had anticipated that all the institutions from whom bids were invited would be able to purchase shares of the value of around RS 2000-2500 crores against DPE's estimated value of over Rs 6000 crores.

When the financial limits of the financial institutions / mutual funds were generally known to the Government, offering shares in excess of the purchasing capacity of such institutions appears to be a financially imprudent decision. The apprehension regarding inadequate purchasing / bidding power was confirmed on opening of bids as only 710 bids for 533 bundles for a total value of Rs 2300.84 crores were received and the value of each bundle quoted was far below Rs 5 crores. This shows that planning in the disinvestment process was inadequate and incomplete.

The DPE stated that to sell a new commodity in the market for the first time it was considered prudent to make wider offer to sell lesser quantity. This argument is not convincing as with inadequate purchasing / bidding power of the buyers, offering of shares much in excess only led to uncompetitive bidding.

5.7 Non-competitive tenders in the first phase of disinvestment in December 1991

The Government invited tenders for the sale of 825 bundles of shares of 31 PSEs from 10 institutions on 10th December 1991 which were opened on 18th December 1991. 710 bids were received from 9 institutions for 533 bundles as under :

		No of bundles	*No of bids*	*Percentage to total bundles*
i)	No of bundles for which one bid was received	387	387	72.61
ii)	No of bundles for which two bids were received	122	244	22.89
iii)	No of bundles for which three bids were received	19	57	3.56
iv)	No of bundles for which four bids were received	3	12	0.56
v)	No of bundles for which five bids were received	2	10	0.38
		533	710	

72.61 per cent of the bundles had only one bidder. In 4.50 per cent cases only 3 or more bids were received. This clearly showed non competitiveness of the bids received.

Out of a total number of 710 bids for 533 bundles, one of the institutions submitted 389 bids valuing Rs 1267.42 crores which accounted for 55 per cent of the total bids received. Another financial institution offered 152 bids valuing Rs 449.34 crores which represented 21 per cent of the total bids received. The remaining 7 institutions / mutual funds together contributed only 24 per cent of the total bids valuing 584.08 crores. This indicated unequal bidding power of the institutions / mutual funds and the obvious corollary was that a couple of institutions had virtually dictated the prices.

After evaluating the above bundles with reference to the revised reserve prices fixed for PSE shares as outlined in Para 3.9, bids could be accepted only for 406 bundles of which 289 bundles were single bids representing 71 per cent of the total bundles sold. The position regarding allocation of these accepted bundles was as under :

Sl No	*Name of the institution / mutual fund*	*No of bundles allotted*	*Amount accepted (Rs Crores)*
1	Unit Trust of India	225	775.76
2	Canara Bank Mutual Fund	25	131.22
3	General Insurance Corporation	66	211.96
4	Life Insurance Corporation	59	184.31
5	Life Insurance Corporation Mutual Fund	9	27.37
6	Punjab National Bank Mutual Fund	1	3.60
7	State Bank of India Capital Market	21	93.19

The DPE stated that when the bidders were uneven in terms of financial strength, bids naturally would not be even.

5.8 Extent of variation in prices of PSE shares in bundles sold with reference to original reserve prices

A scrutiny of the records of DPE revealed that there was

no comparative statement on record indicating the amount of bids received with those worked out with reference to the original prices fixed for each PSE share. A test check conducted by Audit in this regard revealed the position as under :

Value in Rs Lakhs

Bundle No	*Value of shares in the bundle on the basis of Reserve Price originally fixed by the Government for shares of each PSE.*	*Bid price of the bundle accepted by the Government*	*Variation*
74	868.17	317.00	551.17
90	894.59	303.76	590.83
262	860.62	330.00	530.62
277	860.62	330.00	530.62
364	898.33	306.81	591.52
385	898.33	306.81	591.52
404	898.33	306.81	591.52
460	909.78	317.14	592.64
550	965.27	367.00	598.27
580	939.60	351.00	588.60
610	976.48	477.00	499.48
674	979.04	355.00	624.04
756	963.71	497.00	466.71
788	1286.14	338.05	948.09
807	1110.66	308.71	801.95
821	1291.23	327.77	963.46
Total	15600.90	5539.86	10061.04

The above study revealed that the Government accepted bids substantially lower (ie. 64 per cent) than the original reserve prices resulting in potential gains to the financial institutions / mutual funds at the cost of the Exchequer. The Department did not, however, bring out the above position in full details while seeking the approval of the Government for reducing reserve prices.

The DPE stated that different methodologies including futuristic projection of DCF method resulting in higher reserve prices were specifically discussed and the pricing method finally accepted by Government was pragmatic. The reply does not clarify why the effect of lowering of the reserve prices to the extent of around 64 percent of the original reserve prices was not specifically brought to the notice of the Government at the time of seeking approval to the revision of the original reserve prices of the shares of the PSEs for acceptance of the tender bids of the MFs / FIs.

5.9 Unjustified reduction in the reserve prices of PSE shares made after the opening of tenders

The original 'reserve' prices for the sale of selected PSE shares were determined by the DPE in consultation with the PSE concerned, Ministry of Finance, Administrative Ministry of the PSE between 14th to 18th December 1991, on the basis of the data furnished by PSEs for the three methods of NAV, PECV, DCF as well as the valuation done by the consultants appointed by the Government.

On opening the tenders on the 18th December 1991, it was found by the DPE that no tender could be accepted if the bid for each bundle of shares was valued with reference to the reserve prices fixed. The Department attributed the shortfall in the bid prices vis-à-vis the reserve prices to the fact that the FIs and MFs did not share the PSEs optimistic expectations about future cash flows. The DCF method was, therefore, given up by the Government and the shares of PSEs were evaluated only with reference to the CCI formula, the PECV being calculated at a uniform capitalisation rate of 10 per cent which implied prices being determined at 10 times the Earning Per Share. Further, reduction of 10 per cent, if necessary, in the reserve price of the bundle arrived at with reference to reserve price of PSEs shares so fixed, was also stipulated. This revised criteria of valuation of shares resulted in reduction of the reserve prices ranging from 21.95 per cent to 86.67 per cent. In 24 of the 31 cases, the reduction in valuation was above 50 per cent.

The details are given in Annexure II.

Such substantial reduction in reserve prices was not justified for the following reasons :

(i) The valuation committee and the government had earlier rejected the CCI formula as being too conservative and inapplicable for valuation of PSE shares. The CCI formula provides for suitable adjustment in the capitalisation rate on the basis of the stock market price of share. Under the CCI regime premium was allowed only to existing listed companies. Since the PSEs were not listed on the stock exchanges, the adoption of the CCI formula would have required their share value worked out with appropriate adjustment / of the capitalisation rate having regard to the reserves, profitability and market presence. In the earlier valuation exercise the PECV had been arrived at by adopting the appropriate Industry Capitalisation Rate for each PSE. Whereas these ranged from 4.65 to 7.78 per cent in a majority of the cases the Government finally adopted a uniform rate of 10 per cent for all PSEs which is not rational.

(ii) The reduction in the reserve prices to bring them in consonance with the market response was also not reasonable. The bids received were in fact highly non-competitive in nature. For 72.61 per cent bundles only single bids had been received. Only in 4.50 per cent bundles 3 or more bids were received. 55 per cent of the bids were tendered by only one institution namely the UTI. Such non-competitive response could not be taken to reflect the market perception of the fair value of the PSEs shares. These aspects had not been adequately considered by the Government while deciding to reduce the reserve prices.

(iii) While the earlier reserve prices had been determined by the DPE in consultation with the Administrative Ministries and the Chief Executives of the PSEs concerned, the subsequent proposal to the Government for revising the criteria in refixing reserve prices was done without consulting them.

Considering the factors detailed in the preceding para it would have been appropriate for the Government to attempt negotiations with the bidders who were Public Sector financial institutions / mutual funds by explaining / justifying the basis on which the original reserve prices had been fixed.

The DPE stated that it was not required to negotiate with the bidders as it would tantamount to retendering and that all factors were taken into account and the price was fixed as per principles finally approved by Government. The reply is not convincing. The original reference price was fixed by the Government based on the valuation of shares by consultant and also keeping in view the methods mentioned above. These methods of valuations could not, therefore, be discarded only on the ground that the MFs / FIs had quoted lower rates for bundle of shares within their available means of resources. Negotiation or retendering could have facilitated obtaining of reasonable prices for the shares.

5.10 Fixation of Reserve Price for the second tranche of disinvestment of PSEs shares in bundles in February 1992.

The second tranche of disinvestment of PSEs shares in bundles was undertaken in February 1992. Some PSEs were withdrawn from the second tranche on the advice of the ICICI. Out of shares of 31 PSEs offered in the first phase, unsold shares of only 16 PSEs were offered in fresh 120 bundles to all the Public Sector financial investment institutions, mutual funds and merchant banks. The reserve price of Rs 10.08 crores of each bundle for the second phase was based on the valuation of shares of each of the 16 PSEs done by Industrial Credit and Investment Corporation of India (ICICI). The reserve price of Rs 10.08 crores of each bundle was made known to all the bidding parties in the notice inviting bids.

A scrutiny of the 'advice' of ICICI revealed that their

recommendations had not taken into account the following parameters.

(i) Profitability projections made by the PSEs.

(ii) Major changes contemplated by the PSEs in the future plans.

(iii) Any future major restructuring of the PSEs.

(iv) Impact of decontrol of steel on the profitability of SAIL.

The reserve price thus recommended were not based on relevant factors and were much lower than the reserve prices of shares of PSEs originally fixed.

The unjustified reduction in the reserve prices in response to lower bids received in two tranches of sale resulted in under-realisation of receipts aggregating Rs 3441.71 crores to Government as detailed in Annexure IV.

The DPE stated that ICICI, who were one of the expert agencies in the field in the country, recommended reserve price after taking into consideration all those factors provided by the PSEs and the DPE. It was further stated that subsequent to disinvestment of PSE shares, these did not show any remarkable recovery except some sporadic higher quoting in very limited off loading. In fact most of the scrips were not being traded regularly and based on hypothetical calculations, even notional losses to Government could not be taken as logical.

As already stated in the para above, the ICICI had not taken a number of relevant factors for the valuation of shares of PSEs. Their valuation was much lower than the reserve prices originally fixed. It may also be stated that as per Annexure III of this Report, the market price of some of the PSEs as on 30th October 1992 were much higher than the prices recommended by ICICI. The extent of benefit availed of by the FIs/MFs of the high prices prevailing at this time by selling the shares of 10 PSEs, held by them is not ascertainable. In a test check of 19 PSEs listed on the stock exchanges it was seen that in March (2nd-6th) and April (7th) 1993, the prices quoted for their shares were much higher than the average prices realised in the two tranche of disinvestment.

5.11 Uncompetitive biddings of PSEs shares in the second tranche of disinvestment in February 1992.

In the second tranche of disinvestment, bids for 120 bundles of PSEs shares were invited on 11th February 1992 which were opened on 24th February 1992. 273 bids were received from 19 institutions / mutual funds / merchant banks for all the 120 bundles.

Analysis of the bids received from different parties indicated the position as under :

Bundles	*No of bundles*	*No of bids*	*Percentage to total bundles*
i) No of bundles for which only one bid was received	30	30	25
ii) No of bundles for which only two bids were received	48	96	40
iii) No of bundles for which only three bids were received	27	81	22.5
iv) No of bundles for which only four bids were received	9	36	7.5
v) No of bundles for which only five bids were received	6	30	5

It would be seen from the above that only in 35 per cent cases three bids or more had been received which showed lack of competition even in the second tranche of disinvestment despite the fact that the number of bidders had been increased by including merchant banks.

Out of the 273 bids received, 120 bids were received from a single financial institution amounting to Rs 1580.75 crores. The other three bidders contributed 66 bids valued at Rs 768.65 crores. Thus these four bidders contributed 68 per cent of the total bids and this represented 69 per cent of the total value of the bids amounting to Rs 3416.50 crores. The contribution of the remaining 15 bidders taken together was, therefore, insignificant. This clearly showed that in the second phase also there was lack of competition.

The DPE stated that when the bidders were uneven in terms of financial strength, the bids made by them were bound to have high variations. It may, however, be stated that in the second phase of disinvestment though the scope of inviting tenders from parties was enlarged but the number of shares included in each bundle was so large that the reserve price of each bundle was fixed at Rs 10.08 crores whichwas very high. Further, though the number of PSEs was reduced in the second phase from 31 to 16, the shares offered for sale was high and could not be expected to generate better competition keeping in view the limited investible resources of the bidders.

5.12 Market price of disinvested shares.

A scrutiny of the market prices as prevalent at the end of October 1992 of 10 PSEs shares since listed as given in Annexure III, revealed that the potential gain to the financial institutions/ mutual funds / banks ranged between 126.62 per cent to 615.53 per cent over the average price at which these shares were sold in the two phases of disinvestment during 1991-92. The response of the stock market to the PSEs shares also revealed that the reserve prices for PSEs shares fixed by taking an average of NAV + PECV at 10 per cent capitalisation or at ICICI valuation rate, was grossly under estimated. In fact in 6 out of the 10 PSEs listed in the stock exchanges so far, the reserve prices originally fixed under NAV, PECV, DCF and Consultant's method were also lower than the ruling market price.

To save the Government from substantial under-realisation from such sales, it was necessary that a 'claw-back' provision should have been incorporated in the terms and conditions for the sale of shares to the effect that as and when these shares were subsequently sold by the financial institutions / mutual funds to the general public, a reasonable fixed percentage of the gain on these sales would be transferred back to the

Exchequer. Since the government had no past experience and was disinvesting its shares in PSEs for the first time and most of them were not listed, it was all the more necessary to include such a special clause.

The Chief Advisor (cost), Ministry of Finance as well as the Chief Executive of BPCL had in fact suggested, in August 1991, stipulation of a clause that as and when these shares are offered to the general public, 90 per cent of the difference of the price gained by the financial institutions / mutual funds should be transferred back to the Central Government.

The DPE sated that stipulation of claw-back provision was not practicable and FIs/MFs might have desired inclusion of a similar provision for Government meeting their losses or reduced profits in the subsequent sales of shares by them. The incorporation of a claw-back provision has to be viewed in the context that the disinvestment exercise was undertaken for the first time. A claw-back provision was an assurance that in the event of windfall profits obtained by the FIs/MFs on off-loading these shares in the market within a short given period, a part of profits would flow back to the Government. Inclusion of a suitable claw-back provision was also suggested by the Chief Adviser (Cost). Non inclusion of a claw-back provision cannot be considered to be in the best interest of the tax payer.

5.13 Irregular forward trading of shares of PSEs after disinvestment.

While approving the first round of disinvestment the Government had also decided that the shares of the selected PSEs would be listed on the stock exchanges to enable the financial institutions / mutual funds to off-load them to the general public at the appropriate time. The terms and conditions on which bids were invited from the financial institutions, mutual funds and merchant banks for sale of shares of selected PSEs also specified that the purchasers would be free to off-load their share-holding in these PSE's through the normal stock exchanges transactions. Securities and Exchange

Board of India (SEBI) had intimated to all the stock exchanges in the country that the shares of PSEs should be listed by the stock exchanges and traded only after disclosure documents were submitted and approved by the SEBI and stock exchanges.

It was brought to the notice of the Government that some banks and financial institutions which had purchased shares of PSEs had subsequently sold them in transactions outside the stock exchanges violating the terms and conditions of the sale. The Ministry of Finance sought comments on such forward trading of PSEs shares from the DPE. The DPE, however, held the view that the purchasers were not debarred from effecting any forward sale of shares of PSEs before their actual listing on the stock exchanges as the sale of shares from the Government to the institutional buyers in the public sector was a purely commercial deal.

As already stated above the purchasers were free to off-load their share holding in these PSEs only through the normal stock exchange transactions. The view held by the DPE that the purchasers were not debarred to sell shares before actual listing on the stock was thus contrary to the decisions taken at the outset by the Government and terms and conditions prescribed for sale of shares as well as the instructions issued by the SEBI to all stock exchanges in April 1992.

The DPE stated that for any violation of stock exchange regulations the empowered organs like SEBI etc. were to take necessary action and not the DPE.

5.14 Non achievement of objectives of disinvestment

The objectives behind partial disinvestment of its shares in the selected public sector enterprises, as stated in the statement of Industrial Policy and the Budget speech for 1991-92 of July 1991, were to raise non inflationary resources, encourage wider public participation and promote greater accountability of these enterprises.

The Budget Estimates for 1991-92 provided capital receipt of Rs 38174 crores including Rs 2500 crores to be realised from disinvestment of PSE shares and capital expenditure at Rs 32039 crores. The estimated surplus on the capital account was, therefore, Rs 6135 crores. As against this the estimated deficit on the revenue account was Rs 13854 crores. Instead of containing the revenue expenditure and utilising the capital receipts for enhancing availability of resource of PSEs or for any other productive purposes, Rs 3038 crores realised from the sale of PSEs shares during 1991-92 was in effect intended to reduce the revenue deficit of the budget. Thus, capital assets were disposed of to meet partial revenue expenditure and the levels of revenue expenditure not having been reduced, the objective of raising non inflationary resources by means of sale of shares of PSEs for enhancing the availability of resources of PSEs was not realised.

The sale of PSEs shares only to limited number of financial institutions / mutual funds / merchant banks excluding the workers / employees of the PSEs and the general public could also not be considered as wider public participation. The disinvestment served only to contain the fiscal deficit.

5.15 Analysis of selected cases : SAIL

Audit conducted a detailed analysis of a few cases to determine the factors responsible for low value realisations.

Steel Authority of India Ltd (SAIL) was formed in January 1973 as a holding company for the steel and associated input industry. As on 31st March 1991 the share capital of SAIL was Rs 3985.89 crores owned fully by the Government of India.

SAIL was selected as one of the PSEs for disinvestment of Government's equity holding during 1991-92. At the time of finalization of the PSEs whose shares were to be disinvested the Ministry of Steel suggested the exclusion of SAIL for the following reasons.

(i) The response to offer of SAIL's shares and market perceptions would improve after 2-3 years as a result of decontrol of Iron and Steel prices and completion of the on-going modernisation of projects which would enhance the profitability of the company.

(ii) The Government of India would stand to lose in the then prevalent state of affairs of the company as none of three methods suggested for valuation of shares would reflect the real worth of shares of the company.

(iii) SAIL had already drawn-up plans for disinvestment of equity in 1994-95 when the accruals were expected to go up.

After considering the above points the Government decided in November 1991 that only 5 per cent of the shares of the company would be disinvested as against the original proposal of 20 per cent.

In the two phases of disinvestment carried out in December 1991 and February 1992, a total of 1990.75 lakhs shares of face value of RS 10/- were sold to the financial institutions / mutual funds / merchant banks at an average price of Rs 13.24 per share.

A detailed study of the disinvestment of shares of SAIL revealed the following :

(i) Although the total disinvestment was only 5 per cent it actually represented around 23 per cent of the total number of shars of all the 30 PSEs sold during 1991-92. This was due to the higher paid up capital of the company at Rs 3985.89 crores. In the light of the suggestion of the Ministry of Steel, even 5 per cent disinvestment of the shares of this company proved to be on the very high side.

(ii) While recommending valuation of share of SAIL at Rs 10-12 / for the second tranche of disinvestment, the ICICI had / observed (January 1992) that reassessment of value of SAIL's shares was possible after scrutiny of the impact of steel decontrol which was likely to facilitate a higher issue price. Decontrol of steel prices had already been announced on 16th January 1992 before the recommendations of ICICI were received. Despite the recommendations of ICICI and the decontrol of steel prices before the second tranche of disinvestment, the government did not raise the reserve price of shares of SAIL above Rs 12/-. This happened despite the tremendous stock market enthusiasm in respect of the share price of a comparable private sector steel plant viz., TISCO's share price which jumped by almost Rs 50 (20 per cent) immediately after decontrol.

(iii) The proposal for disinvestment in the second tranche did not also indicate that in view of the announcement of decontrol of steel prices it would be advisable to disinvest the shares of SAIL only after impact of decontrol on the valuation of the shares was fully analysed.

(iv) Out of the total number of 1990.75 lakhs shares of SAIL sold in the two phases of disinvestment made in December 1991 and February 1992, 909.66 lakhs shares were sold in the first phase. From the information received in the middle of January 1992 by the government from the financial institutions / mutual funds who purchased the shares of SAIL, the Government was aware that in the majority of the cases the shares of SAIL were purchased by them at the face value of Rs 10/- per share. This was a clear indication that further disinvestment of SAIL shares was inadvisable. The Government did not, however, consider all these factors and disinvested further shares of 1081.09 lakhs of this company in the second phase in February 1992.

(v) In the background of the enthusiasm created by the decontrol of steel prices in respect of the Steel Industry and the general boom in the stock market, SAIL was listed at the DSE in April 1992 at a price of Rs 200, reaching a high of Rs 240. Thus, it was clear that the Government had failed to assess the positive impact of decontrol of steel pricing and distribution.

The DPE stated that since the shares were sold in bundles, it was not possible to work out average realisation per scrip. Therefore, to compare the disclosure statement's average share price of any PSE like SAIL included in the bundle with reserve price was not relevant and was misleading.

It may be stated that though disinvestment of the shares was effected through bundling of shares of PSEs, the consideration paid for the shares of individual PSEs was crucial for effecting their transfer, listing, etc. The comparison of the average share price given in the disclosure statements with the reserve price is, therefore, not only relevant but is essential for computing the under-realisation.

5.16 Analysis of selected cases Indian Petro Chemicals Corporation Limited (IPCL)

IPCL started its operations in 1973 at Baroda (Gujarat). Today it has one more petrochemical complex at Nagothane (Maharashtra). A complex is planned at Gaudhar (Gujarat).

IPCL has an investment plan for over Rs 4600 crores during 1990-95 which includes the proposed Gaudhar project with a capital investment of Rs 3485 crores. One of the conditions of the setting up of this project is that IPCL will have to raise resources without recourse to budgetary support. The equity capital of the company at Rs 186 crores had not been raised after 1977 despite the fact that new assets amounting to Rs 2050 crores had been created. If the fresh investment of Rs 4619 crores from 1990-95 were also to be implemented through borrowings it would result in high debt equity ratio which could create debt servicing problem in the long run.

In the light of the above position, the IPCL requested the DPE in August 1991 that instead of the Government diluting its equity holdings by selling the shares to mutual funds and institutions etc. it might be permitted to issue fresh equity shares to the public to the extent which could dilute Government holding in the overall equity capital of the company to 50 per cent over a period say by 1995. Permission was also sought to increase the authorised capital of the company to RS 400 crores. The company also pointed out that they had the experience of raising funds from public through bonds and debentures and they had been advised by experts that their shares market value would be significantly higher than its book value. Despite these observations the DPE went ahead and disinvested 20 per cent of equity representing 372 lakh shares of face value Rs 10 amounting to Rs 37.20 crores in the two disinvestments carried out in December 1991 and February 1992 at an average price of Rs 65.24 per share.

For the sale of its shares in IPCL in the first phase of disinvestment in December 1991 the Government originally fixed a reserve price of Rs 175/- per share which was reduced to RS 37/- after the tenders were opened. For the second phase of disinvestment the reserve price was, however, refixed at Rs 60/- on the basis of the valuation done by ICICI.

A study of the consideration paid by various institutions indicated that the price per share ranged from RS 35 to Rs 140.60. In the second phase of disinvestment the price per share paid by three parties was less than the reserve price of Rs 60/- which resulted in the under-realisation of Rs 232.77 lakhs to the Government.

Sl No	*Name of the institution*	*No of shares sold*	*Revised Reserve Price per share 2nd phase*	*Price at which shares were sold*	*Loss per share*	*Total loss (Rs. lakks)*
1	Indian Bank Mutual Fund	336700	60	48.96	11.04	37.17
2	Allahabad Bank	335000	60	52.00	8.00	26.80
3	Corporation Bank	675200	60	35.00	25.00	168.80
	Total					232.77

Subsequently IPCL raised Rs 320 crores from the public by sale of fresh equity shares of Rs 10/- each for cash at a premium of RS 150/- per share.

The public issue of IPCL opened on 16th November 1992 and despite the stock market being bearish it was fully subscribed closing on the earliest closing date viz., 19th November 1992. The public issue was preceded by prolonged publicity in News Papers, Magazines, Television etc. about the strength of the company as well as its future plans. The offer was made directly to the public without fixing any minimum limits. Not only has the IPCL succeeded in raising resources for financing its future plans but also widened its equity holding. The public issue of IPCL of November 1992 at a price almost 3 times realized in the earlier dis-investment has highlighted the following major short-comings of the latter.

(a) Disinvestment was not preceded by adequate public exposure of the PSEs.

(b) The offer for sale was restricted to MFs/FIs, the minimum size of bundles being Rs 3 to Rs 3.5 crores in the first tranche and Rs 10.08 crores in the second.

(c) The concerned PSEs were not associated with the dis-investment exercise thereby foregoing the benefit of their expertise and the confidence in their respective organisations in determining realistic reserve price.

6. Summing up

- The disinvestment exercises was not preceded by adequate preparatory study. No efforts were made to generate enthusiasm among financial institutions / mutual funds about PSE shares to encourage good response (Paragraph 5.1)
- Some PSEs like SAIL, IPCL were included against the advice of these PSEs/Administrative Ministries resulting in under realisation of share value in respect of shares disinvested in the PSEs (Paragraphs 5.1, 5.15 and 5.16).

- The method of sale of shares of PSEs in bundles had the effect of depressing the value realisation of 'very good / good' PSEs shares as a result of clubbing together with 'average' PSEs. The disinvestment of shares of Cochin Refineries and Andrew Yule which were listed on the stock exchange to financial institutions / mutual funds in the first tranche was contrary to Government decision (Paragraph 5.3).
- Making bundles before fixation of reserve prices of shares of PSEs resulted in failure to contain the value of each bundle to around Rs 5 crores as approved by the Government. There was also appreciable variation in the value of bundles ranging between Rs 8.61 crores to Rs 12.91 crores. By quoting rates of bundles below Rs 5 crores the financial institutions / mutual funds made adventitious gains at the cost of the Exchequer (Paragraph 5.5).
- Despite being aware that the financial institutions / mutual funds would be able to purchase shares only around Rs 2000-2500 crores in the first phase of disinvestment in December 1991, the Government offered shares whose value on the basis of reserve prices was around Rs 8000 crores, ie., far in excess of the perceived investible resources with the institutions / mutual funds (Paragraph 5.6).
- Tenders received in the first phase of disinvestment were non-competitive. 72.61 per cent of the bids received had only one bidder. Out of 406 bundles sold, 289 bundles were single bids representing 71 per cent of the total bundles sold (Paragraph 5.7).
- In 16 bundles test checked at random in Audit the extent of variation in prices of PSEs shares in bundles accepted with reference to the original prices fixed in the first phase of disinvestment in December 1991 amounted to Rs 10061.04 lakhs (Paragraph 5.8).
- Reserve prices were reduced ranging between 21.95 per cent to 86.67 per cent. In 24 out of 31 cases reduction in

valuation was above 50 per cent. The reduction in original reserve price resulted in under-realisation of share value to the extent of Rs 3442 crores (Paragraphs 5.9 and 5.10).

- In the second phase of disinvestment also the tenders received were uncompetitive. There was also unequal bidding power. Four out of 19 bidders contributed 68 per cent of total bids received (Paragraph 5.11).
- Non incorporation of claw back provision in the terms and conditions of the sale resulted in Government not being able to realise a part of the huge profits made / likely to be made by the buyers in after sale of shares of the PSEs (Paragraph 5.12).
- The off-loading of shares after purchase by some institutions otherwise than through the normal stock exchanges was violative of Government policy and the terms and conditions of the sale (Paragraph 5.13).
- The disinvestment served only to contain the fiscal deficit (Paragraph 5.14).

Annexure – I
(Referred to in Paragraph 3.6)
List of Disinvested Public Sector Enterprises

S No	*Name of PSEs*	*Percentage of Disinvestment*
1	Hindustan Petroleum Corporation Ltd (HPCL)	20.00
2	Indian Railway. Construction Co. Ltd (IRCON)	00.27
3	Minerals & Metals Trading Corporation (MMTC)	00.67
4	Bharat Petroleum Corporation Ltd (BPCL)	20.00
5	Bharat Earthmovers Ltd (BEML)	20.00
6	Videsh Sanchar Nigam Ltd (VSNL)	20.00
7	State Trading Corporation (STC)	07.98

(Contd...)

8	Bharat Heavy Electricals Ltd (BHEL)	20.00
9	Shipping Corporation of India (SCI)	20.00
10	Indian Petrochemicals Corporation Ltd (IPCL)	20.00
11	HMT Ltd (HMT)	05.43
12	Dredging Corporation of India Ltd (DCI)	01.44
13	Bharat Electronics Ltd (BEL)	20.00
14	Cochin Refineries Ltd (CRL)	10.01
15	Indian Telephone Industries (ITI)	20.00
16	Andrew Yule (AY)	13.57
17	Hindustan Organic Chemicals Ltd (HOCL)	20.00
18	Hindustan Cables Ltd (HCL)	03.64
19	Madras Refineries Ltd (MRL)	20.00
20	Mahanagar Telephone Nigam Ltd (MTNL)	20.00
21	Rashtriya Chemicals & Fertilisers Ltd (RCFL)	05.64
22	Steel Authority of India Ltd (SAIL)	05.00
23	Neyveli Lignite Corporation (NLC)	05.00
24	National Aluminium Co Ltd (NALCO)	02.72
25	Hindustan Zinc Ltd (HZL)	20.00
26	Bongaigaon Refineries & Petrochemicals Ltd (BRPL)	20.00
27	National Fertilizers Ltd (NFL)	02.28
28	Fertilizers & Chemicals (Travancore) Ltd (FACT)	01.54
29	Hindustan Photo Films Manufacturing Co Ltd (HPF)	16.05
30	CMC Ltd (CMC)	16.69

(*Source*: Annexure IV of Annual Report of Department of Public Enterprises for the year 1991-92)

Annexure – II

(Referred to in Paragraph 5.9)

Statement of fixation of reserve prices for PSE shares in the first phase of disinvestment in December 1991.

(Face Value – Rs 10/-)

S.No.	Name of Public Sector Enterprises	Price Recommended by the Consultant appointed by Government			Reserve Price Fixed by Government during 14th-18th December 1991	Reserve Price refixed by Government as an average of NAV Plus PCEV at 10 per cent	Reduction in Percentage in the value of share in Column 5 with Reference to Col. 4
		High	*Low*	*Average*			
1	AY	92.14	82.72	87.43	82.00	39.00	52.44
2	BEML	242.72	228.17	235.45	225.00	133.00	40.89
3	BEL	104.22	58.66	81.44	80.00	29.00	63.75
4	BHEL	56.10	47.82	51.96	66.00	37.00	43.94
5	BPCL	351.50	333.32	342.41	350.00	181.00	48.29
6	BRPL	68.18	51.09	59.64	55.00	18.00	67.27
7	CMC	82.03	67.51	74.77	75.00	10.00	86.67
8	DCI	148.70	115.65	132.18	132.00	36.00	72.73
9	FACT	80.85	53.77	67.31	70.00	10.00	85.71
10	HCL	39.29	30.24	34.77	70.00	29.00	58.57

(Contd...)

11	HOCL	147.08	115.22	131.15	132.00	46.00	65.15
12	HPCL	238.88	222.10	230.49	305.00	191.00	37.38
13	HPF	96.12	77.16	86.64	70.00	10.00	85.71
14	HZL	93.77	83.74	88.76	85.00	16.00	81.18
15	HMT	60.94	52.30	56.62	46.00	21.00	54.35
16	IPCL	107.14	101.30	104.22	175.00	37.00	78.86
17	IRCON	250.00	208.00	229.00	440.00	303.00	31.14
18	ITI	80.80	69.38	75.09	100.00	35.00	65.00
19	MRL	73.95	56.55	65.25	65.00	32.00	50.77
20	MTNL	79.57	68.18	73.88	57.00	22.00	61.40
21	MMTC	225.17	210.33	217.75	204.00	93.00	54.41
22	NALCO	35.18	21.17	28.18	38.00	10.00	73.68
23	NLC	84.47	72.38	78.43	57.00	11.00	80.70
24	RCF	94.37	66.30	80.34	64.00	13.00	79.69
25	SCI	63.58	36.44	50.01	75.00	22.00	70.67
26	NFL	63.88	38.27	51.08	65.00	10.00	84.62
27	STC	74.96	63.17	69.07	123.00	96.00	21.95
28	SAIL	35.00	35.00	35.00	35.00	10.00	71.43
29	VSNL	264.24	249.62	256.93	220.00	77.00	65.00
30	CRL	NOT RECOMMENDED			145.00	58.00	60.00

Annexure III
(Referred to in Paragraph 5.12)

Statement showing the market price vis-à-vis the average price at which the shares of selected PSEs were disinvested

Sl. No.	Name of the PSE	Reserve Price of Share Originally Fixed During 14th-18th December 1991	Revised Reserve Price Fixed for 1st Stage of Disinvest-ment in December 1991 / NAV + PECV at 10% Cap. rate	Reserve Price Fixed Second Phase of disinvest-ment in February 1992 (ICICI)	Average Price at which Share Value of Rs. 10/- was sold	Market Price as per Economic Times 31.1092				Gain to Financial Institutions Mutual funds/banks on Lowest of Closing Price on 30.12.92 or Average of 52nd Week	
						Closing price 30.10.92	52nd week			Gain per share	Percent-age of gain
							High	Low	Average		
		Rs.	Rs.	Rs.	Rs.	Rs.	Rs.	Rs.	Rs.	Rs.	Rs.
1	2	3	4	5	6	7	8	9	10	11	12
1	BPCL	350	181	300	243.89	750	1275	650	962.50	506.11	207.52

(Contd...)

2	BHEL	66	37	37	38.05	140	200	130	165.00	101.95	267.94
3	HCL	70	29	-	25.17	65	65	60	62.50	37.33	148.31
4	HOCL	132	46	46	56.92	143.75	220	135	177.50	86.83	152.55
5	HPCL	305	191	225	242.70	550	1200	550	875	307.30	126.62
6	HZL	85	16	17	21.65	58.75	65	47.50	56.25	34.60	159.82
7	HMT	46	21	-	18.11	80	85	67.50	76.25	58.14	321.04
8	SAIL	35	10	12	13.24	42	80	41.25	60.62	28.76	217.22
9	RCPL	64	13	-	9.87	43.75	55	41	48	33.88	343.26
10	NLC	57	11	11	11.46	82	NA	NA		70.54	615.53

Annexure - IV
(Referred to in Paragraph 5.10)
Statement showing under-realisation of value of PSEs shares in the first and second phase of disinvestment during 1991-92

Sl. No.	*Name of PSE*	*No. of Shares dis-invested (Face value Rs. 10 (In lakhs)*	*Percent-age of disinvest-ment to equity*	*Original Reserve Price per share fixed Rs.*	*Average Reali-sation per share Rs.*	*Under Reali-sation per share Rs.*	*Total amount under-realised (Rs. in Lakh)*
1	AY	10.15	13.57	82	NA	-	-
2	BPCL	100.00	20.00	350	243.89	106.11	10611.00
3	BHEL	489.52	20.00	66	38.05	27.95	13682.08
4	BEL	160.00	20.00	80	30.00	50.00	8000.00
5	BRPL	399.61	20.00	55	30.75	24.25	9690.54
6	BEML	60.00	20.00	225	148.31	76.69	4601.40
7	CRL	42.19	10.01	145	98.40	46.60	1966.05
8	CMC	25.28	16.69	75	8.00	67.00	1693.76
9	DCI	4.02	1.44	132	10.00	122.00	490.44
10	FACT	52.32	1.54	70	10.00	60.00	3139.20
11	HPCL	127.68	20.00	305	242.70	62.30	7954.46
12	HCL	16.69	3.64	70	25.17	44.83	748.21
13	HMT	42.68	5.43	46	18.11	27.89	1190.35
14	HPF	191.90	16.05	70	8.00	62.00	11897.80
15	HZL	807.46	20.00	85	21.65	63.35	51152.59
16	HOCL	98.70	20.00	132	56.92	75.08	7410.40
17	IPCL	372.00	20.00	175	65.24	109.76	40830.72
18	IRCON	0.13	0.27	440	225.00	215.00	27.95
19	ITI	175.38	20.00	100	49.45	50.55	8865.46

(Contd...)

20	MTNL	1200.00	20.00	57	46.26	10.74	12888.00
21	MRL	193.16	20.00	65	39.63	25.37	4900.47
22	MMTC	3.34	0.67	204	93.00	111.00	370.74
23	NALCO	351.00	2.72	38	13.13	24.87	8729.37
24	NFL	111.63	2.28	65	8.46	56.54	6311.56
25	NLC	717.91	5.00	57	11.46	45.54	32693.62
26	RCFL	311.36	5.64	64	9.87	54.13	16853.92
27	STC	23.93	7.98	123	67.00	56.00	1340.08
28	SCI	522.46	20.00	75	34.41	40.59	21206.65
29	SAIL	1990.75	5.00	35	13.24	21.76	43318.72
30	VSNL	120.00	20.00	220	123.29	96.71	11605.20
TOTAL		8721.25					344170.74

Index

A

Administrative Reforms Commission, 94, 95, 96

Aggregates, 16

Apple by committee, 30

Autonomy and control, 5, 41, 142
- autonomy and accountability of public enterprise, 143
- government executive and the public enterprise, 143
- public sector performance evaluation, 142
- role of memorandum of understanding in public enterprise management, 142

B

Bureau of Industrial Costs and Prices, 35

C

Capacity of utilisation in Public enterprises, 104

Capital Electricity Regulatory Commission, 19

Capital expenditure, 5

Capital markets, 13

Central PEs (CPEs), 1, 8, 17

Coalition politics on public enterprise activity, 21-23

Committee on disinvestment of shares in public sector enterprises, 215
- criteria for selection of public sector enterprise disinvested during 1992-93, 217-219
- criteria for valuation of equity shares of public sector enterprises, 227-230
- limits on the percentage of equity to be disinvested, 219-223
- *modus operandi* of disinvestment, 224-227
- other issues, 233-237
- target clientele for disinvestment, 230-233

Committee on Public Undertakings (COPU), 31, 77, 78, 85, 86, 90, 92, 93, 214
- constitution, 169-170
- working of the committee, 170-202

Committee to review policy for public enterprises, 203
- accountability of public enterprises, 207
- accountability of public enterprises: performance evaluation, 207-208
- executive appointments and remuneration, 206-207
- financial performance, 208
- financial viability of loss making units, 211-212

pricing in public sector, 212-213
productivity and cost reduction, 208-209
project implementation, 209-210
relations with the parliament, 210
technical change, 209
technology upgradation, 210-211
wage policy in public enterprises, 205-206

Commonwealth secretariat, performance of public enterprise
criteria, 117
financial control, 118-119
financial requirements, 119
government control, 117
organization control, 118
policies and objectives, 117
project control, 118

Comptroller and Auditor General of India (CAG), 78, 82, 88, 89, 91, 92, 97, 214, 238

Corporate governance, Boards, 164
some issues for management, 164-165

Corporate planning, 40

Country-specific experiences, 157
basic issues in performance contracting systems with special reference to Indian case, 158-159
contract plan experience in Africa, 161-162
improving Korea's public enterprise evaluation efforts, 158
memorandum of understanding and the Korean performance evaluation system, 164
memorandum of understanding, 161
methodological issues relating to recent changes in the MOU policy, 163
methods for controlling public enterprises, 161
new public enterprise policy and efficiency improvement, 163
observations in the South Korean system for performance evaluation of public enterprises, 160
past experiences with public performance evaluation system in India, 157
performance contracting system on Bangladesh, report submitted to ministry of France, 160-161
performance evaluation of public enterprises, 162
public enterprise performance evaluation system in Pakistan, 162
public enterprises in India, 163-164
setting targets for improving cost efficiencies in public enterprises, 159
system for evaluating the performance of government invested enterprises in the republic of Korea, 159-160
towards a performance evaluation methodology for public enterprises, 157-158

D

Deficit of PEs, 35
Disinvestment, 17, 18
analysis of selected cases Indian Petro Chemicals Corporation Limited (IPCL), 272-274
analysis of selected cases: SAIL, 269-272
appointment of consultant for valuation of shares, 243-244
approach to disinvestment lacked necessary preparatory work, 247-251
arrangement for valuation and sale of shares of PSEs, 242-247
audit findings and conclusions, 247-274
classification of PSEs – basis inadequate, 254-256
commission, 6, 7
committee on, 215-237
constitution of bundles and inviting of bids without valuing the shares, 256-257
department, 9, 29
during 2001-02, 18
extent of variation in prices of PSE shares in bundles sold with reference to original reserve prices, 259-261
fixation of reserve price for the second tranche of disinvestment of PSEs shares in bundles on February 1992, 263-265
formulation of guidelines for valuation- inadequacies, 251-252
formulation of guidelines for valuation of shares of PSEs, 243
government shareholding, 240
in public sector undertakings, 17
invitation of bids, fixation of reserve pries, 245
irregular forward trading of shares of PSEs after disinvestment, 267-268
market price of disinvested shares, 266-267
minister for, 9
modus operandi for sale of shares, 244-245
non-achievement of objectives of disinvestment, 268-269
non-competitive tenders in the first phase of disinvestment in December 1991, 258-259
offer of shares for sale in excess of the perceived investible resources with the institutions, 257-258
organizational set up, 241-242
revision of reserve prices, 245-246
scope of audit, 247
second tranche of disinvestment, 246-247
summing up, 274-283
uncompetitive biddings of PSEs shares in the second tranche of disinvestment in February 1992, 265-266
unjustified reduction in the reserve prices of PSE shares made after the opening of tenders, 261-263

effect of bundling of shares on prices of very good/ good PSEs, 253-254

Distribution of number, total assets, sales/turnover and profit before tax of public enterprises, 103

E

Economic Administrative Reforms Commission, 30

Estimates Committee, 86, 87

Experts, 39

Financial performance, 10, 17
ratios, 99

Forms of organization of PEs in India, 98

Free standing institutions, 97

G

Global advisors, 5

Gorwala Committee, 30

Government-enterprise interface, 144
- accountability of enterprises, 146
- accountability of public enterprises to parliament, 144
- interface between government and state enterprises, 150-151
- leading issues in public enterprise management on autonomy and accountability of public enterprises, 145

Government-enterprise interface
- public enterprise autonomy form the legislative legislature's point of view, 148-149
- public enterprise autonomy from the legislature's point of view, 147-148
- public enterprises and autonomous agencies in govt. budgeting and expenditure control, 145-146
- state government enterprise, 149-150
- striving for autonomy, 144

I

IMF, 31

Incentive schemes, 5

Indian Electricity Act, 20

Industrial Policy Resolution (IPR) of 1948, 29, 30

Investment on in top ten public enterprises, 98

J

Joint venture, 5

K

Krishna Menon Committee, 30

M

Management development and training, 151
- human resource development in public enterprises, 152-153
- improving public enterprise performance through appraisal, training and management development, 153
- management of public sector enterprise in India, 152
- professionalisation among

managers in industrial organisation in public sector, 151
recruitment and training in public sector, 151
Management of Pes, 28-47
Market shares, 20
Mini-*Ratnas*, 31
Mobilisation of funds, 5
Mohan Committee, 7
Mohd. Fazal Committee, 38

N

National Renewal Fund (NRF), 8
Navartna and *miniratna* PEs, 24-25, 31

P

Pathak Committee, 30
PE executives, 31
management, 30
performance evaluation
accountability through annual reports, 82-83
accountability through audit, 82
accountability to parliament/state legislatures, 77-79
development of techniques and agencies involved in performance evaluation, 85-89
efficacy of performance evaluation system, 89-90
efficacy of performance evaluation system: measuring techniques, 90
efficacy of performance evaluation system: methods for reporting, 90-91
efficacy of performance evaluation system: responding mechanism, 91-92
efficacy of performance evaluation system: impact of PE performance, 92-93
efficacy of performance evaluation system: views and suggestions on evaluation process, 93-97
interface relationships, 76
nature of public enterprise activity, 74-76
overview of performance evaluation system, 83-84
overview of performance evaluation system: financial techniques, 84
overview of performance evaluation system: economic techniques, 84-85
relationship with the government, 79
–administrative ministry, 81
–board appointments, 80
–circulars and office orders, 80
–Department of Public Enterprises (DPE), 81
–finance ministry, 81
–other ministries and departments, 81-82
–power to issue directions, 80

–power of investigation, 80-81
–prior approval, 79
–reports, returns and meetings, 80

Performance contracting for state owned enterprises, 165
commentaries on state enterprise control problems, 165
contracts between the state and it's enterprises, 166-167
control systems for SOE's, 166
linking managers with ministries, 167
MOU's for the state level public enterprises in India, 166
performance contracts with state owned public enterprises, 165-166

Performance evaluation of philosophy and policy issues
action learning programme, 135-136
commonwealth secretariat, performance of public enterprise, 116-117
comparative impact of monetary incentives on productivity in public and private enterprises, 138-139
concept of political will in the context of evolving a suitable performance evaluation system for public enterprises, 132
conceptual review of public enterprises, 130
control of public enterprises in India, 128
curriculum development for evaluating public enterprise performance, 112-113
draft on revamping PSUs: government identifies 58 sick units, 113
dynamics of management of public enterprises, 115
evaluation as a positive activity, state enterprises, 114
excellent management in public sector, 114
image of public sector, 132-133
legal reforms must for efficient PSU working, 115-116
macroeconomic impact of public sector enterprises, 121-122
managerial effectiveness in public enterprises, 119
nature of public enterprise, 129
operational efficiency of public enterprises in India, 140
operative perception on performance appraisal in public enterprise, 116
organizational energy- a diagnostic exercise, 112
performance evaluation of public enterprise in India, 120
performance appraisal of public enterprises in India, 136-137
performance of public enterprises as a model employer in India, 137-138

performance of public enterprises in India, 139-140
perspective for understanding effectiveness, 141-142
political economy of India's public sector, 122-123
productivity in public enterprises, 133
promise and performance: a study for creditable system of evaluating the efficiency of public enterprise, 124
public enterprises policy and performance, 119-120
public enterprise performance in north eastern region, 120-121
public enterprise performance evaluation, 121
public enterprise management strategies for success, 125-127
public enterprises in the third world countries, 127-128
public enterprise: studies in organisational structure, 128-129
public enterprise and the developing world, 129
public enterprise in Britain, 129-130
public enterprise: how it is different from the private sector, 135
public enterprise policy and reform measures, 138
public sector performance evaluation, 123-124
public sector-promises programmes, performances and prospects, modern management, 130-132
role and achievement of public enterprises, 122
social commitment and efficiency in Indian public enterprises, 133-134
social performance of public enterprises, 134
some lessons for management of public enterprises, 115
transnational corporations and public enterprises in India, 113

Performance evaluation, 40, 153
basic purpose of a performance contract, 154-155
efficacy of public enterprise, 155
enterprise contract system in public enterprise management, 155-156
improving public enterprise performance, 154
more memorandum less understanding, 153-154
performance evaluation of public enterprises in India, 153
public enterprise reform and privatisation, 157
theory and practice of contractual approach, 156

Performance evaluation
philosophy and policy issues, 105
changing efficiency of public enterprises in India, 107-108
evaluation of public

enterprises performance, 105-107
evaluation of training, 112
public enterprise sector and development lessons from international experience, 108
public enterprise in developing countries, 109-111
public enterprise in developing countries: impact of environment, 109-110
public enterprise in developing countries: institutionalized norms, 110
public enterprise in developing countries: size and structure, 110-111
structural changes in human relationship between manager and worker, 108

Plan investment by central public sector enterprises, 13

Plan
Eighth Five-year, 30
Fifth Five-year, 30
First Five-year, 30
Ninth Five-year, 31
Second Five-year, 30
Seventh Five–year, 30
Third Five-year, 30

Planning Commission, 45

Policy measures (2000-02)
budget, 2000-01, 8
budget, 2001-02, 8-9
performance, 9

Policy measures in 1990s
accountability and autonomy, 5-6
approach global financial institutions for stabilisation (1991-96), 2
Board for Industrial and Financial reconstruction, 3
disinvestments and public participation, 3-4
governing boards, 4
mobilisation of funds, 3-4
Portfolio, 2-3
up grading of technology, 4

Policy measures in 1997
disinvestment commission, 5
disinvestment process, 5
distribution of dividends, 6
guidelines, 6
navratnas and *miniratnas*, 5-6
privatisation, 7
redefining the scope of the disinvestment commission, 6
rehabilitation package, 6

Policy measures in 1999
competition, 7
salaries and wages, 7

Price preference, 213
award of contracts, 213
BPE guideline, 214
expenditure on township and residential quarters, 213-214

Privatisation, 6, 7, 19-24

Productivity measures of public sector units, 14-15

Profitability, trend of, 11-12

Public Accounts Committee, 31

Public enterprise policy, 1

Public sector's contribution in total industrial production, 9-10

Public sector - promises programmes, performances and prospects, modern management: standing conference of public enterprises, 131-132

R

Raj committee, 34

Retrenchment compensation, 8

S

Sengupta Committee, 30, 41, 96, 203-214

Share-holding, 1, 5

Sick Industrial Companies Act, 1985, 30

State Electricity regulatory Commission, 20

State PEs (SPEs), 1, 8, 17, 33, 34, 92

T

Trend of profitability, 101

Trend of profitability, 11-12

U

United nation publications, 167
  a handbook for managers, 167
  bureaucrats in business, 167-168
  department of development and support management services, 168

V

Vital committee, 6

Voluntary retirement scheme (VRS), 8

Voluntary Separation Scheme (VSS), 8

W

Worker's representation, 4, 37

Working capital, 34

World Bank, 31, 97

❑❑❑